Apple Pro Training Series

OS X Server
Essentials

Arek Dreyer and Ben Greisler

Apple
Certified

Apple Pro Training Series: OS X Server Essentials
Arek Dreyer and Ben Greisler
Copyright © 2013 by Peachpit Press

Published by Peachpit Press. For information on Peachpit Press books, go to: www.peachpit.com

To report errors, please send a note to errata@peachpit.com. Peachpit Press is a division of Pearson Education.

Apple Series Editor: Lisa McClain
Production Coordinator: Kim Elmore, Happenstance Type-O-Rama
Technical Editor: David Colville
Apple Reviewer: John Signa
Apple Project Manager: John Signa
Copy Editor: Darren Meiss
Proofreader: Darren Meiss
Compositors: James D. Kramer, Craig Johnson; Happenstance Type-O-Rama
Indexer: Jack Lewis
Cover Illustration: Kent Oberheu
Cover Production: Cody Gates, Happenstance Type-O-Rama

ISBN 13: 978-0-321-88733-7   ISBN 10: 0-321-88733-6
9 8 7 6 5 4 3 2 1 Printed and bound in the United States of America

Acknowledgments

We extend a big thank you to Steve Jobs. He will be missed, and he will continue to inspire us.

Thank you to all the people at Apple for getting Mountain Lion and OS X Server out the door.

Thank you to all the people who continue to help their users get the most out of OS X and iOS. Keep learning, and don't expect the pace of change to let up any time soon.

Thanks to the amazingly capable Lisa McClain for gently making sure these materials made it into your hands, and to Darren Meiss and Kim Elmore for working their editorial and production magic.

Thank you, also, to the following people. Without your help, this book would be much less than what it is:

Craig Cohen	Adam Karneboge	Joel Rennich
David Colville	Andrina Kelly	Schoun Regan
Gordon Davisson	Bob Kite	Anthony Robinson
LeRoy Dennison	Andre LaBranche	John Signa
John DeTroye	Judy Lawrence	Chris Silvertooth
Kevin Dunn	Pam Lefkowitz	David Starr
Josh Durham	Ben Levy	Frank Valletutti
Charles Edge	Tip Lovingood	Cindy Waller
Eugene Evon	Jussi-Pekka Mantere	Jeff Walling
Ben Harper	Nader Nafissi	Kevin White
Michael Gauss	Masayuki Nii	Simon Wheatley
Patrick Gallagher	Tim O'Boyle	Josh Wisenbaker
Phil Goodman	Timo Perfitt	Kaoru Yamakawa
H Göck	John Poyner	Eric Zelenka
Eric Hemmeter	Mike Reed	

Dedications

Arek Dreyer

Thanks to my lovely wife, Heather Jagman, for her cheerful support.

Ben Greisler

My love and appreciation to my wife, Ronit, and my children, Galee and Noam, for being there for me throughout this project.

Contents at a Glance

Implementing Deployment Solutions

Providing Network Services

Using Collaborative Services

Table of Contents

Implementing Deployment Solutions

Providing Network Services

Using Collaborative Services

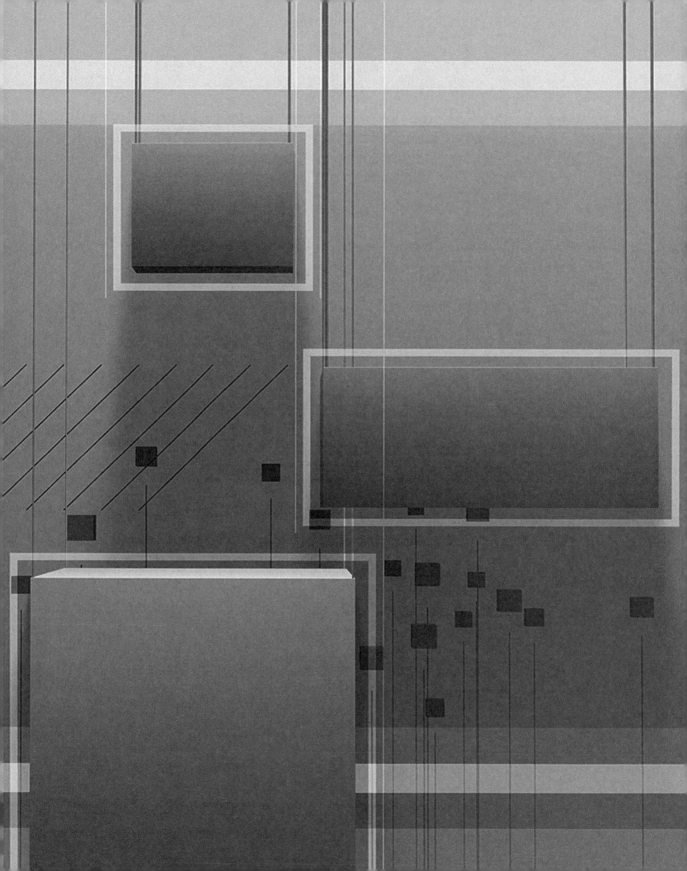

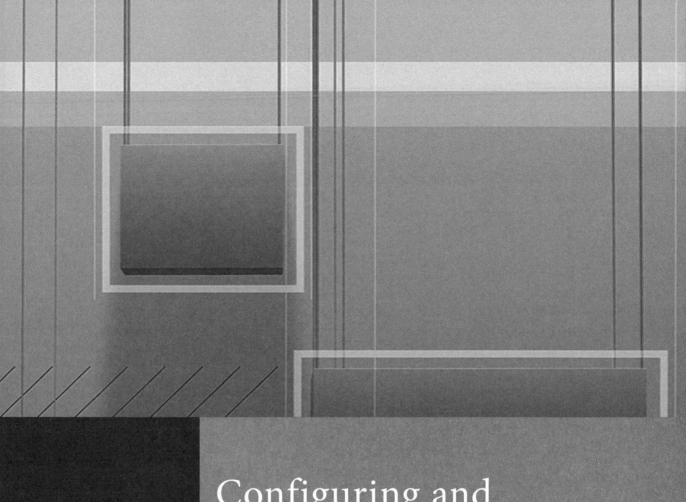

Configuring and
Monitoring OS X Server

Lesson 1
About This Guide

This guide serves as a tour of the breadth of functionality of OS X Server and the best methods for effectively supporting users of OS X Server systems. In addition, this guide is the curriculum for the Apple official training course, Mountain Lion 201: OS X Server Essentials 10.8, a three-day, hands-on course that provides an intense and in-depth exploration of how to configure and troubleshoot OS X Server for Mountain Lion. This course is facilitated by an Apple Certified Trainer and is organized into multiple lessons, each containing instructor presentations followed by related student exercises. In other words, this guide is for both self-paced learners working independently and those participating in an instructor-led course.

GOALS

► Understand how this guide is organized to facilitate learning

► Set up an environment for self-paced exercises

► Introduce Apple Authorized Training and Certification

The primary goal of this guide is to prepare technical coordinators and entry-level system administrators for the tasks demanded of them by OS X Server; you will learn how to install and configure OS X Server to provide network-based services, such as configuration profile distribution and management, file sharing, authentication, and collaboration services. To help you become truly proficient, this guide covers the theory behind the tools you will use. For example, not only will you learn how to use the Server app—the tool for managing services and accounts—but you will also learn about the ideas behind profile management, how to think about access to and control of resources, and how to set up and distribute profiles to support your environment.

You will learn to develop processes to help you understand and work with the complexity of your system as it grows. Even a single OS X Server computer can grow into a very complicated system, and creating documentation and charts can help you develop processes so that additions and modifications can integrate harmoniously with your existing system.

This guide assumes that you have some knowledge of OS X, because OS X Server is now just an app that you install on top of OS X (Mountain Lion). Therefore, you should be comfortable with basic navigation, troubleshooting, and networking in OS X. When working through this guide, a basic understanding and knowledge of OS X is preferred, including knowledge of how to troubleshoot the operating system. Refer to *Apple Pro Training Series: OS X Support Essentials* from Peachpit Press if you need to develop a solid working knowledge of OS X.

> **NOTE** ▸ Unless otherwise specified, all references to OS X refer to version 10.8.2 or later, and references to OS X Server refer to version 2.1.1, which was the most current version available at the time of writing. Due to subsequent upgrades, some screen shots, features, and procedures may be slightly different from those presented on these pages.

Learning Methodology

Each lesson in this guide is designed to give technical coordinators and entry-level system administrators the skills, tools, and knowledge to implement and maintain a network that uses OS X Server by

- ▸ Providing knowledge of how OS X Server works
- ▸ Showing how to use configuration tools
- ▸ Explaining troubleshooting and procedures

The exercises contained within this guide are designed to let you explore and learn the tools necessary to manage OS X Server v10.8. They move along in a predictable fashion, starting with the installation and setup of OS X Server and moving to more advanced topics such as performing multiprotocol file sharing, using access control lists, and permitting OS X Server to manage network accounts. It is required that you start from a Mac that is not yet running OS X Server, and that you do not use this server as a production server.

This guide serves as an introduction to OS X Server and is not meant to be a definitive reference. Because OS X and OS X Server contain several open source initiatives, it is impossible to include all the possibilities and permutations here. First-time users of OS X Server and users of other server operating systems who are migrating to OS X Server have the most to gain from this book; still, others who are upgrading from previous versions of OS X Server will also find this book a valuable resource.

OS X Server is by no means difficult to set up and configure, but how you use OS X Server should be planned out in advance. Accordingly, this book is divided into seven parts:

▶ Part 1, "Configuring and Monitoring OS X Server," covers planning, installation, initial configuration, and monitoring of OS X Server.

▶ Part 2, "Configuring Accounts," defines authentication and authorization, access control, and Open Directory and the vast functionality it can provide.

▶ Part 3, "Managing Devices with Configuration Profiles," covers managing devices with the Profile Manager service.

▶ Part 4, "Providing File Services," introduces the concept of sharing files over multiple protocols and controlling access to files with access control lists.

▶ Part 5, "Implementing Deployment Solutions," teaches you how to effectively use deployment services, NetInstall, and the Software Update service.

▶ Part 6, "Providing Network Services," introduces the network services, including the Time Machine, VPN, DHCP, and websites.

▶ Part 7, "Using Collaborative Services," focuses on setting up collaboration services together, starting with Mail, moving through Wiki, Calendar, and Messages, and finishing with the Contacts service.

Lesson Structure

Each lesson in this guide contains a reference section followed by an exercise section.

NOTE ▶ "Note" resources, like this one, offer important information to help clarify a subject. For example, to avoid confusion you should know that this first lesson is the only one in the guide without a specific exercise section.

The reference sections contain initial explanatory material that teaches essential concepts. The exercise sections augment your understanding of concepts and develop your skills through step-by-step instruction for both self-paced learners and the hands-on portions of an instructor-led course.

TIP "Tip" resources, like this one, provide helpful hints, tricks, or shortcuts. For example, each lesson begins with an opening page that lists the learning goals and necessary resources for the lesson.

MORE INFO ▶ The "More Info" resources, like this one, provide ancillary information. These resources are merely for your edification, and are not considered essential for the coursework.

Each lesson includes a list of additional resources, including relevant Apple Knowledge Base articles and recommended documents related to the topic of the lesson. Knowledge Base articles (www.apple.com/support) are free resources that contain the very latest technical information on all the Apple hardware and software products. We strongly encourage you to read the suggested documents and search the Knowledge Base for answers to any problems you encounter. You are encouraged to explore two additional resources that Apple provides specifically for OS X Server: OS X Server documentation (www.apple.com/osx/server/specs/) and OS X Server: Advanced Administration (http://help.apple.com/advancedserveradmin/mac/10.8/).

Finally, each lesson closes with a short review that recaps the lesson through a series of questions that reinforce the material you learned in the guide. Try to answer each question yourself before looking at the answer. You can refer to various Apple resources, such as the Knowledge Base, and OS X Server documentation, as well as the lessons themselves, to help you answer these questions.

Exercise Setup

This guide is written so that an Apple Authorized Training Center (AATC) attendee, a student at an educational institution, or a self-paced learner can complete most of the exercises using the same techniques. Those attending at an AATC will have the appropriate exercise setup provided as part of the training experience. On the other hand, self-paced learners attempting these exercises will have to set up an appropriate environment using their own equipment.

> **NOTE** ▶ Some of these exercises can be disruptive—for example, turning on the DHCP service may prevent devices on the local network from being able to browse Internet— and some exercises, if performed incorrectly, could result in data loss or damage to files. As such, it's recommended that you perform these exercises on an isolated network, using Mac computers that are not critical to your daily productivity. Apple, Inc., and Peachpit Press are not responsible for any data loss or any damage to any equipment that occurs as a direct or indirect result of following the procedures described in this guide.

Mandatory Requirements

Here's what you will need to complete the lessons in the book:

▶ Two Mac computers, each with OS X Mountain Lion. One Mac is referred to as your "administrator computer," and the Mac on which you will install OS X Server is referred to as your "server computer." After you are done using your server computer with this guide, you should erase and reinstall OS X on its startup volume before using it again in a production environment.

NOTE ▶ OS X Server does not require the use of Ethernet, except to provide NetInstall services; therefore, if you do not want to perform the NetInstall exercise, you can use Macs that do not have built-in Ethernet interfaces.

▶ An Apple ID that is associated with a verified email address so you can obtain Apple Push Notification service (APNs) certificates for Server app notifications and for the Profile Manager service. You can create the Apple ID at the appropriate time during an exercise if you don't already have an Apple ID.

▶ A valid licensed copy of OS X Server from the Mac App Store.

▶ An Internet connection is required for obtaining APNs certificates for alerts and for the Profile Manager service.

▶ An isolated network or subnet with an exercise-specific configuration. This can be facilitated with something as simple as a small network Wi-Fi router with multiple Ethernet ports. For example, Apple AirPort Extreme would be a good choice (www .apple.com/airportextreme/). You can find instructions for the general setup of an exercise network and specific instructions for the configuration of AirPort Extreme at www.apple.com/airportextreme/features/easy-setup.html.

▶ A router (such as AirPort Extreme) to connect the small isolated network to the Internet.

▶ To complete the NetInstall exercises, you need two Ethernet network cables; each Ethernet cable will connect a Mac to the Ethernet switch.

▶ Student Materials demonstration files, which you can download after registering your book with Peachpit. Instructions for registration and download are included in Exercise 2.1.

Optional Add-Ons

If a specific resource is required for an optional exercise, it will be listed as a prerequisite at the beginning of that exercise. For example:

▶ An iOS device to test access to OS X Server services.

▶ A Wi-Fi access point (preferably the same AirPort base station) to provide wireless access for iOS devices to your private network.

▶ For Exercise 15.2, "Create NetBoot and NetRestore Images": to make an image of your administrator computer's startup volume, your server computer and your administrator computer must both have the same kind of port: either a FireWire port, or a Thunderbolt port, and you must have the appropriate FireWire cable or Thunderbolt cable to connect the two computers.

▶   For Exercise 19.1, "Configure DHCP Service (Optional)": to provide DHCP on an extra isolated network: either an additional built-in Ethernet port on your Mac (for example, if your server computer is a Mac Pro), or a USB to Ethernet adapter, or a Thunderbolt to gigabit Ethernet adapter; and an extra Ethernet network switch.

If you lack the equipment necessary to complete a given exercise, you are still encouraged to read the step-by-step instructions and examine the screen shots to understand the procedures demonstrated.

Network Infrastructure

As was previously stated, the exercises require an isolated network. You should replicate the instructor-led classroom environment, which is described in the next sections, as closely as possible, so that you do not need to translate between the exercise instructions and your situation.

IPv4 Addresses

The instructor-led environment provides an IPv4 network with a gateway of 10.0.0.1 and subnet mask of 255.255.255.0; if possible, configure your internal network with the same parameters.

Many consumer-level routers are configured with a gateway of 192.168.1.1 and a subnet mask of 255.255.255.0. You might not be able to change this on your router; in many cases you will be able to replace the "10.0.0" portion of an IPv4 address in the exercise with a value appropriate for your isolated network (for example, 192.168.1.171 instead of 10.0.0.171 for a server address for student 17). You will need to remember to substitute your network prefix throughout the exercises.

DHCP

The classroom DHCP service provides IPv4 addresses in the range of 10.0.0.180 to 10.0.0.254; if possible, configure your internal network's DHCP service with the same parameters.

If DHCP service is available on your isolated network, your Mac computers will use DHCP during the initial setup, but you will then configure them to use static IP addresses.

If you can configure your isolated network's DHCP service, configure it to use a similar range of IPv4 addresses. If you are unable to change the range of IPv4 addresses, there is a possibility that the DHCP service will assign to a device an IPV4 address already in use by your server computer or your administrator computer. This is another reason to keep your network isolated; do not introduce new devices to it.

Domain Name

The exercises in this guide use the Internet domain pretendco.com, which is for learning environments only.

The exercises are written in a way that any existing DNS service on your isolated network will be ignored, so that you can experience your server setting up the DNS service for itself.

Advanced Administrators

If you already have advanced server administration skills, you may choose to use different settings, including your organization's Internet domain (instead of pretendco.com), your organization's DNS service, and a different IPv4 address scheme, but be warned that this introduces a high level of variability that the exercises cannot address in the given space, and be prepared to modify the exercises on your own as necessary.

Exercise Order

The exercises in this guide are designed to be relatively independent of each other, so that you can perform them out of order or skip exercises you are not interested in. However, some exercises you must perform in the correct order, and where appropriate, an exercise lists the prerequisites for that exercise.

► You must perform all the exercises in Lesson 2, "Installing OS X Server," to install OS X Server and configure your administrator computer before performing any other exercises.

► You must perform Exercise 9.1, "Configure Your Server to Manage Network Accounts," and Exercise 10.1, "Create and Import Network Accounts," to create users that you will use in later exercises; otherwise, if the prerequisites section for an exercise lists the user accounts used in the lesson, you can simply create those user accounts with the Server app's Users pane.

► You must create additional DNS records in Lesson 3, "Providing DNS," before performing the exercises in Lesson 20, "Hosting Websites."

Apple Certification

After following this guide, you may want to take the OS X Server Essentials 10.8 Exam. Passing both this exam and the OS X Support Essentials 10.8 Exam earns Apple Certified Technical Coordinator 10.8 (ACTC) certification. This is the second level of the Apple certification program for Mac professionals, which includes:

▶ Apple Certified Support Professional 10.8 (ACSP)—Ideal for help desk personnel, service technicians, technical coordinators, and others who support OS X Mountain Lion customers over the phone or who perform Mac troubleshooting and support in schools and businesses. This certification verifies an understanding of the OS X core functionality and an ability to configure key services, perform basic troubleshooting, and assist users with essential Mac capabilities. To receive this certification, you must pass the OS X Support Essentials 10.8 Exam. This guide is designed to provide you with the knowledge and skills to pass that exam.

▶ Apple Certified Technical Coordinator 10.8 (ACTC)—This certification is intended for OS X technical coordinators and entry-level system administrators tasked with maintaining a modest network of computers using OS X Server. Since the ACTC certification addresses both the support of Mac clients and the core functionality and use of OS X Server, the learning process is correspondingly longer and more intensive than that for the ACSP certi-fication, which addresses solely Mac client support. This certification requires passing both the OS X Support Essentials 10.8 Exam and the OS X Server Essentials 10.8 Exam.

> **NOTE** ▶ Although all the questions in the OS X Server Essentials 10.8 Exam are based on material in this guide, simply reading it will not adequately prepare you for the exam. Apple recommends that before taking the exam, you spend time actually setting up, configuring, and troubleshooting OS X Server on Mountain Lion systems.

Apple hardware service technician certifications are ideal for people interested in becom-ing Mac repair technicians, but also worthwhile for help desk personnel at schools and businesses, and for Mac consultants and others needing an in-depth understanding of how Apple systems operate:

▶ Apple Certified Macintosh Technician (ACMT)—This certification verifies the ability to perform basic troubleshooting and repair of both desktop and portable Mac systems, such as iMac and MacBook Pro. ACMT certification requires passing the Apple Macintosh Service Exam and the OS X Troubleshooting Exam. To learn more about hardware certification, visit http://training.apple.com/certification/acmt.

> **MORE INFO** ▶ To learn more about Apple Certification, visit http://training.apple.com/certification/osx.

Lesson **2**

Installing OS X Server

OS X Server on Mountain Lion helps your users collaborate, communicate, share information, and access the resources they need to get their work done, whether in business or education.

To keep things simple, OS X Server is an app that runs on a Mac running Mountain Lion; if your Mac can run Mountain Lion, it can run OS X Server.

You can divide working with OS X Server into four phases:

GOALS

▶ Understand the requirements for OS X Server

▶ Perform the initial installation and configuration of OS X Server

1. Planning and installation—Plan how the server will be set up, verify and configure the hardware, and install the OS X Server software; this is covered in this lesson.

2. Configuration—Use the Server app to configure your server; all the lessons in this guide use the Server app to configure your server.

3. Monitoring—Use the Server app to monitor the status of your server, and optionally to specify an email address to receive notifications of specific alerts, which is covered in Lesson 6, "Using Status and Notifications."

4. Ongoing maintenance—Use the Server app to perform ongoing server and account maintenance and monitoring.

This lesson begins with planning and continues into the initial installation and configuration of OS X Server.

Reference 2.1
Evaluating OS X Server Requirements

Before you install the software, take the time to evaluate the server needs of your organization and the OS X Server hardware requirements.

Understanding Minimum Hardware Requirements

You can install the OS X Server application on any Mac computer running OS X Mountain Lion, with at least 2 GB of RAM and 10 GB of available disk space.

In order to run Mountain Lion, your Mac must be one of the following models or newer:

- ▶ iMac (Mid 2007 or newer)
- ▶ MacBook (Late 2008 Aluminum, or Early 2009 or newer)
- ▶ MacBook Pro (Mid/Late 2007 or newer)
- ▶ MacBook Air (Late 2008 or newer)
- ▶ Mac mini (Early 2009 or newer)
- ▶ Mac Pro (Early 2008 or newer)
- ▶ Xserve (Early 2009)

Some features of OS X Server require an Apple ID, and some features require a compatible Internet service provider.

Verifying System Requirements

Before you install OS X Server, confirm that your system meets the hardware requirements. You can find this information on the label attached to the box of every Mac sold, or you can find it with the About This Mac and System Information applications.

To check if a Mac can run Mountain Lion, you can start with the About This Mac application. The next few figures are taken from a Mac running a previous version of OS X, and they walk you through the process of determining whether this Mac can run OS X Server on Mountain Lion.

In the About This Mac window, click More Info to move on to the System Information application, which contains all the information you need in a single application. The Overview pane displays your Mac system's model and memory.

The Storage pane displays information about available storage.

Additional Hardware Considerations

Typical considerations when choosing server systems include network and system performance, disk space and capacity, and RAM. You may find that using multiple servers, running a few services on each server, results in better performance than running all the services on a single server.

Network

Be sure to consider the speed of the network interface when making a server hardware decision. Many Apple products support Gigabit Ethernet; if your Mac ships with a built-in Ethernet port, that port supports Gigabit Ethernet. If your Mac is equipped with a Thunderbolt port, you can use the Apple Thunderbolt to Gigabit Ethernet adapter.

You can combine two Ethernet interfaces to act as one, to aggregate network throughput for services such as Apple file sharing.

For learning and testing scenarios only, you could consider using Wi-Fi as your server's primary network connection. This opens the possibility of using a MacBook Air, which does not have a built-in Ethernet port. In this instance, you could use Wi-Fi, the Apple USB Ethernet adapter for MacBook Air (which provides 10/100 Base-T Ethernet), or the Thunderbolt to Ethernet adapter. These options are adequate for the purposes of learning and testing.

> **NOTE ▶** Ethernet is required to provide NetInstall service. See Lesson 15, "Leveraging NetInstall," for more information.

Disk

Be sure you have enough disk space to hold the data for the services you plan to offer. If the services you plan to offer are disk intensive, for example, the Mail service with a high volume of mail, consider using a faster physical disk, or even an external disk system. Although you can change the location where your server stores the service data for many of its services, as you will learn in Lesson 4, "Exploring the Server App," it is recommended to specify a location *before* populating your server with data, because moving the service data location stops services, then moves the data, before starting services again.

RAM

In general, more RAM results in better system performance, but exactly how much RAM is ideal for your situation is impossible for this guide to prescribe.

Availability

In order to help ensure that OS X Server stays up and running, you can enable the Energy Saver system preference setting labeled "Start up automatically after a power failure" (not available on all Macs).

> **NOTE** ▶ If you use an external volume, do not enable the checkbox for "Start up automatically after a power failure," because you cannot guarantee that an external volume will be powered up correctly after a power failure.

Reference 2.2
Preparing to Install OS X Server

> **NOTE** ▶ This reference section describes the process of installing OS X Server in a general way; the exercises offer detailed step-by-step instructions, so do not perform any actions until you reach the exercises, which are at the end of this lesson.

It is possible to purchase a Mac with OS X Server preinstalled. However, you may find yourself upgrading an existing Mac with OS X Snow Leopard, Snow Leopard Server, or Lion to OS X Server (Mountain Lion). Before you purchase OS X Server on the Mac App Store, confirm that your Mac is indeed eligible to run OS X Server.

Formatting/Partitioning Drives

After you confirm that your computer meets the hardware requirements, you can simply install Mountain Lion on your existing hard disk, or you can install Mountain Lion on another disk. You can also begin making decisions surrounding the devices and subsequent formatting of those devices prior to actually installing the software.

Disk Utility is located in the Utilities folder, which is in the Applications folder. Using this utility, you can divide a hard disk into one or more partitions. Doing so allows you to first choose a partition scheme for your disk. Your choices are as follows:

▶ GUID Partition Table—Used to start up Intel-based Mac computers

▶ Apple Partition Map—Used to start up PowerPC-based Mac computers

▶ Master Boot Record—Used to start up DOS and Windows-based computers

> **NOTE** ▶ In order to install OS X Server on a volume, that volume's disk must be for-
> matted with the GUID Partition Table. You can examine a disk's partition scheme
> with the Disk Utility application, which lists this information as the Partition Map
> Scheme, and with the System Information application, which lists this information as
> Partition Map Type.

Once you choose a partition scheme, you can divide your disk into as many as 16 logical
drives, each with its own format. Each logical drive is called a partition. Once you format
a partition, it contains a volume. See *Apple Pro Training Series: OS X Support Essentials* for
further information about the available volume formats.

In order to install OS X Server on a volume, it must have one of the two following journaled formats:

▶ Mac OS X Extended (Journaled)

▶ Mac OS X Extended (Case-Sensitive/Journaled)

Unless you have a compelling reason to use Case-Sensitive/Journaled format, use Mac OS X
Extended (Journaled).

You can use the other, nonjournaled formats for data partitions, but journaling eliminates
the need for a lengthy disk check on a volume after a power outage or other failure.

By using separate partitions, you can segregate your data from the operating system. You
may decide to store user data on a separate volume. Having the operating system on its
own volume conserves space by keeping user files and data from filling up the boot volume. In case you need to perform a clean install of OS X and OS X Server at a later time,
you can erase the entire boot volume and install the operating system without touching
the data on the other volumes.

> **NOTE** ▶ OS X Server stores data for many of its services in /Library/Server on the
> boot volume by default, but as you will see later in this lesson, you can use the Server
> app to change the service data location. In any event, make sure you have a good
> backup of your server before erasing your server boot volume.

To create multiple partitions on a single hard disk, simply select your hard disk, choose the number of partitions from the Partition Layout menu, and choose the following for each partition:

▶ Name of partition—Using lowercase alphanumeric characters and removing spaces in volume names may help reduce troubleshooting of share points later down the road.

▶ Format of partition—See the previous list for various acceptable OS X Server partition formats.

▶ Size of partition—Again, OS X Server requires at least 10 GB of available disk space for installation.

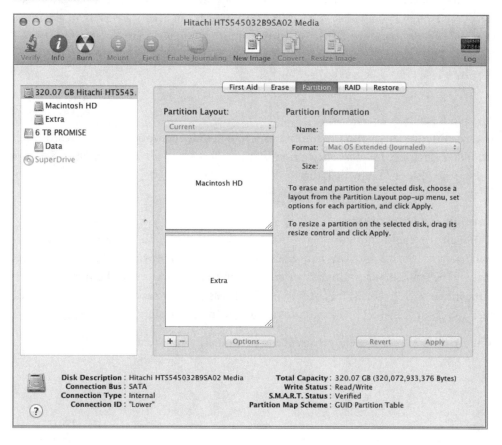

Before you click Apply, remember: *All previous data on the disk may be erased!*

Having multiple partitions does not increase speed, but installing multiple drives may increase server performance. Installing the operating system on one drive and installing additional drives to store user data can reduce connection times to the operating system and to data. If you add the second drive on a separate bus, the server can read and write to each of those buses independently.

RAID (Redundant Array of Independent Disks)

In order to provide increased availability or performance, it is possible to install OS X on a RAID volume before installing OS X Server. However, because an OS X Recovery system partition cannot exist on a RAID volume, you may want to create an external OS X Recovery system from which you can start up in order to access a variety of administration and troubleshooting utilities. For further information, you may wish to read *Apple Pro Training Series: OS X Support Essentials,* Lesson 4, "OS X Recovery," particularly Exercise 4.3, "Create a Full OS X Recovery Disk."

FileVault 2 Full Disk Encryption

Because full disk encryption requires a user to enter an encryption password after the computer starts up, full disk encryption isn't recommended for use with OS X Server for the startup disk or for any disk that stores service data.

Configuring Networking

Although you could configure networking during your initial installation and configuration using the Server app, you may want to configure the networking for the computer that will be your server computer before you run the Server app for the first time, so you can confirm DNS records. It is best to manually assign your server an IPv4 address, rather than to rely on a DHCP service to provide a dynamically assigned IPv4 address.

You use the Network system preference to set your IPv4 address.

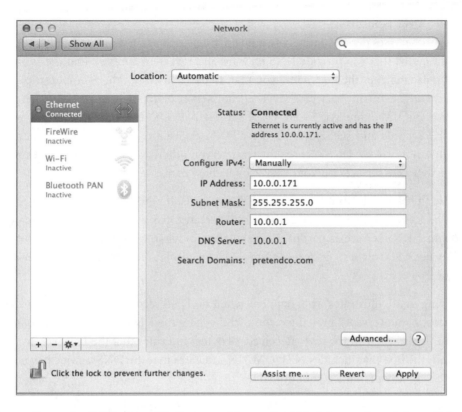

To configure the DNS server(s) that your Mac uses, click Advanced, and then click the DNS tab.

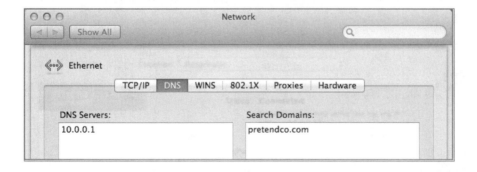

MORE INFO ► OS X automatically appends the contents of the Search Domains field to the DNS names you enter in apps like Safari.

Confirming DNS Records

Because many services depend on having a host name (such as server17.pretendco.com), it is recommended that you provide DNS forward and reverse records so that the IPv4 address you use matches the host name you plan to use. This way, other computers can use your server's host name to access services your server offers. If you don't have DNS records available at the time you install OS X Server, that's OK, because OS X Server will provide DNS records for itself. However, if the DNS service for all the devices on your network does not provide DNS records for your server, other computers and devices will not be able to access services on your server by its host name.

You can use the Network Utility to confirm DNS records. If DNS records don't exist for your IPv4 address, OS X Server will automatically create DNS records and automatically start providing DNS service as part of the installation process. However, other computers and devices will use these DNS records unless you configure them to use your server's DNS service.

The following figure illustrates what happens when no DNS records are available for the intended host name server17.pretendco.com, while using the DNS service from 10.0.0.1. The output that starts with the text "Received 40 bytes" indicates that the DNS service did respond; the line that includes NXDOMAIN indicates that the DNS service has no records at all for any pretendco.com domain.

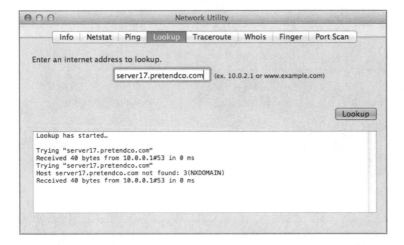

The next figure illustrates a record from the DNS service at 10.0.0.200. Note that the answer is listed directly under the line "ANSWER SECTION": server17.pretendco.com's IPv4 address is 10.0.0.171.

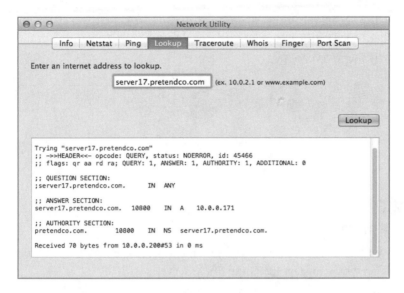

This figure illustrates a successful reverse DNS record lookup. The query for the address 10.0.0.171 results in the answer of server17.pretendco.com.

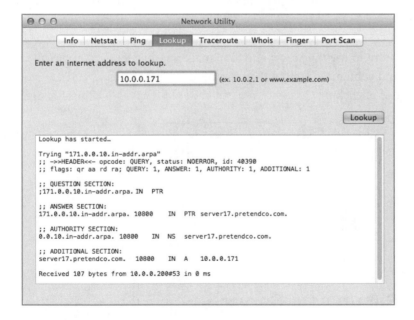

Downloading OS X Server

Download OS X Server from the Mac App Store, or if you've already downloaded it on another Mac, copy the Server app (in the Applications folder) to your Mac.

NOTE ▶ It's called OS X Server in the Mac App Store, and it's called Server in your Applications folder (once it finishes downloading from the Mac App Store), and this guide refers to it as the "Server app."

Reference 2.3
Installing OS X Server

Once you've configured OS X on your server computer, and have the Server app installed on your server computer, you can start installing OS X Server.

Open the Server app; you can click Launchpad in the Dock and click Server, or open the Server app from your Applications folder, or even open it with a Spotlight search. From the introductory window, when you click Continue, you start the process of installing and configuring OS X Server.

NOTE ▶ If you want to use the Server app to manage another server that has already been installed and configured (rather than installing and configuring OS X Server on this Mac), instead of clicking Continue you can choose Manage > Connect to Server.

License Pane

As soon as you click Continue, you have to agree to the terms of the software license agreement. You must have a valid license for each copy of OS X Server you install and configure. You can use the Server app on as many OS X computers as you like for the purpose of remotely configuring, managing, and monitoring OS X Server.

Once you click Agree, you need to provide local administrator credentials.

Multiple Networks Detected Pane

If your server is connected to more than one active network, you will see the Multiple Networks Detected pane. Choose the primary network connection from the pop-up menu, and the Server app uses that network connection to determine your server's host name.

Accessing Your Server Pane

You have three choices at the Accessing Your Server pane.

If your server never needs to be accessed by anyone outside of your local private network, you could select Local Network. Computers and devices on your local network will access your server with a host name ending in .local.

> **NOTE ▶** Do not confuse this .local with an Active Directory domain that ends in .local, a decreasingly common Active Directory configuration.

The second option, "Local Network and using VPN" might be appropriate if you install OS X Server with a private IPv4 address on a network that allows computers and devices to use a Virtual Private Network (VPN) to gain access to that network. Computers and devices will access your server with a host name ending in .private.

If you want computers and devices not on your organization's internal network to be able to access services offered by your server, select Domain Name. This is what you will use for this guide.

Connecting to Your Server Pane

This pane allows you to set your computer name and host name, and offers a shortcut to the Network system preference.

When you configure OS X Server, be sure to have an active network connection, even if it is only to a network switch that doesn't have anything else connected to it. The host name gets automatically updated if you edit the Network Address (see the following section), so you may want to click Edit to update or confirm your network settings before specifying your host name.

In the following figure, the Server app automatically provided a computer name based on your OS X computer's computer name set in the Sharing system preference (by default, the computer name is based on the initial user name you configure in OS X).

The Network Address

If you click Edit in the "Connecting to Your Server" pane, the Server app opens the Network system preference so you can modify your network setup.

Choosing a manual address for your servers is highly recommended, because dynamic addressing will reduce the number of services you can offer, and most services require a statically assigned address.

Apple servers can use multiple interfaces for network access. Examples include computers with Wi-Fi cards installed and Mac Pro computers with dual Gigabit Ethernet ports.

The Network system preference displays any interfaces it finds, so you can select whether TCP/IP should be enabled for each interface. You are prompted for detailed configuration information for each selected interface on subsequent panes.

The following figure shows how each Ethernet interface is displayed for configuration. Each interface has its own IP settings—for hosting different server services or dividing the amount of traffic supported over any one interface, including the ability to disable IPv6 and set your Ethernet interface to match the speed of your switch, should the need arise. You can also manually configure multiple interfaces or reconfigure network information later using the Network preferences.

If the DNS Server you specify in the DNS Server field of the Network preferences does not supply forward and reverse DNS records for the address you specify in the IP Address field, the Server app automatically configures and starts the DNS service on your server, and updates the DNS Server field to use its own DNS service in addition to the DNS service you specify.

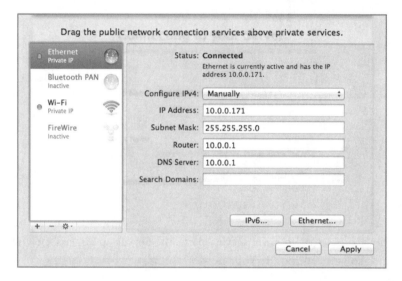

After you click Apply, the "Connecting to Your Server" pane reappears, with the Network Address updated.

Configure the Computer Name

The computer name is used by clients who use the Apple Filing Protocol (AFP) to access AFP share points and Screen Sharing services on the server. The computer name can contain spaces.

Although you do not see it in this pane, the Server app automatically generates a local hostname based on the computer name you assign. Your server uses Bonjour to advertise its services on its local subnet. The local hostname is a name that ends in .local and follows the rules for DNS names. The Server app automatically removes any special characters and replaces any space character with a dash in the local hostname.

After the server is done being configured, if your server offers file- or screen-sharing services, Mac users in the same broadcast domain (usually a subnet) will see your server's computer name in the Shared section of the Finder sidebar.

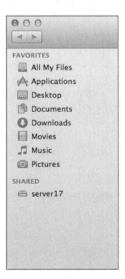

Configure the Host Name

The host name, or the primary DNS host name, is a unique name for your server, histori-cally referred to as the fully qualified domain name, or FQDN. Some services on OS X Server require a working FQDN or will work better if one is available. Computers and devices can access services on your server by using your server's DNS host name, even if they are not on the same local subnet.

The Server app automatically enters the DNS host name in the Host Name field, if there is a DNS record for your server computer's primary IPv4 address. This happens regardless of whether you manually assigned an IPv4 address, or if your server computer acquired its primary IPv4 address via DHCP.

However, if the Server app does not detect a DNS name for your server computer's pri-mary IPv4 address, it leaves the Host Name field blank. In this case, you must either quit the Server app and ensure that DNS records are provided, or you must continue and enter a host name in the Host Name field, which causes the Server app to do the following:

▶   Configure the DNS service on your server computer to provide a forward DNS record for your primary DNS name and a reverse DNS record for its primary IPv4 address.

▶   Start the DNS service.

▶   Configure your server computer's primary network interface to use 127.0.0.1 (the loopback address that always points back to the computer itself) as the primary DNS service, in addition to whatever DNS server(s) were provided before.

This ensures that your server will always be able to resolve its host name to its IPv4 address, and its IPv4 address to its host name.

Xsan Pane

If your server has a Fibre Channel card installed, you will be presented with an Xsan configuration pane. This guide does not cover configuring Xsan. Unless you understand the implications of configuring Xsan at this point, click "Do not install Xsan."

AirPort Management Pane

If your local network has an Apple AirPort device such as an AirPort Extreme or a Time Capsule, you can allow Server Admin to update that AirPort device's configuration when you enable certain services, such as Contacts or Mail. This is a powerful feature that allows the Server app to modify the Network Address Translation (NAT) port mappings so that certain services are available to the public, even if your server has a private IPv4 address.

Apple Push Notifications Pane

If you supply your Apple ID, the Server app will automatically generate APNs certificates for your server and send you an email notification that they have been successfully generated. See Lesson 6, "Using Status and Notifications" and Lesson 11, "Configuring OS X Server to Provide Device Management" for more information about APNs and the Profile Manager service.

> **NOTE** ► After you finish the initial installation and configuration of OS X Server, you can use the Server app to enter an Apple ID for Apple Push Notifications.

Congratulations Pane

After you have successfully configured OS X Server, you see the Congratulations pane. Congratulations, indeed!

Reference 2.4
Upgrading or Migrating to OS X Server

If you have an existing Lion Server or Mac OS X Server v10.6 Snow Leopard, and your computer meets the hardware requirements for OS X Server, you can *upgrade* to OS X Server on Mountain Lion. Otherwise, you can *migrate* from your old server to OS X Server on Mountain Lion on a Mac that meets the hardware requirements for OS X Server by first installing OS X Mountain Lion, and then using the Mountain Lion Setup Assistant or the Migration Assistant, and then installing OS X Server.

To upgrade to OS X Server on Mountain Lion, first you need to upgrade to Mountain Lion, and then you can install OS X Server. Remember, it is always best practice to back up any existing setup prior to running the upgrade so you can restore should anything go wrong.

Use the following steps:

1   Make sure your Mac can run Mountain Lion.

2   Make sure you have Lion Server or the latest version of Snow Leopard Server. If you have Snow Leopard Server, use Software Update to update to the latest version of Snow Leopard Server v10.6.8.

3   Download OS X Mountain Lion from the Mac App Store.

4   Open Install Mac OS X Mountain Lion to perform the upgrade to OS X Mountain Lion.

5   Download OS X Server from the Mac App Store.

6   Open Server from the Launchpad or in the Applications folder to install OS X Server.

> **NOTE ▶** Upgrading the server software should be a planned event. Always run updates on a test system before rolling out into production. In some cases, third-party solutions have not continued to operate smoothly with the new software. You should preflight the update in isolation first and roll out the update once you have tested your implementation.

> **MORE INFO ▶** See the Knowledge Base document HT5381, "OS X Server: Upgrade and Migration" for detailed instructions.

Reference 2.5
Updating OS X Server

When an update for OS X Server becomes available, you can download and install it using the Mac App Store.

You may notice that the App Store icon in the Dock displays a badge with a number indicating the number of updates available.

To install the update, open the App Store, click Updates in the toolbar, and then click Update for the OS X Server update.

If the Server app is running when you apply the update, you must quit the Server app before continuing. If you aren't already signed in to the Mac App Store, you will be prompted to do so.

With newer versions of OS X Server, even though you see a message that services have been stopped, you'll find that all your services are still running.

NOTE ► With early versions of OS X Server, if your server provides DNS service for itself, and the DNS Server field in the Network pane of System Preferences contains 127.0.0.1 only, updating OS X Server leaves the DNS Server value empty. In this case, you must enter a DNS Server value in the Network preferences in order to obtain DNS service until you open the Server app to start your server's services (including DNS service) again.

Reference 2.6
Troubleshooting

One common problem found in server installations is incompatibility with third-party hardware and software configurations. Isolate the changes to your system when you run into problems, and keep the variables to a minimum.

Inspecting Logs

Mountain Lion and OS X Server log events to various log files. You can view logs in the Console application or select Logs in the sidebar of the Server app. In the following figure, the Console app displays the contents of system.log; the user pressed Command-F to find a word, and entered a search term in the search field in the upper-right corner; the Console app highlights one instance of the string.

Throughout this guide, you will view various logs with the Console application or the Logs pane of the Server app.

Exercise 2.1
Configure OS X Before Installing OS X Server on Your Server Computer

▶ **Prerequisite**

   ▶ You must have a Mac running OS X Mountain Lion, which has never had OS X Server installed on its startup volume, and is qualified to run OS X Server.

In this exercise, you will configure your server computer in preparation for installing OS X Server on it.

You'll use one of two options to configure a local administrator account, depending on whether you are performing these exercises independently or are in an instructor-led environment with a Mac computer that already has been set up..

In both situations, you'll use System Preferences to configure Network, Sharing, Software Update, and Energy Saver settings. You will also download student materials that you'll use throughout this class. Finally, you will apply any necessary system software updates.

Establish Your Student Number

In this exercise you will use a student number to provide unique names and addresses for your computers.

1   If you are in an instructor-led environment, obtain your student number from the instructor.

    If you are performing the exercises independently, you can use any number between 1 and 17, but this guide uses student number 17 in its examples, so you might consider choosing 17 as your student number.

Configure OS X

It is most convenient to start out with fresh installation of OS X, but if you need to use an existing OS X system, you can use Option 1. Otherwise, if your Mac is at the Welcome pane when you turn it on, skip to Option 2.

Option 1: Configure an Existing OS X System for Your Server Computer

This option is designed only for those performing the exercises independently, whose computer is already set up with an existing administrator account.

> **NOTE** ▶ You may not use a Mac whose startup volume has already had OS X Server installed.

If your computer has not been set up (that is, if the initial administrator account has not been created), perform Option 2, "Configure OS X on Your Server Computer with Setup Assistant," instead.

Create a new administrator account in System Preferences.

1   If necessary, log in with your existing administrator account.

2   From the Apple menu, choose System Preferences.

3   In System Preferences, click Users & Groups.

4   In the lower-left corner, click the lock icon.

5   In the dialog that appears, enter the password for your existing administrator account and click Unlock.

6   Click the Add (+) button under the user list.

7   In the dialog that appears, enter the following information:

> **NOTE** ▶ It is important that you create this account as specified here. If you do not, future exercises may not work as written. If you already have an account named Local Admin or ladmin, you will have to use a different name here and then remember to use your substitute name throughout the rest of the exercises. Highlighted text is used throughout this guide to indicate text that you should enter exactly as shown.

> ▶ New Account: choose Administrator
> ▶ Full Name: Local Admin
> ▶ Account Name: ladmin

If your server is not accessible from the Internet, enter ladminpw in the Password and Verify fields.

If you are performing the exercises independently, you can select a more secure password for the Local Admin account. Be sure to remember the password you have chosen, as you will need to reenter it periodically as you use this computer.

You may provide a password hint if you want to.

NOTE ▶ In a production environment, you should always use a strong password.

8 Click Create User.

9 At the bottom of the user list, click Login Options.

10 If an account is selected for Automatic Login, use the pop-up menu to switch it to Off.

11 Close System Preferences and log out.

12 At the login screen, select the Local Admin account and enter its password (ladminpw, or whatever you chose earlier).

13 Press Return to log in.

14 When you are prompted to enter an Apple ID, click Skip, and then click Skip in the confirmation dialog.

15 If a Thank You pane appears, click Start Using Your Mac.

Please skip the Option 2 section, and continue at the section "Confirm Your Computer Is Qualified to Run OS X Server."

Option 2: Configure OS X on Your Server Computer with Setup Assistant

This option is necessary only if your server computer has not already been set up, which is the situation in an instructor-led environment. If you are using a Mac with existing accounts, perform Option 1, "Configure an Existing OS X System for Your Server Computer," instead.

Ensure that you have Mountain Lion installed on your server computer. If it isn't already installed, install it now using the Mac App Store, the Recovery HD, or other method specified by your instructor, and then continue when you reach the Welcome pane.

In this section, you'll step through the OS X Setup Assistant for initial system configuration of your server computer.

1   Ensure that your computer is connected to a valid network connection.

2   If necessary, turn on your Mac that will run OS X Server.

3   In the Welcome pane, select the appropriate region and click Continue.

4   Select the appropriate keyboard layout and click Continue.

The Setup Assistant will evaluate your network environment and try to determine if you are connected to the Internet. This can take a few moments.

5   If asked to Select Your Wi-Fi Network or "How Do You Connect to the Internet," this indicates that either there is no active Ethernet connection or there is no connection to the Internet.

If you are performing the exercises in an instructor-led environment, ask your instructor how you should configure your computer; it is possible that the classroom DHCP service is not enabled, or that your administrator computer is not connected to the classroom network.

If you are performing the exercises independently and you plan to use Wi-Fi as your primary network connection, select an appropriate Wi-Fi network and click Continue. Keep in mind that in order to perform the NetInstall exercises, your server needs an Ethernet connection.

6   When asked about transferring information from another Mac to this Mac, select Not Now and click Continue.

7   At the Enable Location Services pane, you can select or deselect the "Enable Location Services on this Mac" option; it will not impact the exercises. Click Continue.

8   When prompted for an Apple ID, leave both fields empty at this time and click Skip, and then click Skip to confirm that you want to skip signing in with an Apple ID. Note that if you do not click Skip, some figures may look slightly different, and there may be extra steps.

9   In the Terms and Conditions pane, you may click the right-arrow button next to the OS X Software License Agreement to read it. When you have finished reading, click Continue.

10 In the dialog that appears, click Agree.

Create your local administrator account.

> **NOTE** ▶ It is important that you create this account as specified here. If you do not, future exercises may not work as written. Highlighted text is used throughout this guide to indicate text that you should enter exactly as shown.

11 In the Create Your Computer Account pane, enter the following information:

  ▶ Full Name: **Local Admin**

  ▶ Account Name: **ladmin**

  ▶ Password: **ladminpw**

  ▶ Verify: **ladminpw**

  ▶ Require password when logging in: Leave this option selected.

  ▶ Password Hint: Leave blank.

If you are performing the exercises independently, and if your server is accessible from the Internet, you can select a more secure password for the Local Admin account. Be sure to remember the password you have chosen, as you will need to reenter it periodically as you use this computer.

If you are performing the exercises independently, you may provide a password hint if you want to.

> **NOTE** ▶ In a production environment, you should always use a strong password.

12 Click Continue.

13 If an exclamation point appears because you did not include a Password Hint, click Continue.

Finish up the initial configuration.

14 In the Select Time Zone pane, click your time zone in the map, or choose the nearest location in the Closest City pop-up menu, and then click Continue.

15 If you see the Register pane, click Skip; you won't be entering registration information at this time.

16 When asked if you are sure you don't want to register, click Skip.

17 If you are presented with a Finishing Up pane with information about using multi-touch scrolling, follow the instructions to complete the introduction.

18 If you are presented with the Thank You pane, click Start Using Your Mac.

19 If you are prompted to install software updates, click Not Now.

This is the end of Option 2; everyone should continue with the next section.

Confirm Your Computer Is Qualified to Run OS X Server

Before you go to the trouble of installing OS X Server, make sure your computer meets the technical requirements to run OS X Server. The first requirement is a Mac computer running Mountain Lion. The next two requirements are 2 GB of memory and 10 GB of available disk space.

1 From the Apple menu, choose About This Mac.

2 Confirm that you have at least 2 GB of memory.

3   If your Mac computer has more than one volume, About This Mac displays the name of your startup disk. Make a note of the name of your startup disk.

4   Click More Info.

5   Click the Storage tab.

6   For your Startup Disk, confirm that you have at least 10 GB free disk space.

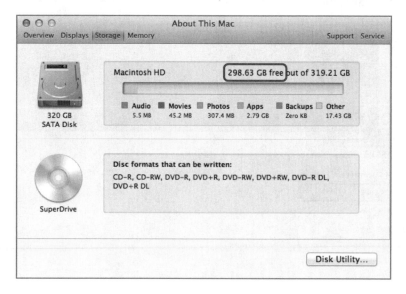

7   If your Mac computer has only one volume, make a note of its name—it is the name of your startup volume.

8   Press Command-Q to quit System Information.

Optional: Change Your Startup Volume Name

In the last section, you made a note of your startup volume name. Before you install OS X Server, confirm that your server computer's startup volume is what you would like it to be. You can change that name now, because you should avoid changing your startup volume name after you install OS X Server. If you need to change your server computer's startup volume name after you install OS X Server, you should reboot your server after making the change.

1   In the Finder, choose Go > Computer.

The Finder window displays the volumes.

2   Select your startup volume.

3   Press Return to edit the name.

4   Enter a name for the startup volume.

5   Press Return to save the name change.

6   Press Command-W to close the Finder window

Set the Computer Name and Turn On Remote Management

In an environment with more than one student, because every student has entered the same account name information, and because OS X uses the account name and computer model name as the basis for the initial computer name and local host name, all student computers may have the same computer name. To distinguish your computer on the network, you need to set a unique computer name. Additionally, OS X won't allow duplicate local host names on the same subnet, so you may see an alert message indicating that your local host name has been incremented from Local-Admins-*computer model*.local to Local-Admins-*computer model-n*.local, where *n* is a semirandom number (not your student number).

You will specify a computer name associated with your student number.

You will also enable Remote Management so the instructor can assist you if necessary by enabling him to observe your computer, control your keyboard and mouse, gather information, copy items to your computer, and otherwise help you if necessary.

NOTE ▶ Even though you know administrator credentials for other students' computers, and have the technical ability to remotely control their computers, please do not use that ability to interfere with their classroom experience.

1   In your Dock, open System Preferences.

2   Open Sharing.

3   Set the Computer Name to servern, replacing *n* with your student number.

     For example, if your student number is 17, the computer name should be server17, all lowercase and no spaces.

4   Press Return.

     Notice that the name listed under the Computer Name field, which is the local host name, updates to match your new computer name.

Enable your instructor (and yourself) to remotely manage your server computer from another Mac computer using Apple Remote Desktop or Screen Sharing.

5   Select the Remote Management checkbox.

6   In the dialog that appears, leave all the checkboxes deselected and click OK for now, as this controls access for all local users, and you will configure access for one user only next.

     You want to allow only certain users.

7   In "Allow Access for," select "Only these users."

8   Click the Add (+) button, select Local Admin, and click Select.

9   In the dialog that appears, hold down the Option key while selecting the Observe checkbox, which results in automatically selecting all the checkboxes, as shown in the following figure.

10 Click OK.

11 Click Show All to return to the main System Preferences pane.

Set Energy Saver Preferences

Prevent your server computer from going to sleep while you use it for the exercises. You can set the display sleep to whatever setting you prefer.

1 In System Preferences, open Energy Saver.

2 If you have a portable computer, you have two tabs: Battery and Power Adapter. Click Power Adapter to configure the settings while using the power adapter.

3 Set the computer to never sleep by dragging the "Computer sleep" slider to the far right.

   This prevents the computer from going to sleep while installing software updates.

4 When the "Your computer may use more energy with these settings" message appears, click OK.

5 Drag the "Display sleep" slider to a value of your choice. You can leave the other settings at their defaults.

6 Click Show All to return to the main System Preferences pane.

Configure Software Update

If you are performing the exercises in an instructor-led environment, you should disable Software Update from automatically checking for updates, so that you do not unnecessarily use bandwidth.

1 In System Preferences, click Software Update.

2 Deselect the checkbox "Automatically check for updates."

3 Click Show All to return to the main System Preferences pane.

Configure Network

Although you can configure your network interfaces during your initial installation and configuration of OS X Server, you will configure them now so you can check DNS records.

> **NOTE ▶** The exercises are written for only one network interface to be active, but if you decide to use multiple network interfaces, this will not significantly impact your ability to complete the exercises.

1 In System Preferences, click Network.

2 In the instructor-led environment, configure your Mac computer's built-in Ethernet port to be the only active network service.

If you are performing the exercises independently, you may leave additional interfaces active, but be aware that this may cause differences between the way the exercises describe the windows and what you actually see.

In the list of network interfaces, select each network interface you will not use in the exercise, which should be all interfaces except one built-in Ethernet port, click the Action (gear icon) pop-up menu, and choose Make Service Inactive.

3 If you will use multiple network interfaces, click the Action (gear icon) pop-up menu, choose Set Service Order, drag services to an appropriate order so that your primary interface is at the top of the list, and click OK.

4 In the instructor-led environment, enter the following information to manually configure the Ethernet interface (IPv4) for the classroom environment:

   ▶ IP Address: **10.0.0.**n**1** (where n is your student number; for example, student1 uses 10.0.0.11, student 6 uses 10.0.0.61, and student 15 uses 10.0.0.151.)

▶ Subnet Mask: **255.255.255.0**

▶ Router: **10.0.0.1**

If you are performing the exercises independently and choose to use different network settings, see the "Exercise Setup" section in Lesson 1.

5 Click Advanced, and then click the DNS tab.

6 In the instructor-led environment, under the DNS Servers field, click Add (+) and enter **10.0.0.1**.

If you are performing the exercises independently, under the DNS Servers field, click Add (+) and enter the value or values appropriate for your environment.

7 Under the Search Domains field, click Add (+) and enter **pretendco.com**.

If you are performing the exercises independently, enter a value appropriate for your environment.

8 Click OK to close the Advanced sheet.

9 Review the settings, and then click Apply to accept the network configuration.

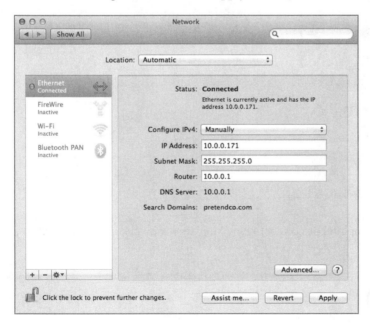

10 Quit System Preferences.

Option 1: Download Student Materials and Apply Software Updates in the Instructor-Led Environment

If you are performing the exercises independently, skip to "Option 2: Download Student Materials and Apply Software Updates for the Independent Reader."

If you are in an instructor-led environment, you will connect to the classroom server and download the student materials used for the course. To copy the files, you'll drag the folder to your Documents folder.

1 In the Finder, choose File > New Finder Window (or press Command-N).

2 In the Finder window sidebar, click Mainserver.

If Mainserver does not appear in the Finder sidebar, in the Shared list click All, and then double-click the Mainserver icon in the Finder window.

Because Mainserver allows guest access via Apple Filing Protocol (AFP), your administrator computer logs in automatically as Guest and displays the available share points.

3 Open the Public folder.

4 Drag the StudentMaterials folder to the Documents folder in the Finder window sidebar.

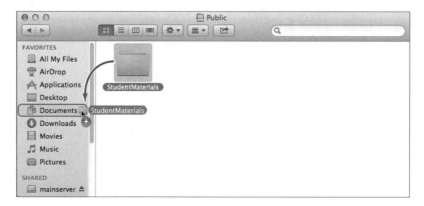

5 Once the copy is complete, disconnect from Mainserver by clicking Eject next to the Mainserver listing.

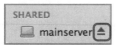

6 In the Finder window sidebar, click the Documents folder and open the StudentMaterials folder.

7 If there is a Software Updates folder inside the StudentMaterials folder, open it and install any OS X updates it contains. To install a software update, double-click the disk image file to open it, and then run the installer that appears on the screen. Restart if necessary.

In this exercise you configured your server computer in preparation for installing OS X Server. You have completed this exercise; skip the Option 2 section that follows.

Option 2: Download Student Materials and Apply Software Updates for the Independent Reader
If you are in the instructor-led environment, skip this section.

If you are performing the exercises independently, download the materials from Peachpit's site, place them in your Documents folder, and then run Software Update.

1 Go to this guide's webpage at www.peachpit.com/apts.osxservermountainlion.

2 Click the "Register your product" link.

3 Enter this guide's13-digit ISBN and click Submit.

The Registered Products page of your account appears.

4 Click the Access Bonus Content link to access the course material.

5 Download the course material, which places the material in your Downloads folder.

6 In the Finder, choose File > New Finder Window (or press Command-N).

7 Choose Go > Home.

8 Open your Downloads Folder.

9 Drag the StudentMaterials folder from your Downloads folder to the Documents folder in the Finder window sidebar.

10 Choose Software Update from the Apple menu, and install any OS X software updates.

In this exercise you configured OS X on your server computer in preparation for installing OS X Server.

Exercise 2.2
Perform the Initial Installation of OS X Server on Your Server Computer

> **Prerequisite**
>
> ▸ Exercise 2.1, "Configure OS X Before Installing OS X Server on Your Server Computer"

Now that you have OS X configured on your server computer, it's time to install OS X Server on it and configure it so you can administer it remotely.

There are two ways to obtain the Server app:

▸ Download OS X Server from the Mac App Store.

▸ Copy the Server app from another Mac.

As part of the license agreement when you purchase OS X Server, you can install the Server app on as many administrator computers as you like, and use it to administer other OS X Servers, but you must purchase a copy of OS X Server for each Mac computer you configure to run OS X Server.

> **TIP ▸** You must use the same Apple ID used for the original purchase in order to avoid being charged again.

If you are performing the exercises independently, purchase and download OS X Server from the Mac App Store, which automatically places the Server app in your Applications folder. If you have already purchased the Server app and have it available on a removable volume, drag the Server app from your removable volume into your Applications folder.

In the instructor-led environment, the classroom server has the Server app available in the StudentMaterials folder; move the Server app to the Applications folder on your server computer with the following steps:

1 In the Finder on your server computer, open a new Finder window, click Documents in the Finder window sidebar, open the StudentMaterials folder you downloaded, and then open the Lesson2 folder.

2   Drag the Server app into the Applications folder in the Finder window sidebar.

Once you have the Server app installed in the Applications folder, open the Server app.

1   In your Dock, click Launchpad.

2   You may need to swipe to the next page in Launchpad to see the Server app (hold down the Command key and press the Right Arrow key, or if you have a trackpad, swipe to the left with two fingers to get to the next page in Launchpad).

3   Click Server to open the Server app.

4   At the "Set up your Server" pane, click Continue.

5   At the license agreement pane, click Agree.

6   Provide local administrator credentials and click Allow.

7   If you see the Multiple Networks Detected pane, choose the appropriate network service and click Continue. This should be the network service that has the IPv4 address for which DNS records are configured; if no DNS records are available for this IPv4 address, the Server Assistant creates DNS forward and reverse records for this IPv4 address.

8   In the Accessing Your Server pane, select Domain Name and click Continue.

9   If necessary, set the Computer Name to **servern**, where *n* is your student number.

10   Next to the Network Address field, click Edit.

11 Confirm your network interfaces are configured as you want them configured.

The settings should be as follows:

▶ IP Address: **10.0.0.n1** (where *n* is your student number)

▶ Subnet Mask: **255.255.255.0**

▶ Router: **10.0.0.1**

▶ DNS Server: **10.0.0.1**

▶ Search Domains: **pretendco.com**

12 Click Apply to accept the network configuration.

Enter an appropriate value in the Host Name field in the "Connecting to Your Server" pane.

13 In the Host Name field, enter **servern.pretendco.com** (where *n* is your student number).

14 Click Continue to accept the names and network address.

15 If your server has a Fibre Channel card installed, an Xsan configuration pane appears. Click "Do not install Xsan."

16 If your isolated network has an AirPort wireless device, you will see the AirPort Management pane. The ability to use the Server app to manage an AirPort device is a great feature, but it is not practical for each student's server to manage the AirPort in a classroom setting. Therefore, deselect the checkbox labeled "Use Server to manage this AirPort wireless device," and then click Continue.

If you are not in an instructor-led environment, you may select the checkbox labeled "Use Server to manage this AirPort wireless device." Be aware that when you turn on various services, the Server app will ask if you want to allow access to that service from the Internet, and you can reply to the question as you wish at that time.

17 In the Apple Push Notifications pane, leave the fields blank for now and click Continue.

You will configure an Apple ID for Apple Push Notifications in the Server app in Lesson 12, "Managing with Profile Manager."

18 In the Congratulations pane, click Finish.

Finally, configure your server so that you can administer it with the Server app on your administrator computer. After you click Finish in step 18, the Server app window automatically opens.

1   In the Server app window, click the Settings tab.

2   If necessary, select the checkbox "Allow remote administration using Server."

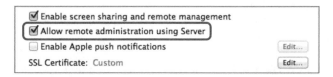

3   Because you're going to open the Server app on your administrator computer next, press Command-Q to quit the Server app.

It's recommended that you administer your server with only one instance of the Server app at a time; if you have the Server app open while logged in on your server, quit the Server app before opening the Server app on your administrator computer.

In this exercise you used the Server app to configure your server with OS X Server, and you enabled remote administration using the Server app, which leads nicely to the next exercise, which is to configure your administrator computer.

Exercise 2.3
Configure Your Administrator Computer

▶ **Prerequisites**

- ▶ Exercise 2.1, "Configure OS X Before Installing OS X Server on Your Server Computer"

- ▶ Exercise 2.2, "Perform the Initial Installation of OS X Server on Your Server Computer"

- ▶ You must have a Mac running OS X Mountain Lion, which has never had OS X Server installed on its startup volume.

Your "administrator computer" is a Mac on which you will open the Server app and use it to administer your computer running OS X Server. Remember that your administrator computer must be running OS X Mountain Lion in order to administer OS X Server (Mountain Lion).

In this exercise, you will configure your administrator computer in preparation for using it to administer your server and to remotely access services from your server.

This exercise is very similar to Exercise 2.1, but you will configure your administrator computer to use:

- ▶ A different computer name
- ▶ A different primary IPv4 address
- ▶ Your server's DNS service

You'll use one of two options to configure a local administrator account, depending on whether you are performing these exercises independently or are in an instructor-led environment.

In both situations, you'll use System Preferences to configure Network, Sharing, and Energy Saver settings. You will also download student materials that you'll use throughout this class. Finally, you will apply any necessary system software updates, and then use the Server app to confirm that you can use it to connect to your server.

Option 1: Configure an Existing OS X System for Your Administrator Computer

This option is designed only for those performing the exercises independently, whose computer is already set up with an existing administrator account.

> **NOTE ▸** You may not use a Mac whose startup volume has already had OS X Server installed.

If your computer has not been set up (that is, if the initial administrator account has not been created), perform Option 2, "Configure OS X on Your Administrator Computer with Setup Assistant," instead.

Create a new administrator account in System Preferences.

1 If necessary, log in with your existing administrator account.

2 From the Apple menu, choose System Preferences.

3 In System Preferences, click Users & Groups.

4 In the lower-left corner, click the lock icon.

5 In the dialog that appears, enter the password for your existing administrator account and click Unlock.

6 Click the Add (+) button under the user list.

7 In the dialog that appears, enter the following information:

> **NOTE ▸** It is important that you create this account as specified here. If you do not, future exercises may not work as written. If you already have an account named Local Admin or ladmin, you will have to use a different name here and then remember to use your substitute name throughout the rest of the exercises. Highlighted text is used throughout this guide to indicate text that you should enter exactly as shown.

▶ New Account: choose Administrator

▶ Full Name: Local Admin

▶ Account Name: ladmin

If you are performing the exercises in an instructor-led environment, enter **ladminpw** in the Password and Verify fields.

If you are performing the exercises independently, you can select a more secure password for the Local Admin account. Be sure to remember the password you have chosen, as you will need to reenter it periodically as you use this computer.

You may provide a password hint if you want to.

NOTE ▶ In a production environment, you should always use a strong password.

8   Click Create User.

9   At the bottom of the user list, click Login Options.

10   If an account is selected for Automatic Login, use the pop-up menu to switch it to Off.

11   Close System Preferences and log out.

12   At the login screen, select the Local Admin account and enter its password (**ladminpw**, or whatever you chose earlier).

13   Press Return to log in.

14   When you are prompted to enter an Apple ID, click Skip, and then click Skip in the confirmation dialog.

15   If a Thank You pane appears, click Start Using Your Mac.

Please skip the Option 2 section, and continue at the section "Set the Computer Name and Turn On Remote Management."

Option 2: Configure OS X on Your Administrator Computer with Setup Assistant

This option is only necessary if your administrator computer has not already been set up, which is the situation in an instructor-led environment. If you are using a Mac with existing accounts, perform Option 1, "Configure an Existing OS X System for Your Administrator Computer," instead.

Ensure that you have Mountain Lion installed on your administrator computer. If it isn't already installed, install it now using the Mac App Store, the Recovery HD, or other method specified by your instructor, and then continue when you reach the Welcome pane.

In this section, you'll step through the OS X Setup Assistant for initial system configuration of your administrator computer.

1   Ensure that your administrator computer is connected to a valid network connection.

2   If necessary, turn on your administrator computer.

3   In the Welcome pane, select the appropriate region and click Continue.

4   Select the appropriate keyboard layout and click Continue.

    The Setup Assistant will evaluate your network environment and try to determine if you are connected to the Internet. This can take a few moments.

5   If asked to Select Your Wi-Fi Network or "How Do You Connect to the Internet," this indicates that you don't have an active Ethernet connection or you don't have a connection to the Internet

    If you are performing the exercises in an instructor-led environment, ask your instructor how you should configure your computer; it is possible that the classroom DHCP service is not enabled, or that your administrator computer is not connected to the classroom network.

    If you are performing the exercises independently and you plan to use Wi-Fi as your primary network connection, select an appropriate Wi-Fi network and click Continue. Keep in mind that in order to perform the NetInstall exercises, your server needs an Ethernet connection.

6   When asked about transferring information from another Mac to this Mac, select Not Now and click Continue.

7   At the Enable Location Services pane, you can select or deselect "Enable Location Services on this Mac" option; it will not impact the exercises. Click Continue.

8   When prompted for an Apple ID, leave both fields empty at this time and click Skip, and then click Skip to confirm that you want to skip signing in with an Apple ID.

9   In the Terms and Conditions pane, you may click the right-arrow button next to the OS X Software License Agreement to read it. When you have finished reading, click Continue.

10 In the dialog that appears, click Agree.

Create your local administrator account.

> **NOTE** ▶ It is important that you create this account as specified here. If you do not, future exercises may not work as written. Highlighted text is used throughout this guide to indicate text that you should enter exactly as shown.

11 In the Create Your Computer Account pane, enter the following information:

  ▶ Full Name: **Local Admin**

  ▶ Account Name: **ladmin**

  ▶ Password: **ladminpw**

  ▶ Verify: **ladminpw**

  ▶ Require password when logging in: Leave this option selected.

  ▶ Password Hint: Leave blank.

  If you entered your Apple ID, you can select or deselect the checkbox "Allow my Apple ID to reset this user's password," it does not have a major effect on the exercises.

12 Click Continue.

13 If an exclamation point appears because you did not include a password hint, click Continue.

Finish up the initial configuration.

14 In the Select Time Zone pane, click your time zone in the map, or choose the nearest location in the Closest City pop-up menu, and then click Continue.

15 If you see the Register pane, click Skip; you won't be entering registration information at this time.

16 When asked if you are sure you don't want to register, click Skip.

17 If you are presented with a Finishing Up pane with information about using multi-touch scrolling, follow the instructions to complete the introduction.

18 If you are presented with the Thank You pane, click Start Using Your Mac.

19 If you are prompted to install software updates, click Not Now.

This is the end of Option 2; everyone should continue with the next section.

Set the Computer Name and Turn On Remote Management

You will specify a computer name associated with your student number. If you are per-forming the exercises independently, you can choose to skip this section.

You will also enable Remote Management so the instructor can assist you if necessary by enabling him to observe your computer, control your keyboard and mouse, gather infor-mation, copy items to your computer, and otherwise help you if necessary.

1   In your Dock, open System Preferences.

2   Open Sharing.

3   Set the Computer Name to client*n*, replacing *n* with your student number.

For example, if your student number is 17, the computer name should be server17, all lowercase and no spaces.

4   Press Return.

Notice that the name listed under the Computer Name field, which is the local host name, updates to match your new computer name.

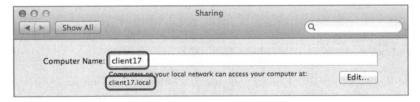

Enable you and your instructor to remotely manage your administrator computer; this also allows you to use Screen Sharing from another Mac.

5   Select the Remote Management checkbox.

6   In the dialog that appears, leave all the checkboxes deselected and click OK for now, as this controls access for all local users, and you will configure access for one user only next.

You want to allow only certain users.

7   In "Allow Access for," select "Only these users."

8   Click the Add (+) button, select Local Admin, and click Select.

9   In the dialog that appears, hold down the Option key while selecting the Observe checkbox, which results in automatically selecting all the checkboxes.

10   Click OK.

11   Click Show All to return to the main System Preferences pane.

Set Energy Saver Preferences

Prevent your administrator computer from going to sleep while you use it for the exercises. You can set the display sleep to whatever setting you prefer.

If you are performing the exercises independently, you can choose to skip this section.

1   In System Preferences, open Energy Saver.

2   If you have a portable computer, you have two tabs: Battery and Power Adapter. Click Power Adapter to configure the settings while using the power adapter.

3   Set the computer to never sleep by dragging the "Computer sleep" slider to the far right.

This prevents the computer from going to sleep while installing software updates.

4   When the "Your computer may use more energy with these settings" message appears, click OK.

5   Drag the "Display sleep" slider to a value of your choice. You can leave the other settings at their defaults.

6   Click Show All to return to the main System Preferences pane.

Configure Software Update

If you are performing the exercises in an instructor-led environment, you should disable Software Update from automatically checking for updates, so that you do not unnecessarily use bandwidth.

1   Open Software Update.

2 Deselect the "Automatically check for updates" option.

3 Click Show All to return to the main System Preferences pane.

Configure Network

Configure your administrator computer to use your server's DNS service.

> **NOTE ▶** The exercises are written for only one network interface to be active, but if you decide to use multiple network interfaces, this will not significantly impact your ability to complete the exercises.

1 In System Preferences, click Network.

2 In the instructor-led environment, configure your Mac computer's built-in Ethernet port to be the only active network service.

In the list of network interfaces, select each network interface you will not use in the exercise (which should be each interface except for one Ethernet interface), click the Action (gear icon) pop-up menu, and choose Make Service Inactive.

If you are performing the exercises independently, you may leave additional interfaces active, but be aware that this may cause differences between the way the exercises describe the windows, and what you actually see.

3 If you will use multiple network interfaces, click the Action (gear icon) pop-up menu, choose Set Service Order, drag services to an appropriate order so that your primary interface is at the top of the list, and click OK.

4 Enter the following information to manually configure the Ethernet interface (IPv4) for the classroom environment:

   ▶ IP Address: 10.0.0.n2 (where n is your student number; for example, student1 uses 10.0.0.12, student 6 uses 10.0.0.62, and student 15 uses 10.0.0.152.)

   ▶ Subnet Mask: 255.255.255.0

   ▶ Router: 10.0.0.1

If you are performing the exercises independently and choose to use different settings, see the "Network Infrastructure" section in Lesson 1, and be prepared to substitute network values that are appropriate for your environment throughout all the exercises in this guide.

5   Click Advanced, and then click the DNS tab.

6   Under the DNS Servers field, click Add (+) and enter the IPv4 address of your server computer (10.0.0.*n*1, where *n* is your student number; for example, student1 uses 10.0.0.11, student 6 uses 10.0.0.61, and student 15 uses 10.0.0.151.).

7   Under the Search Domains field, click Add (+) and enter pretendco.com.

8   Click OK to close this pane.

9   Click Apply to accept the network configuration.

10   Click Apply to save the changes.

11   Quit System Preferences.

Confirm DNS Records

Use Network Utility to confirm that your administrator computer can access your server's DNS service.

1   In your Dock, click Launchpad.

2   Click the Folder named Other.

3   Open Network Utility.

4   Click the Lookup tab.

5   Enter your server's primary IPv4 address in the field (10.0.0.*n*1, where *n* is your student number) and click Lookup.

6   Confirm that your server's host name appears in the results field.

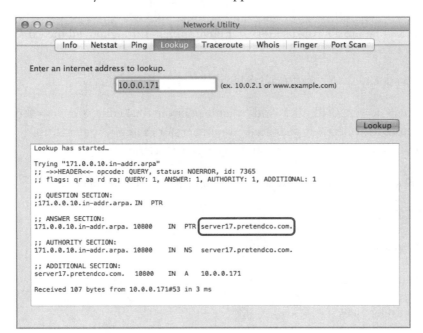

7   Enter your server's host name in the field and click Lookup.

8   Confirm that your server's primary IPv4 address appears in the results field.

9   Press Command-Q to quit Network Utility.

Option 1: Download Student Materials and Apply Software Updates in the Instructor-Led Environment

If you are in an instructor-led environment, you will connect to the classroom server and download the student materials used for the course. To copy the files, you'll drag the folder to your Documents folder.

If you are performing the exercises independently, skip to the next section, "Install the Server App."

1   In the Finder, choose File > New Finder Window (or press Command-N).

2   In the Finder window sidebar, click Mainserver.

If Mainserver does not appear in the Finder sidebar, in the Shared list click All, and then double-click the Mainserver icon in the Finder window.

Because Mainserver allows guest access via Apple Filing Protocol (AFP), your administrator computer logs in automatically as Guest and displays the available share points.

3   Open the Public folder.

4   Drag the StudentMaterials folder to the Documents folder in the Finder window sidebar.

5   Once the copy is complete, disconnect from Mainserver by clicking Eject next to the listing for Mainserver.

6   In the Finder window sidebar, click the Documents folder and open the StudentMaterials folder.

7   If there is a Software Updates folder inside the StudentMaterials folder, open it and install any updates it contains. To install a software update, double-click the disk image file to open it, and then run the installer that appears on the screen. Restart if necessary.

Skip Option 2 which follows, and resume with the section "Install the Server App."

Option 2: Download Student Materials and Apply Software Updates for the Independent Reader

If you are performing the exercises independently, copy the Student Materials from your server, or download the materials from Peachpit's site, and place them in your Documents folder, then run Software Update.

If you have a USB, FireWire, or Thunderbolt disk, you can connect it to your server, copy the StudentMaterials folder from your local administrator's Documents folder to the volume, eject the volume, connect the volume to your administrator computer, and drag the StudentMaterials folder to your Documents folder in the Finder window sidebar.

Alternatively, you can download the files from Peachpit again using the following steps:

1   Go to this guide's webpage at www.peachpit.com/apts.osxservermountainlion.

2   Click the "Register your product" link.

3   Enter this guide's 13-digit ISBN and click Submit.

The Registered Products page of your account appears.

4 Click the Access Bonus Content link to access the course material.

5 Download the course material, which places the material in your Downloads folder.

6 In the Finder, choose File > New Finder Window (or press Command-N).

7 Choose Go > Home.

8 Open your Downloads Folder.

9 Drag the StudentMaterials folder from your Downloads folder to the Documents folder in the Finder window sidebar.

10 Choose Software Update from the Apple menu, and install any OS X software updates.

Everyone should continue with the next section, "Install the Server App."

Install the Server App

On your server computer you ran the Server app to configure your server computer as a server. However, on your administrator computer, you will run the Server app to remotely administer your server.

If you are performing the exercises independently, you should have already purchased OS X Server by the time you have completed Exercise 2.2; if this is the case, open the Mac App Store from your Dock or from the Apple menu, log in with the Apple ID you used to purchase OS X Server, and download OS X Server, which automatically places the Server app in your Applications folder. If you have already purchased the Server app and have it available on a removable volume, drag the Server app from your removable volume into your Applications folder.

In the instructor-led environment, the classroom server has the Server app available in the StudentMaterials folder; move the Server app to the Applications folder on your server computer with the following steps:

1 In the Finder on your server computer, open a new Finder window, click Documents in the Finder window sidebar, open the StudentMaterials folder that you downloaded, then open the Lesson2 folder.

2   Drag the Server app into the Applications folder in the Finder window sidebar.

Use the Server App to Administer Your Server

Using your administrator computer, open the Server app, connect to your server and accept its SSL certificate.

1   On your administrator computer, open the Server app.

2   Choose Manage > Connect to Server.

3   In the "Choose a Mac" window, select your server and click Continue.

4   Select the "Remember this password in my keychain" checkbox so the credentials you provide will be saved in your keychain (a secure store of passwords) so you do not need to provide credentials again.

5   Provide the administrator credentials (Administrator Name ladmin and Administrator Password ladminpw).

6   Click Connect.

7   Because your server is using a self-signed SSL (Secure Sockets Layer) certificate that has not been signed by a Certificate Authority (CA) that your administrator computer is configured to trust, you'll see a warning message that you are connecting to a server whose identity certificate is not verified. See Lesson 5, "Configuring SSL," for more information on SSL.

   NOTE ▶ In a production environment, you might want to address this situation as soon as possible by using Keychain Access on your server computer to configure your server to use a valid SSL certificate for the com.apple.servermgrd identity, which is used to communicate with a remote instance of the Server app. This is outside the scope of this guide.

8   Click Show Certificate.

9   Select the checkbox to always trust com.apple.servermgrd when connecting to your server.

10 Click Continue.

11 You must provide your login credentials in order to modify your keychain.

Enter your password (**ladminpw**) and click Update Settings.

After you click Update Settings, the Server app connects to your server.

In this exercise you prepared your administrator computer to remotely administer your server and to access services from your server.

Additional Resources

The following documents provide more information about installing OS X Server.

Many other documents are available at www.apple.com/osx/server/specs/.

OS X Server Administration Guides

OS X Server: Advanced Administration http://help.apple.com/advancedserveradmin/mac/10.8/

Apple Knowledge Base Documents

You can check for new and updated Knowledge Base documents at www.apple.com/
support/.

Document HT1310, "Startup Manager: How to select a startup volume"

Document HT1782, "Using Disk Utility to verify or repair disks"

Document HT4718, "OS X: About OS X Recovery"

Document HT4886, "Mac mini Server (Mid 2011): How to install OS X Server on a software RAID volume"

Document HT5300, "OS X Server: Steps to take before upgrading or migrating the Open
Directory database"

Document HT5381, "OS X Server: Upgrade and migration"

Document HT5382, "OS X Server: Upgrading Websites service from previous versions"

Document HT5387, "OS X Server: Share points are not preserved when migrating from
Lion Server"

Document HT5412, "OS X Server: About the DHCP Service"

Document HT5413, "OS X Server: About the Firewall service"

Document HT5414, "OS X Server: About the NAT Service"

Document TS4331, "OS X Server: Where to find Podcast data after upgrading"

Document TS4353, "OS X Server: Cannot administer AirPort base station after upgrading
to Mountain Lion"

Lesson Review

1. What are the minimum RAM and hard drive requirements for installing OS X Server?

2. What tool do you use to perform an installation and initial configuration of OS X
   Server?

3. If you are installing OS X Server on a Mac, what's one configuration step you should
   take before installing?

4.   What are two kinds of names associated with your server, and what are they used for?

5.   How can you install the Server app on an administrator computer?

Answers

1.   The minimum RAM and hard disk requirements for OS X Server are:

     2 GB of RAM (more for high-demand servers running multiple services)

     10 GB of available disk space

2.   You use the Server app to perform an installation and initial configuration of OS X Server.

3.   Configure your Mac with OS X to use a manually assigned IPv4 address.

4.   You can use the Server app to configure these two names:

     Computer name—This is what appears in the Finder sidebar for other Macs if your server offers file sharing services.

     Host name—Computers and devices can access services offered by your server by using your server's DNS host name, even if they are not on its local network, as long as the host name corresponds with an IPv4 address that is reachable and not blocked by firewalls.

5.   You can use the Mac App Store to download OS X Server, or just copy the Server app to your Applications folder.

Lesson 3
Providing DNS

The Domain Name System (DNS) is a critical service. It is so critical in fact that OS X Server will set up its own DNS service if one is not provided for it. Without proper working DNS, many problems can occur and as a result, it is important to understand what DNS is and how to manage it for OS X and other computers.

Although there are many aspects of DNS, this lesson concentrates on what is needed to make OS X work properly.

GOALS

► Using OS X Server as a DNS server

► Understand the how and why of DNS

Reference 3.1
What Is DNS?

In its most basic form, DNS is the system that helps identify computers, servers and other devices on a network via an IPv4 number or name. For example:

server17.pretendco.com = 10.0.0.171

10.0.0.171 = server17.pretendco.com

UNIX operating systems such as OS X rely on DNS to keep track of resources on the network, including themselves. They are constantly doing "lookups" or finding out about the IP addresses and hostnames they need to contact, including their own information. The lookups can be triggered by authentication requests, access to resources, or almost anything else a server may be asked to do.

Typical trouble caused by bad or nonexistent DNS includes:

► Resources that can't be connected to over the network such as websites, wikis, calendars, and file shares

► Not being able to log into a computer that uses Open Directory hosted by the server

▶ Single sign-on (SSO) via Kerberos not working

▶ Authentication problems

There are a number of pieces to the DNS system, including but not limited to:

▶ Requestor—The computer looking for information

▶ DNS server—The service that provides all or some of the information the requestor asks for

▶ Records—The information defining information relating to the DNS zone, such as machines and nameservers

▶ Zone files—The text-based files that contain the DNS records. These files reside in /var/named.

▶ Primary zone—A group of records for a domain

▶ Secondary zone—A replica of a primary zone, typically on another DNS server, that has its records created by a zone transfer

▶ Zone transfer—Sending a copy of a primary zone to another server for use with a secondary zone

▶ Forwarding server—Where requests are sent if the DNS server doesn't have the zone information to answer the request

Reference 3.2
Evaluating OS X DNS Hosting Requirements

When first configuring OS X Server, the Server app checks to see if a DNS hostname correlating to the computer's IPv4 address is being provided by the DNS server listed in Network preferences. If it is, the computer is named with the hostname information contained in the DNS records. If DNS information for the computer's IPv4 address is not provided, the Server app will set up the DNS service on that computer. This process guarantees that at least enough DNS information is available to the server to function properly. You can tell if DNS service was turned on by a green status indicator next to the DNS service in the Server app list of services, and that in Network preferences, the value for the DNS server is 127.0.0.1.

Here are three typical scenarios for DNS services as they relate to OS X Server:

▶ Automatically configured DNS—If the server has its own DNS running and working, leaving it that way and not configuring the DNS service beyond that point may be appropriate. This may be when the server is the only server on the network, as might be the case in a small office. The client computers will contact the server via Bonjour for those services that support it. This assumes that the server is on the same segment (subnet) of the network as the client. This configuration is viable and might work very well.

▶ Externally provided DNS—Other configurations may require externally provided DNS. An example of this is when the server will be connected to an Active Directory (AD) system for user and groups information. In this situation it is best to place a record for the server into the DNS service used by the Windows server hosting the AD. Make sure there is an A record, used for forward lookups, server17. pretendco.com = 10.0.0.171, and a reverse or PTR record, 10.0.0.171 = server17. pretendco.com. Check these details using Network Utility or command-line tools before configuring your server to use this external DNS server.

NOTE ▶ Windows DNS service prior to 2008 R2 commonly doesn't provide a reverse zone. While making an A record there is a checkbox to automatically make a PTR record, but unless the appropriate reverse zone exists, the PTR record will not be made.

▶ OS X Server hosted DNS—This differs from the automatically configured DNS as it is manually set up by the administrator and can be used by other computers and devices on the network to get DNS information. The DNS service on the server has new DNS zones set up and populated with records representing the computers, servers, and other devices on the network. This style of providing DNS is used when there are larger needs than simply identifying one server on the network, and all computers on your network will use your server for DNS information.

Reference 3.3
Configuring DNS Service in OS X Server

Prior to setting up DNS services in OS X Server, you need to collect certain information. This includes:

▶ The domain you want to host. In this guide you'll be using pretendco.com.

▶ The hostnames you want to have records for. In this example use server17 as the hostname, but it could also include records for devices like printer01 or winserver02. These are used for the A records or forward lookups, which map a DNS name to an IPv4 address.

▶ The IPv4 addresses for all the hostnames you want to include. These are used for the PTR records or reverse lookups, mapping IPv4 addresses to DNS names.

▶   The IPv4 address of upstream DNS servers that will answer DNS requests the DNS server you are setting up doesn't have the answers for. This is called a forwarder.

▶   The range of IPv4 addresses or networks you want your DNS server to provide DNS lookups for. This prevents unwanted networks from using your DNS server.

The general flow of setting up a DNS server includes defining the domain or domains that the server will be responsible for. The DNS service that is responsible for the "official" DNS information about a domain is called the Start of Authority (SoA) of the domain and is contained in the DNS records. If you are hosting DNS records strictly for your internal domains, this is not a critical piece of information, but if you were hosting DNS for a domain that is accessible to the Internet, it is critical.

Reference 3.4
Troubleshooting DNS Service in OS X Server

Since DNS is a critical service it helps to understand the basics of troubleshooting it:

▶   Is the server, computer, or device set up to use the proper DNS server? Many problems are related to the wrong information being delivered via a wrongly defined DNS server.

▶   Are DNS services available on the defined DNS server? Check that the DNS service is running on the defined server. In Terminal, run the command telnet *<IPv4 address of server>* 53 and see if a connection is made (after a successful connection, press Control-], then type quit to close the connection). Port 53 is the port used by DNS.

▶   Are the proper DNS records available from the DNS server? Check all the pertinent records, forward and reverse, using Terminal commands or Network Utility. Make sure both the forward and reverse records are available and match.

Exercise 3.1
Configure DNS Services

When you performed the initial installation and configuration of OS X Server in Lesson 2's exercises, the DNS service you configured OS X to use did not contain records for your server's primary IPv4 address. This resulted in DNS service being turned on and hosting a domain called server*n*.pretendco.com (where *n* is your student number) with one A (forward) record in it. While this is fine for a single host system, if you want to host multiple devices in your DNS, you need to build a new zone to host the pretendco.com domain. In this exercise, you will configure your DNS service to multiple hostnames.

Collect DNS Configuration Data

Prior to setting up the DNS service, gather the following information:

▶ Domain name (such as pretendco.com)

▶ IPv4 addresses and associated hostnames

▶ Forwarder server address

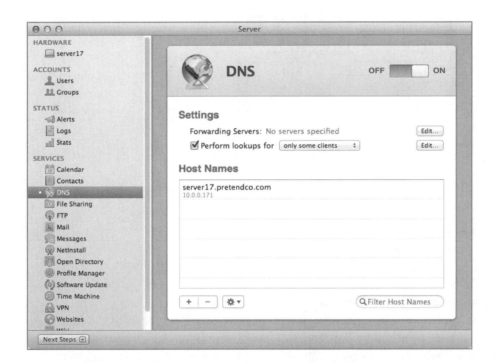

Configure Forwarding Servers

A forwarding server is a configuration that hands off DNS lookups to another DNS server if the DNS server does not have the information regarding the requested domain. The forwarding server is often the DNS server provided by the ISP, which has a much larger cache of entries from the Internet.

> **NOTE ▶** In a classroom situation, your instructor will provide you with the proper IPv4 address and explain why it is being used. If you are performing the exercises independently, use the IPv4 address of a DNS server provided by your ISP.

1   On your server, open the Server app and choose the DNS service in the Services section.

2   To the right of Forwarding Servers, click Edit.

3   Click the Add (+) button.

4   Enter the IPv4 address of the upstream DNS server you want to use and click OK.
A common DNS server to use would be the one provided by the ISP. If you are in a
classroom, your instructor will provide the proper IPv4 address to use.

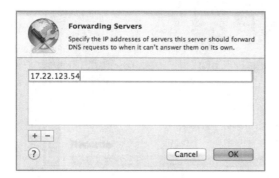

The forwarders are listed in the main DNS service pane.

Configure Lookup Restrictions

You can control what computers or devices can use your DNS server by defining their
IPv4 addresses or networks. Any computer or device not having an IPv4 address in the
defined accepted ranges or hosts will not be granted DNS lookup information. Use the
following steps to configure the DNS service to respond to requests from another network;
you'll use 192.168.0.0 just as an example.

1   If not already selected, select the "Perform lookups for" checkbox.

2   Choose "only some clients" from the pop-up menu, which allows you to define networks that can be served by your server's DNS service.

3   To the right of "Perform lookups for," click Edit.

4   If not already selected, select the checkboxes for "The server itself," "Clients on the local network," and "Clients on the following networks."

5   Click the Add (+) button and enter **192.168.0.0/24**.

This defines the 192.168.0.0 network as also being able to perform DNS lookups using this server, in addition to the 10.0.0.0 "local network" range the server is currently in. A single IPv4 address can be entered also to narrow down the range to a single device.

Configure DNS Hosts

You will replace the limited primary zone of server*n*.pretendco.com (where *n* is your student number) with a new zone for pretendco.com, which can contain a broader set of records. You will also create and configure another primary zone, pretendco.private, to reemphasize the process of configuring zones. Additionally, the machine records you create in the pretendco.private zone are required for the exercises in Lesson 20, "Hosting Websites," which demonstrate the ability to host websites for more than one domain.

1   Click the Action (gear icon) menu at the bottom of the DNS pane and choose Show All Records. This changes the simplified view into a more standard view illustrating the various zones configured.

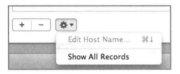

2   Review the records listed in the pane; you can drag the bottom edge of the Server app window to expand the Records field and expose more records. In the following figure, there are two zones: a primary named server17.pretendco.com and a reverse named 171.0.0.10.in-addr.arpa. Each zone has a nameserver record, which defines your server as the authoritative DNS service for that zone. The primary zone has one machine record, and the reverse zone has one mapping record that corresponds to the primary zone's one machine record.

3   Click the Add (+) button and choose Add Primary Zone.

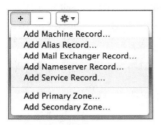

4   In the Name field enter pretendco.com and keep the "Zone data is valid for 24 hours" setting. Do not select the "Allow zone transfers" option. Click Done.

5   In the main DNS pane, click the Add (+) button and choose Add Machine Record.

6   From the Zone menu, choose pretendco.com.

7   In the Host Name field, enter server*n* (where *n* is your student number). Note that you should not enter the domain, just the first part of the host name.

8   Click the Add (+) button and enter your server's IPv4 address, 10.0.0.*n*1 (where *n* is your student number).

9   Click Done.

10 Add a mail exchanger (MX) record. Click the Add (+) button and choose Add Mail Exchanger Record. From the Zone menu, choose pretendco.com. In the Mail Server field, enter server*n*.pretendco.com (where *n* is your student number) and set Priority to 10.

Note that there is now a primary zone for pretendco.com with machine and nameserver entries in it. There is also a reverse zone for 0.0.10.in-addr.arpa with reverse mapping and nameserver entries.

Create an additional zone

Use the following steps to create another zone, specify its nameserver value, and create records in the zone.

1 In the main DNS pane, click the Add (+) button and choose Add Primary Zone.

2 In the Name field, enter pretendco.private. Leave the other settings at their defaults, and click Done.

3 In the main DNS pane, click the Add (+) button and choose Add Nameserver Record.

4 Click the Zone pop-up menu and choose pretendco.private.

5   In the Nameserver field, enter **server*n*.pretendco.com** (where *n* is your student number), then click Done.

6   In the main DNS pane, click the Add (+) button and choose Add Machine Record.

7   Click the Zone pop-up menu and choose pretendco.private.

8   In the Host Name field, enter **www**.

9   In the IP Addresses field, click the Add (+) button and enter **10.0.0.*n*5** (where *n* is your student number).

10 Click Done to save the new record.

11 In the main DNS pane, click Add (+) and choose Add Machine Record.

12 Click the Zone pop-up menu and choose pretendco.private.

13 In the Host Name field, enter **ssl**.

14 In the IP Address field, click Add (+) and enter **10.0.0.*n*3** (where *n* is your student number).

15 Click Done to save the new record.

Your records should look similar to those contained in the following figure.

Remove the redundant zone and confirm records

To prevent confusion in the future, remove the limited zone that the Server app originally created. Then use Network Utility to confirm that your server and your administrator computer can successfully perform lookups on the records you just created.

1   Remove the server*n*.pretendco.com primary zone by choosing it and clicking the Delete (–) button. When prompted, confirm that you do want to delete the zone by clicking Delete. Notice that the corresponding reverse zone, *n*.0.0.10.in-addr.arpa (where *n* is your student number), was automatically removed.

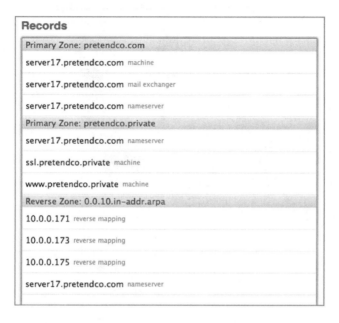

Records

Primary Zone: pretendco.com	
server17.pretendco.com	machine
server17.pretendco.com	mail exchanger
server17.pretendco.com	nameserver
Primary Zone: pretendco.private	
server17.pretendco.com	nameserver
ssl.pretendco.private	machine
www.pretendco.private	machine
Reverse Zone: 0.0.10.in-addr.arpa	
10.0.0.171	reverse mapping
10.0.0.173	reverse mapping
10.0.0.175	reverse mapping
server17.pretendco.com	nameserver

2   On your server, open Network preferences and make sure the DNS Servers field is set to 127.0.0.1 and the Search Domain field is set to pretendco.com. If they are not, change the entries to look like the following figure.

3 Using Network Utility, check that DNS is resolving properly by performing a lookup on **server**n**.pretendco.com** (where *n* is your student number).

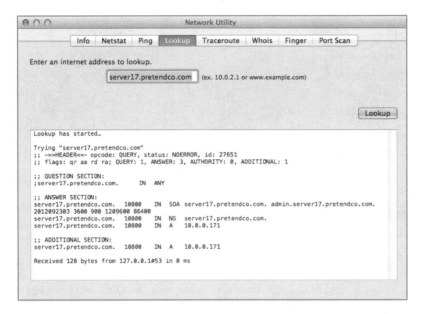

4 Using Network Utility, check that DNS is resolving properly by running a lookup on **10.0.0.**n**1** (where *n* is your student number). The associated machine record is returned, server**n**.pretendco.com.

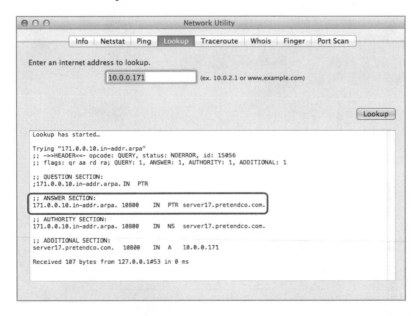

5   Using Network Utility, check the returned information on just the domain
pretendco.com. In the returned information is the MX record and the priority number.

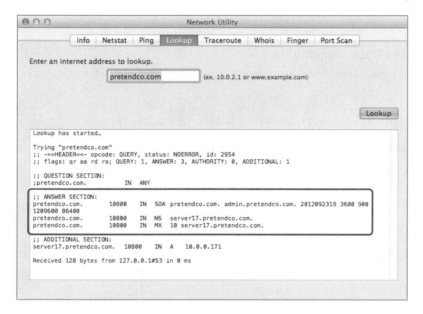

6   Using Network Utility, perform a lookup for ssl.pretendco.private, and confirm
that the answer section returns 10.0.0.*n*3 (where *n* is your student number); perform
a lookup for that same IPv4 address and confirm that the answer section returns
ssl.pretendco.private.

7   On your administrator computer, open Network preferences and confirm that the
DNS Server field is set to 10.0.0.*n*1 (where *n* is your student number) and the Search
Domain field is set to pretendco.com.

8   On your administrator computer, repeat steps 4–6 to use Network Utility to confirm
DNS records.

Additional Resources

The following documents provide more information about DNS in OS X Server.

Many other documents are available at www.apple.com/osx/server/resources/
documentation.html and www.apple.com/osx/server/specs/.

OS X Server Administration Guides

OS X Server: Advanced Administration http://help.apple.com/advancedserveradmin/mac/10.8/

Apple Knowledge Base Documents

You can check for new and updated Knowledge Base documents at www.apple.com/support/.

Document PH11162, "OS X Mountain Lion: Edit DNS and search domain settings"

Document PH10790, "OS X Mountain Lion: Test your DNS server"

Document PH10975, "OS X Mountain Lion: Use a DNS server"

Document HT5343, "OS X: How to reset the DNS cache"

Lesson Review

1. What is the purpose of DNS?
2. If no DNS server is defined when configuring OS X Server, how will the server provide DNS for itself?
3. If you are using an external DNS server to provide DNS for your server, what should you do prior to configuring the server?
4. When might you feel it is OK to leave the automatically configured DNS server running on your server with no modification?
5. When might you want to use a manually configured DNS service on your OS X Server?

Answers

1. To convert host names into IP addresses and IP addresses to host names.
2. A basic DNS server will be configured automatically and turned on.
3. You should check that the DNS server has the proper forward and reverse DNS information configured for your server's host name and IPv4 address.
4. When it is a very simple network with one server, and all the computers and devices are on the same network
5. When you want to have records for multiple computers and devices.

Lesson 4

Exploring the Server App

Once you've completed your initial installation and configuration of OS X Server and you click Finish at the Congratulations pane, the Server app opens its main configuration pane and you can continue configuring it. In this lesson you'll learn about the various panes available in the Server app. You will learn how to enable remote access to the Server app and how to move the location your server uses to store much of its service data.

GOALS

▶ Understand how to use the Server app

▶ Use the Server app to administer a remote computer with OS X Server

▶ Move service data to a different volume

Reference 4.1
Allowing Remote Access

You can certainly administer your server on your server computer, however, even though OS X Server is now an application, rather than an entire operating system, it's still not recommended to use your server for your daily productivity applications. Additionally, your server computer might be located in an inconvenient physical location.

You can use the Server app on a Mac with Mountain Lion to manage OS X Server running on a remote Mac, but only if the checkbox "Allow remote administration using Server" is selected. It is recommended that you do not simultaneously use the Server app on more than one Mac to administer a given server.

> **MORE INFO** ▶ When you select the "Allow remote administration using Server" checkbox, you enable other Macs to use the Server app to configure your server using TCP port 311.

Unlike previous versions of OS X Server, you cannot perform a remote initial installation and configuration of OS X Server with the Server app; you have to use the Server app on the Mac on which you want to install OS X Server, at least for the initial installation and configuration.

However, sometimes you need direct control of your server computer; for example, to perform a series of file or folder copy operations using the Finder. If you select the checkbox "Enable screen sharing and remote management," you can use tools like Screen Sharing (available from the Tools menu in the Server app, and located in /System/Library/Core-Services), and Apple Remote Desktop (available from the Mac App Store) to take control of the Mac running OS X Server.

When you select the "Enable screen sharing and remote management" option, this allows access for any local accounts on the server computer that you configure as an administrator. If you want to allow access for other accounts, or specify a password for software that uses the VNC protocol, configure this in the Sharing preferences on the server computer.

NOTE ▶ If you have the Sharing preferences open when you use the Server app to configure a user account as an administrator, you need to quit System Preferences and reopen the Sharing pane to see the updated list of accounts.

The following figure illustrates the checkbox in the Sharing preferences that is enabled when you enable the checkbox for "Enable screen sharing and remote management."

The "Allow remote login using SSH" checkbox in the Server app has the same effect as the Remote Login checkbox in the OS X Sharing preferences; selecting or deselecting either checkbox has the same effect on the checkbox in the other tool.

When you run the Server app on a remote administrator computer, if the "Allow remote login using SSH" option is selected, an arrow appears next to it. If you click this arrow, the

Server app opens Terminal and attempts to connect to your server using the SSH protocol, with the username of the administrator account that you provided to the Server app to connect to your remote server computer. You must provide the password to successfully open an SSH connection.

Similarly, there is also a shortcut to open a Screen Sharing session with your server. This opens the Screen Sharing application, which allows remote observation and control of the remote server computer.

Of course, the checkbox for "Allow remote administration using Server" is not available for you to configure unless you use the Server app directly at the server.

The following figure illustrates the arrows that are shortcuts to open a connection to the server.

NOTE ▸ At the time of this writing, a reinstallation of OS X Mountain Lion from the Recovery HD results in the Sharing preferences with Screen Sharing enabled for local administrator user accounts, and Remote Login (SSH shell access) enabled for all local user accounts. If you upgrade from OS X v10.6.8 or any version of OS X v10.7, your Mac with OS X Mountain Lion inherits the Sharing settings from the system you upgraded.

Reference 4.2
Using the Next Steps Drawer

The Next Steps drawer is at the bottom of the Server app window, and is a great introduction to the Server app. Once you are more familiar with the Server app, you can click the Next Steps button to close the Next Steps drawer. You can always click the Next Steps button to open the drawer again.

The five sections in the Next Steps drawer are pretty self-explanatory:

Configure Network

You should have already configured your network interfaces the way you want, but the Configure Network pane gives you a quick view of your current network configuration, as well as a shortcut to your server's Network pane in the Server app.

> **NOTE ▸** Changing your server's IP address can have significant unexpected consequences, depending on the services your server provides. Search for "Find or change your server's IP address" in the online "OS X Server: Advanced Administration" for more information.

Add Users

Lessons 8 and 10 delve into managing local users, as well managing local network users. The Add Users pane offers some advice and a shortcut to the Server app's Users pane.

Review Certificates

You will learn about using SSL certificates in the next lesson. One blue link opens Server Help, and the second is a shortcut to the Settings pane where you can configure SSL certificates.

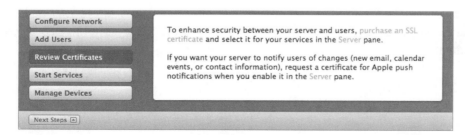

Start Services

This pane lists any currently running services. The Server app sidebar displays a green status indicator next to any service that's running.

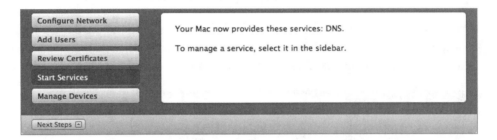

Manage Devices

You will learn more about managing Macs and iOS devices in Lesson 11, "Configuring OS X Server to Provide Device Management," and in Lesson 12, "Managing with Profile Manager."

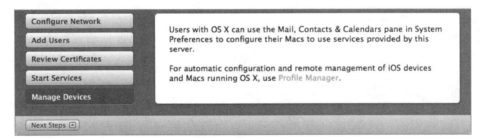

Reference 4.3
Using Server Sidebar Elements

The Server app's sidebar contains four sections, which you'll use over and over throughout this guide.

Hardware

The Hardware section displays your server, as well as an AirPort device if there is one on your subnet.

If you select the AirPort device, and provide authentication to manage the AirPort device, when you use the Server app to start some services for the first time, the Server app asks if you would like to modify the AirPort device's NAT rules to allow outside access to the service. This is convenient if an AirPort device sits between your internal network and your connection to the Internet.

Once you select your server in the Server app sidebar, you see four tabs:

▶ Overview

▶ Settings

▶ Network

▶ Storage

Overview

The Overview pane is the first thing you see after your initial installation and configuration of OS X Server. The arrow next to your Startup Disk is a shortcut to clicking the Storage tab and selecting the startup volume.

Settings

The Settings pane offers a number of options to configure remote access and administration.

This is also where you edit your server's SSL certificates; remember that the Next Steps Review Certificates pane contains a link to this Settings pane.

The last option in the Settings pane allows you to configure your server to store data for various services on a volume other than the boot volume.

Moving Service Data Location

When you click Edit next to the Service Data field, you have the opportunity to change where your server stores some of its service data. Here's what the pane looks like for a server with two internal volumes and one external volume:

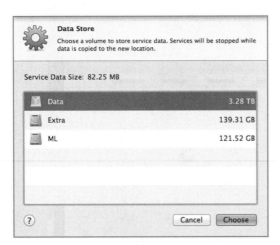

If you use the Server app to choose a different service data volume, it does the following:

▶ Automatically stops the appropriate services

▶ Creates a new folder on the volume you choose (/Volumes/*volume_name*/Library/Server)

▶ Copies the existing service data to the new folder

▶ Configures services to use the new location

▶ Starts the services again

The list of services whose data gets relocated includes:

▶ Calendar and Contacts

▶ Mail

▶ Messages

▶ PostgreSQL databases and backups that services like Profile Manager use

▶ Profile Manager

▶ Software Update

▶ Websites

▶ Wiki

Not all the server's service data is moved. For example, configuration and temporary files (like the Mail spool file) remain on the startup volume, and some services, like FTP, NetInstall, and Websites, offer separate interfaces to choose where to store data for those services.

Just as you should not change the name of your server's startup volume after you start offering services, you should not change the name of the service data storage volume after you designate it in the Server app.

> **MORE INFO** ▶ If you choose to share the Websites root via FTP, it will share the /Library/Server/Web/Data/Sites/ directory on your server's volume, even if you choose a different data volume for your server's service data.

Network

The Network pane shows your current Computer Name and Host Name, as well as the status of your server's network interfaces.

Storage

This Storage pane displays an alphabetical list of the disks connected to your server computer; you can also drill down and edit file ownership, permissions, and access control lists (ACLs). You'll see more about this pane in Lesson 14, "Understanding File Access."

TIP ► If you have multiple volumes attached to your server, only the boot volume has special folder icons for the Applications, Groups, Library, Shared Items, System, and Users folders. Other volumes have regular folder icons.

Accounts

The Accounts section of the Server app sidebar contains the Users and the Groups panes. Lesson 8, "Managing Local Accounts," and Lesson 10, "Managing Local Network Accounts," make extensive use of the Users and Groups panes.

Status

Lesson 6, "Using Status and Notifications," covers using the Alerts, Logs, and Stats panes to proactively monitor your server.

Services

This is a list of the services that OS X Server offers. A green status indicator appears next to the services that are currently running. Select any service to configure it.

MORE INFO ► The "Additional Resources" section of Lesson 2, "Installing OS X Server," contains a list of Knowledge Base articles that address services that have been offered in previous versions of Mac OS X Server but do not appear in this list of services.

Reference 4.4
Using the Manage Menu

The Server app's Manage menu offers three menu items.

"Connect to Server" opens the "Choose a Mac" pane, where you see a list the includes your Mac, servers in your broadcast domain, and Other Mac, which allows you to specify another Mac by its host name or IP address.

The "Import Accounts from File" menu item is covered in Lesson 8, "Managing Local Accounts," and Lesson 10, "Managing Local Network Accounts."

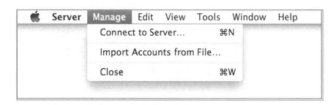

Reference 4.5
Using the Tools Menu

The Tools menu allows you to quickly open four administration applications:

▶   Directory Utility

▶   Screen Sharing

▶   System Image Utility

▶   Xsan Admin

The first three applications are located in /System/Library/CoreServices on every Mac with OS X Mountain Lion. Xsan Admin is located inside a folder in the Server app itself.

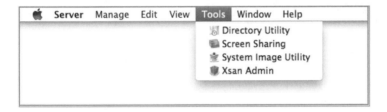

Reference 4.6
Using Help

Don't underestimate the power of the Server Help. After you enter search terms into the Search field, Help displays a list of Server Help resources that match your query.

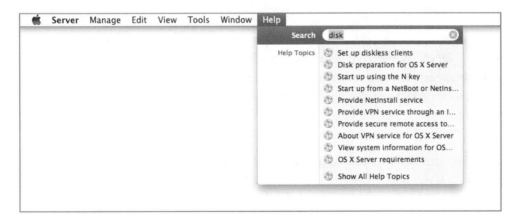

Once you choose a topic from the list of results, the Help Center window stays in the foreground until you close it.

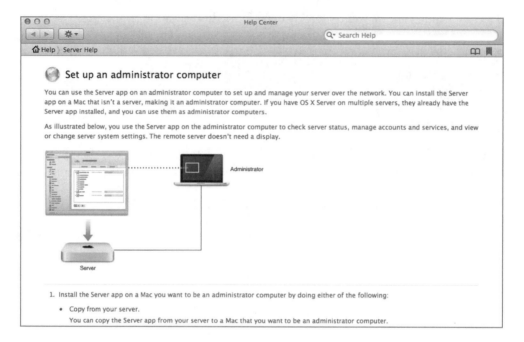

Reference 4.7
Troubleshooting

If your administrator computer does not have DNS records available for a remote server, you will not be able to authenticate to that server with the Server app.

On your server, do not delete the Server app or move the Server app from the Applications folder on your startup volume. If you do, you will see a dialog that all your services have stopped; when you reinstall OS X Server (or just move the Server app back into the Applications folder of the server's startup volume), you will have the opportunity to reenter your Apple ID to renew your Apple Push Notification service certificates, and then your services will start again.

It is recommended that you do not change the name of your server's startup volume, but if you do, you will need to restart your server to restart its services.

Exercise 4.1
Enable Screen Sharing And Remote Management

In Exercise 2.2, you confirmed that your server allows remote administration using the Server app. Now you will enable screen sharing and remote management as well. If you had a copy of Apple Remote Desktop, performing this action would allow you to use it to control your server. In this exercise you will use Screen Sharing to control your server.

Open a connection to your server with the Server app if you don't already have one open.

1   On your administrator computer, open the Server app, and choose Manage > Connect to Server. Select your server and click Continue.

2   Provide administrator credentials (Administrator Name **ladmin** and Administrator Password **ladminpw**).

3   Click Connect.

Enable screen sharing and remote administration.

1   If your server isn't already selected in the Server app sidebar, select your server now.

2   Click the Settings tab.

3   To enable you to open a Screen Sharing session using the Server app on a remote administrator computer, select the checkbox "Enable screen sharing and remote management."

Open a Screen Sharing connection.

1 Click the arrow next to the "Enable screen sharing and remote management."

2 Enter local administrator credentials for your server computer.

NOTE ▸ If you provided your Apple ID when setting up OS X, you will see "Connect as a registered user" and "Using an Apple ID" as two different options in the window. If this is the case, select "Connect as a registered user" and enter credentials for the local administrator on your server.

NOTE ▸ The Name field automatically contains the full name of the currently logged-in user on your administrator computer.

3 Click Connect.

4 Move some windows around to demonstrate that you are controlling your server computer.

5 In the Screen Sharing window, click the close button.

Because you selected the checkbox for "Enable screen sharing and remote management," you were able to take control of your remote server computer using Screen Sharing, right from the Server app's shortcut.

Exercise 4.2
Explore the Next Steps Drawer

The Server app has a helpful Next Steps drawer that helps you determine your next management and monitoring steps.

Like many exercises in this guide, you can open the Server app on your administrator computer, or on your server computer.

1   If it isn't already open, open the Server app and connect to your server.

2   In the Next Steps drawer, click Configure Network. Review the text, which contains information about your IP address and host name and instructions for changing these.

3   In the second sentence, click the blue word "Server," which is a link to the Network pane; this produces the same result as selecting your server in the Server app sidebar and then clicking Network.

4   Unlike earlier versions of OS X Server, if you want to change your IP address or host name, you do not have to use the command line. To access the appropriate interface to change your IP address or host name, click Edit next to the Host Name field.

5   In the Change Host Name pane, click Continue.

6   If you see the Multiple Networks Detected pane, confirm that the pop-up menu contains your primary network connection, and choose Continue.

7   In the Host Name pane, select "Host name for Internet" and click Continue.

8   Review the computer name, host name, and network address. This is where you would make changes when appropriate, but for the purposes of this guide, do not make any changes at this point: Click Go Back as many times as it takes to get back to the Change Host Name pane, and then click Cancel.

9 Click the four other Next Steps buttons and review their content.

10 Click the Next Steps button in the lower-left corner to make the Next Steps drawer disappear.

11 Click the Next Steps button again to make the drawer reappear.

The Next Steps drawer is a great place to start when you're new to administering your server with the Server app, but you can close the Next Steps drawer when you're more familiar with the Server app.

Exercise 4.3
Configure the Service Data Volume

▶ **Prerequisite**

  ▶ Exercise 4.1, "Enable Screen Sharing And Remote Management"

In this exercise, you will go through the procedure to relocate your service data volume but will not actually change it.

Moving the Service Data to a Different Volume

Using the Server app, you can choose a different volume for service data. It's a good idea to perform this task as early as possible, so that you don't have to wait with services disabled while a large amount of data is moved to the new volume.

1 If necessary, on your administrator computer, open the Server app and connect to your server.

2   In the Server app sidebar, select your server and click Settings.

3   Next to the Service Data field, click Edit.

4   Inspect the current Service Data Size, as well as how much space is available on any listed volume. If you have another volume available on which to store the service data, you could select that volume and click Choose.

Because it is possible that you do not have any extra volumes in your test environment, the rest of the exercises for this guide are written with the assumption that the service data is stored on the startup volume. So, for the purposes of these exercises, click Cancel to close the window.

Even though you went through the procedure to relocate your service data volume, you didn't actually change it in this exercise. You can use this procedure in a production environment with an additional storage volume.

Additional Resources

The following documents provide more information about using the Server app to manage and configure OS X Server.

Many other documents are available at www.apple.com/osx/server/resources/documentation.html.

OS X Server Administration Guides

OS X Server: Advanced Administration http://help.apple.com/advancedserveradmin/mac/10.8/

Apple Knowledge Base Documents

You can check for new and updated Knowledge Base documents at www.apple.com/support/.

Document HT1822, "OS X Server: Admin tools compatibility information"

Document HT4974, "OS X Server: Changing the service data storage location"

Document HT4814, "How to administer OS X Server remotely using Server App"

Document HT5359, "OS X Server: Dedicating system resources for high performance services"

Lesson Review

1. Using an administrator computer with the Server app installed, how do you use the Server app to administer a remote server?

2. What option do you need to select in order to allow another Mac to administer your server, and where is its checkbox?

3. What tools does the Tools menu give you quick access to open?

4. Do you have to install extra software to take control of your server's keyboard and mouse?

5. How do you hide the Next Steps drawer?

6. If you use the Server app to choose a different service data volume to a volume called /Volumes/Data, what folder will contain the service data?

7. Do you need to stop all services before using the Server app to change your service data volume?

8. Can you remotely install OS X Server on a brand new Mac computer that comes with OS X Server, without first configuring OS X on that computer?

Answers

1. Open the Server app, choose Manage > Connect to Server, select your remote server from the list (or select Other, and then provide its host name or address), and provide credentials for a local administrator.

2. Select your server in the Server app sidebar (in the Hardware section), click the Settings tab, and then select the option "Allow remote administration using Server."

3. The Tools menu gives you access to these applications:

    Directory Utility

    Screen Sharing

    System Image Utility

    Xsan Admin

4. No, on your server computer, you open the Server app and select your server in the Server app sidebar (in the Hardware section). Click the Settings tab, select the checkbox "Enable screen sharing and remote management," and then on your administrator computer use Screen Sharing to take control of your server computer's keyboard.

5.   Click the Next Steps button, or choose Help > Next Steps Button.

6.   In this case, your service data will be stored in /Volumes/Data/Library/Server.

7.   No, the Server app automatically stops the appropriate services before moving their data to the new service data volume.

8.   No, you need to configure OS X before installing and configuring OS X Server.

Lesson 5
Configuring SSL Certificates

You can definitely use OS X Server without doing any additional work to secure its services. However, you can use SSL (Secure Socket Layer) technology to prove your server's identity to client computers and devices, and to encrypt communication between your server and client computers and devices. This lesson starts out with the basics of SSL, and then shows you how to configure SSL certificates for use with OS X Server.

Reference 5.1
Understanding SSL Certificates

Here's a problem: You want the users who use your server's services to trust your server's identity, and to be able to encrypt network traffic with your server.

The OS X solution is to use Secure Sockets Layer, or SSL, which is a system for the transmission of data securely between hosts. You can configure your server to use an SSL certificate, which will provide the ability to use the SSL system.

An *SSL certificate* (also referred to as simply a *certificate*) is a file that identifies the certificate holder. A certificate specifies the permitted use of the certificate, and has an expiration date. Importantly, a certificate includes a *public key infrastructure* (*PKI*) public key.

PKI involves the use of public and private *keys*. Grossly simplified, a key is a cryptographic blob of data, and within PKI, public and private keys are created in a way that they are mathematically linked: Data encrypted with one key can be decrypted only by using the other key. If you can decrypt data with one key, it proves that the data was encrypted with the other key. The public key is made publicly available, and the private key should be kept private. Fortunately, all of this encryption and decryption happens behind the scenes, and is the basis for establishing secure communications.

GOALS

► Understand the basics of SSL certificates

► Create a self-signed SSL certificate

► Create a certificate signing request

► Import a certificate signed by a certificate authority

► Archive your certificate

► Configure which certificate your OS X Server services use

Back to definitions:

A *digital identity* (or more simply, *identity*) is an electronic means of identifying an entity (such as a person or a server). An identity is the combination of a certificate (which includes the public key) and the corresponding private key. If you don't have your private key, you can't prove your identity. Similarly, if another entity has your private key, that other entity can claim your identity, so be sure to keep your private key private!

Again simplifying, a *digital signature* is a cryptographic scheme that uses PKI private and public keys to demonstrate that a given message (a digital file such as an SSL certificate) has not been changed since the signature was generated. If a message, which has been signed, changes or is otherwise tampered with, it will be clear that the signature no longer matches the underlying data. Therefore, you can use a digital signature on a certificate to prove its integrity.

Coming back to certificates: a certificate must be either self-signed, or signed by a *certification authority* (also known as a certificate authority, or more simply, a CA). In other words, you can sign your own certificate, using your private key (remember that a certificate is a file that identifies the holder of the certificate, and includes the public key), or you can have someone else, namely a CA, use their private key to sign your certificate.

An *intermediate CA* is a CA whose certificate is signed by another CA. So it's possible to have a hierarchical *chain* of certificates, where an intermediate CA, which in turn is signed by yet another CA, signs a certificate. The certificate chain ends with a CA that signs its own certificate, which is called a *root CA*. It is not required to have an intermediate CA involved: you could simply have a root CA sign your certificate, but in practice, an intermediate CA is often involved.

How does one know if she can trust a CA? After all, since a root CA has signed its own SSL certificate, this effectively means that the organization in control of a root CA simply asserts that you should trust that it is who it *claims* to be.

The answer is that trust has to start somewhere. In OS X and iOS, Apple includes a collection of root and intermediate CAs that Apple has determined are worthy of trust (see the Apple Root Certificate Program page in the Additional Resources section for more information on the process Apple uses to do so). Out of the box, your Mac computers and iOS devices are configured to trust those CAs. By extension, your computers are devices that also trust any certificate or intermediate CA whose certificate chain ends with one of these CAs. In OS X, these trusted CAs are stored in the System Roots keychain. (See Lesson 9, "Keychain Management," in *Apple Pro Training Series: OS X Support Essentials*, for more

information about the various keychains in OS X.) You can use Keychain Access to view
this collection of trusted root CAs. Open Keychain Access (in the Utilities folder). In the
upper-left Keychains column, click System Roots. Note that on the following figure, the
bottom of the window states there are 182 trusted CAs or intermediate CAs by default in
OS X Mountain Lion version 10.8.2.

> **MORE INFO** ▶ Some third-party software, like Mozilla Firefox, does not necessarily
> use the System Roots keychain, and has its own mechanism to store CAs that its soft-
> ware is configured to trust.

In Lesson 9, "Configuring Open Directory Services," you will learn that when you configure your server to manage network accounts, also known as configuring your server as an
Open Directory master, the Server app automatically creates a new CA and a new intermediate CA, and uses the intermediate CA to sign a new SSL certificate with your server's
host name as the Common Name (the Common Name value is part of what identified the
certificate holder). It is recommended that if you haven't engaged a widely-trusted CA to
sign an SSL certificate for your server, you should use the SSL certificate signed by your
Open Directory intermediate CA, because in Lesson 11, "Configuring OS X Server to Provide Device Management," you will learn how to use the Trust Profile to configure your
iOS devices and OS X computers to trust your Open Directory CA, the intermediate CA,
and the new SSL certificate.

But what about computers and devices that are outside your control and which you cannot
configure? When people use computers and devices that are not configured to trust your
server's self-signed SSL certificate, or your server's Open Directory CA or intermediate CA,
and they try to securely access services on your server, they will still see a message that the
identity of your server cannot be verified.

One solution to the problem of proving your identity is for your server to use an SSL certificate that's signed by a CA that most computers and devices are configured to trust. The next section shows you how to obtain a certificate that's signed by a widely trusted CA, so that you can use it to prove the identity of your server, and use it to encrypt communications between your server and the users of your server's services.

Reference 5.2
Configuring SSL Certificates

Your server has a default SSL certificate that's self-signed. That's a good start, but no other computers or devices will trust services that use that certificate. In order to get a CA to sign your certificate, you can start with the Server app. Specific steps to accomplish this objective follow in more detail, but generally, they include the following:

▶ Creating a new self-signed SSL certificate

▶ Using the new self-signed certificate to generate a certificate signing request (CSR)

▶ Submitting your CSR to a CA

▶ Replacing the self-signed certificate with the certificate signed by the CA

▶ In cases in which you use a CA that isn't trusted, using Keychain Access to import the CA's certificate

▶ Configuring your OS X Server services to use your newly signed certificate

The CA's process of using your CSR and signing your SSL certificate with its own private key includes verifying your identity (otherwise, why would anyone trust the CA if it signed certificates from unverified entities?) and optionally charging you money.

To finish the story, computers and devices can now use your server's services, without getting a warning that your SSL certificate is not verified, and your server and the users of its services can use your server's SSL certificate in the process of encrypting communications for services that use your SSL certificate.

Viewing Your Server's Default Certificate

You can use Keychain Access to display the default certificate. Because you need to inspect the Keychain that resides on your server, you have to log in directly on your server (or use a screen sharing method to control your server).

Keychain Access is in the /Applications/Utilities folder on your startup volume; you can use Spotlight or Launchpad to search for it (in Launchpad, it is in the folder named Other). Select the My Certificates category to filter the items that Keychain Access displays. In the Keychains column, click System to show items that are for the entire system, not just for the user who is currently logged in.

At least three items are listed (if you provided an Apple ID for push notifications, you will see more items):

▶ com.apple.servermgrd, which is used for remote administration with the Server app

▶ The Server Fallback SSL Certificate

▶ An SSL certificate with the host name of your server

If you select the certificate with your server's host name, you'll see a warning icon with the text "This certificate has not been verified by a third party," as shown in the following figure:

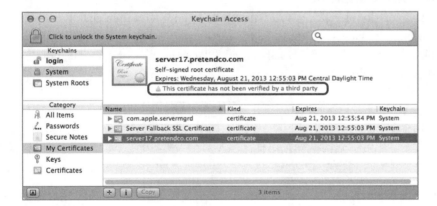

If you double-click the certificate with your host name to open it, you'll see a warning icon and text that states, "This certificate has not been verified by a third party."

If a service on your server uses this self-signed certificate, when users attempt to use services that use that SSL certificate, they may be warned that your SSL certificate is not trusted, as shown in the following figure:

It's recommended to train your users that when they see an SSL warning, they should *not* continue using the service that uses the unverified SSL certificate. Unfortunately, the reality is that some sites users need to use, or want to use, have unverified SSL certificates, and users will visit those sites anyway.

Creating a Self-Signed Certificate

In Keychain Access, if you double-click your certificate to open it, and then click the Details disclosure triangle to view the details for the certificate, you won't see much information in the Subject Name section of this self-signed SSL certificate (for example, no email address and no street address).

If you generate a CSR for this self-signed SSL certificate, any certification authority would reject the request because your request does not have enough information, so the next section starts you on the path of obtaining a signed SSL certificate.

You can use the Server app to create a new self-signed certificate, which is the first step towards getting a signed certificate. See Exercise 5.1, "Create a Certificate Signing Request," for complete instructions.

When you create a new self-signed certificate, you have the opportunity to specify information that a CA can use to verify that you are who you say you are. Use your organization's full legal name for the Organization field, or if it's for personal use, just use your full name. The Organizational Unit field is flexible; you can enter information like your department name, but you should enter some value. The following figure illustrates part of the process of creating a new self-signed certificate.

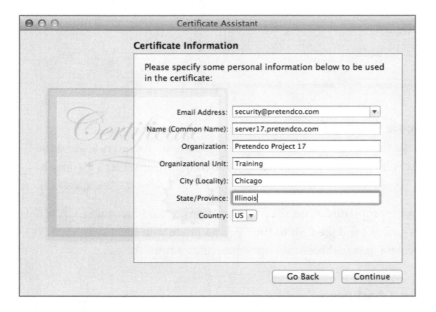

Inspecting the Certificate and Private Key in the System Keychain

You can see your new self-signed certificate in the System keychain of your server computer (the System keychain contains items that are not user specific, and are available to all users of a system). When you double-click the new self-signed certificate to open it, and then click the disclosure triangle for Details, you see the private key associated with the certificate. Remember that you need to keep this private key from falling into the hands of anyone else. You can confirm that it has the values you specified for attributes like Email Address and Organization when you created the new self-signed certificate.

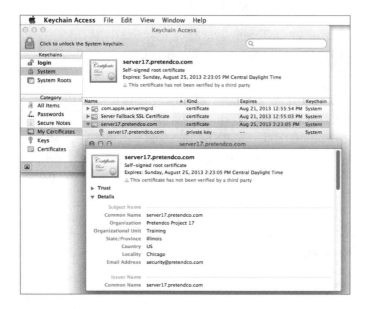

Creating a Certificate Signing Request

You can choose to get a CA to sign your self-signed certificate, so that users around the world can use your server's services without being notified that your server's identity is not verified.

You need to choose an appropriate CA for your organization's needs (choosing a CA is outside the scope of this guide), send the CSR to the CA, and prove your identity to the CA. After some period of time, you will receive a signed certificate from the CA.

Importing the Signed Certificate

After you receive the certificate back from the CA, replace your self-signed certificate with the signed certificate, using the Server app. See the optional Exercise 5.2, "Import a Signed Certificate," for detailed instructions.

Archiving Your Certificate

Whether you have a self-signed certificate, or a certificate signed by a CA, you should take steps to archive your certificate and its private key. You may need to reinstall your server in the future, or an administrator might accidentally remove your certificate and its private key; if you have an archive of your certificate and private key, you can easily use the Server app to re-import your certificate.

You use the Keychain Access app to export your certificate and private key. Keychain Access prompts you to specify a password to protect your private key; it is recommended that you use a strong password.

You use the Server app to import the certificate and private key; you need to provide the password that was entered when the certificate was exported in the first place, otherwise you will not be able to import.

See the optional Exercise 5.3, "Archive Your Certificate," for detailed instructions.

Configuring OS X Server Services to Use a Certificate

Once you've taken steps to create a new self-signed certificate, and optionally obtain a signed certificate, you should use the Server app to configure services to use that certificate. You start in the Server app's Settings pane, and click Edit next to SSL Certificate.

Next, in the Certificate pop-up menu, choose one of the following:

▶   None—None of the services will use SSL.

▶   A specific certificate (server17.pretendco.com – Self-signed is displayed in the following figure)—All the services will use that certificate.

▶   Custom—In the field below the Certificate pop-up menu, for each service displayed, you can choose None, or choose a specific certificate.

Here's an example of setting the Certificate pop-up menu to Custom, and then editing the value for the Websites service:

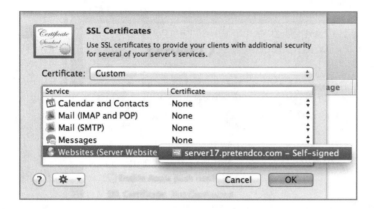

You can use the server app to configure the following OS X Server services to use SSL:

▶ Calendar and Contacts

▶ Mail (IMAP and POP)

▶ Mail (SMTP)

▶ Messages

▶ Open Directory (only appears after starting Open Directory services)

▶ Websites

You will see in Lesson 20, "Managing Web Services," that you can granularly specify an SSL certificate per website you host, and you can use the Profile Manager pane to specify the SSL certificate to use for the Profile Manager service.

At least two other services use SSL, but are not shown in the Server app:

▶ com.apple.servermgrd (for remote administration with the Server app)

▶ VPN

See Exercise 5.4, "Configure Your Server to Use Its New SSL Certificate," for complete instructions.

Following the Certificate Chain

When choosing a CA to use, make sure that it's a root CA that most computers and devices are configured to trust. It's not very useful for you to have a CA sign your certificate, if not many computers or devices will trust that certificate. As an example, here's how an SSL certificate signed by Verisign's trial CA appears in Keychain Access:

You can see that the "Issued by" field near the top of the window is VeriSign Trial Secure Server CA - G2. Note the red X icon and the text, "This certificate was signed by an untrusted issuer." This is a root CA that is not trusted by computers and devices by default, so even if you used this signed certificate for OS X Server services, the people who access your services would experience trouble. In some cases the service might silently fail, or the user may be alerted that the identity of the service cannot be verified. The following figure illustrates that on a client Mac, Safari notifies the user that Safari can't verify the identity of the website.

If you click Show Certificate, Safari displays the certificate chain. The following figure shows what you see when you select the server's certificate at the bottom of the certificate chain.

The following figure illustrates that if you click the Details disclosure triangle, you'll see information about the identity of the certificate holder, as well as information about the issuer (the entity that signed the certificate). In this case, the issuer's Common Name is VeriSignTrial Secure Server CA – G2, which is the same name as is displayed in the certificate chain near the top of the pane.

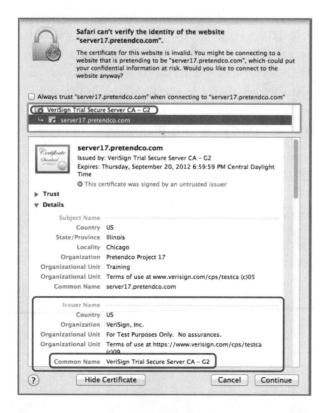

When you select the certificate at the top of certificate chain, you see that this is an intermediate CA; the window states "Intermediate certificate authority," and the Issuer Name information shows you that the Common Name of the issuer (or signer) is VeriSign Trial Secure Server Root CA - G2. Because that root CA is not in this computer's System Roots keychain, this computer doesn't trust the intermediate CA, and doesn't trust the server17 .pretendco.com certificate either.

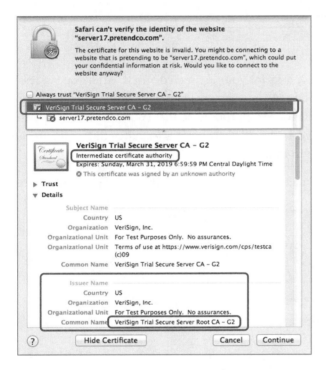

Configuring Trust

Continuing the example of a certificate signed by the trial intermediate CA, you can configure your Mac to always trust this intermediate CA for the currently logged-in user. Start by selecting the CA in the certificate chain, and then selecting the "Always trust" option.

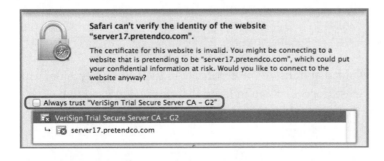

Similarly, for a self-signed certificate, select the "Always trust" option to configure your Mac to trust this self-signed SSL certificate for the currently logged-in user.

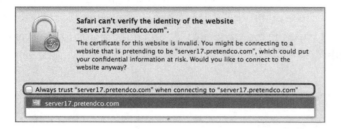

After you select "Always trust," OS X asks for your login credentials. After you successfully authenticate, OS X adds the certificate to your personal keychain, and configures your system to always trust the certificate for SSL purposes, so that your Mac trusts it when you are logged in as the currently logged-in user. This will not affect any other computers or devices, or any other users that log in to that Mac.

Here is a view of the certificate chain after the test root CA has been configured to be trusted.

A further option is to download and install the certificate in the System keychain, with a configuration to "Always trust" for SSL. Keep in mind that this would need to be done for *every* computer or device that uses SSL-enabled services from your server.

See Exercise 5.5, "Configure Your Administrator Computer to Trust an SSL Certificate," for complete instructions.

Reference 5.3
Troubleshooting

The Certificate Assistant uses the IPv4 address of the Mac from which you run the Server app, so if you're using an administrator computer to configure a remote server and generate a new self-signed certificate, be sure to use the server's host name and IP address where appropriate.

When you configure your server as an Open Directory server, if you have a self-signed certificate with your server's host name in the certificate's Common Name field, the Server app will replace the original self-signed SSL certificate with a new certificate. This new certificate will be signed by a newly created intermediate CA associated with your server's Open Directory service.

However, if you have a certificate with your server's host name in the certificate's Common Name field, and the certificate is signed by a CA or an intermediate CA, then the Server app will not replace it with a new one signed by the Open Directory intermediate CA.

Each certificate has an expiration date; if the current date is later than a certificate's expiration date, the certificate is not valid.

> **MORE INFO ▶** Some files associated with certificates are stored in /etc/certificates on your server.

Exercise 5.1
Create a Certificate Signing Request

In this exercise, you will generate a self-signed SSL certificate, and then you will go through the steps of preparing a CSR and importing a signed certificate using the Server app.

If you are reading this guide in order, your server is not yet running any services other than DNS. In this lesson you will not verify that your server services actually use the SSL certificate created in this lesson. However, the lessons in this guide that cover services that do use SSL certificates will refer back to the self-signed SSL certificate that's created in this lesson.

The default SSL certificate does not have enough information for a CA to sign it, so you will create a new self-signed SSL certificate, generate a CSR for this new self-signed SSL certificate, and then use the Server app to import a certificate signed by a CA.

Unfortunately, you will not be able to receive a valid signed certificate for pretendco.com for production use, but you will become familiar with the necessary steps.

1 On your administrator computer, if you are not already connected to your server, open the Server app, connect to your server, and authenticate as a local administrator.

2 In the Next Steps drawer, click Review Certificates.

The Server app displays explanatory text about certificates.

3 Click the blue word "Server" in the second line, which is a link to the Settings pane; this produces the same result as selecting your server in the Server app sidebar and then clicking Settings.

4 Next to the SSL Certificate field, click Edit.

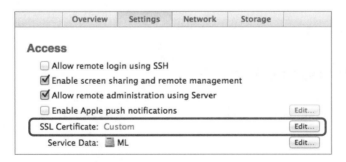

5   Click the Action (gear icon) pop-up menu and choose Manage Certificates.

6   Select the certificate that was generated automatically when you first configured your server; it is the certificate with your server's host name.

7   Click the Details disclosure triangle.

Note that the Common Name and Country fields are filled in, but there is no other information about your organization.

Because it does not have much information, no CA will sign a CSR generated from this automatically created certificate. Because there is also the Server Fallback SSL Certificate, you can remove this default certificate and create a new self-signed certificate.

8   With your server*n*.pretendco.com certificate still selected (where *n* is your student number), click the Delete (–) button.

9   At the warning message, click Delete.

Now only the Server Fallback SSL Certificate is listed.

If you configured the server to send you alerts, you may get an alert that your server doesn't have an SSL certificate. That's fine, because you're about to create a new one.

Create a New Self-Signed Certificate

Start out by choosing to create a new certificate identity.

1   Click the Add (+) button and choose Create a Certificate Identity.

Carefully fill out information for the new self-signed certificate.

2 In the Name field, verify that your server's Host Name, which was automatically populated, is accurate.

3 Confirm that the Identity Type is Self Signed Root.

4 Confirm that the Certificate Type is SSL Server.

5 Select the "Let me override defaults" option so that you can specify additional information, such as your email address, that a CA can use to verify your identity.

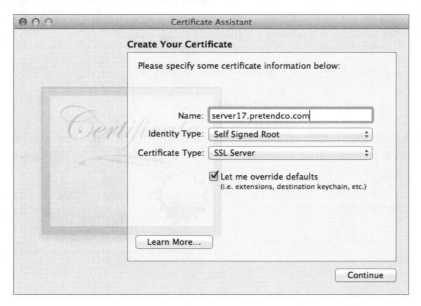

6   Click Continue.

7   At the message alerting you that you are creating a self-signed certificate, click Continue.

8   Accept the defaults for Serial Number and Validity Period, and click Continue.

9   In the Certificate Information pane, enter information appropriate for your situation.

In the Email Address field, enter ladmin@server*n*.pretendco.com (where *n* is your student number).

In a production environment, consider specifying an email address for your organization that will remain active even if you leave the organization, rather than your personal email address.

Normally you should enter valid information for every single field because part of this information may be used as verification of your identity before a CA will sign your certificate. But for this the exercise to actually submit a CSR to a CA is optional, so the information does not need to be real—but it should at least be valid.

10 In the Name (Common Name) field, enter your server's host name: server*n*.pretendco .com (where *n* is your student number).

NOTE ▶ Because you are running the Server app on your administrator computer, the Certificate Assistant automatically populates the Name (Common Name) field with information from your administrator computer.

11 In the Organization field, enter Pretendco Project *n* (where *n* is your student number).

12 In the Organizational Unit field, enter Training.

13 Enter information appropriate for your City and State/Province. To be perfectly compliant with the standards, when you enter your state or province, use its full name, not an abbreviation.

14 Modify the Country field if necessary.

15 After you have completed all the fields and confirmed that the information is correct, click Continue.

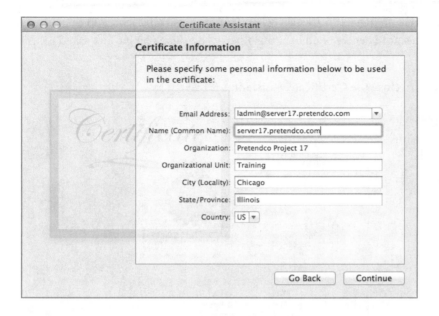

16 Click Continue for the rest of the panes, until you see the Subject Alternate Name Extension pane.

17 The Certificate Assistant uses the IP address of your administrator computer to populate the iPAddress field, so in the iPAddress field, enter the IPv4 address of your server, **10.0.0.**n**1**, where n is your student number, and click Continue.

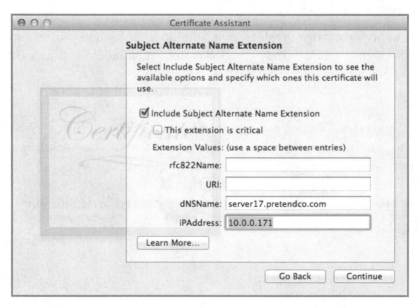

18 In the Conclusion pane, don't worry when you see a warning icon and the text "This certificate has not been verified by a third party," because you haven't asked a CA to sign it yet.

Click Done to close the Certificate Assistant.

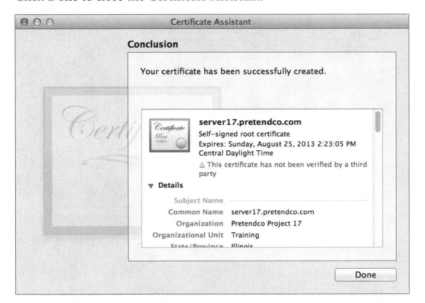

19 When the Server app window appears with "Server wants to export key [your host name] from your keychain," click Allow.

This allows the Server app to move items from your personal login keychain to the System keychain, and to store the new certificate information in /etc/certificates so other services can use the certificate.

Create a CSR

You're now ready to create a CSR that you would send to the CA of your choice. Even if you do not plan to perform the optional exercise to send this CSR to a CA, go ahead with the rest of the exercise to become familiar with the steps required.

1 In the Server app, select the certificate you just created (the certificate with your host name).

2   Click the disclosure triangle for Details to display the details for the SSL certificate.

3   Confirm that you selected the self-signed certificate you just created; you should see additional information that the default self-signed certificate does not contain, such as Organization, Organizational Unit, and State/Province.

4   Click the Action (gear icon) pop-up menu and choose Generate Certificate Signing Request (CSR).

5   You can use the plain text provided to request a signed certificate from a CA.

Click Save to save the file. By default it is saved in your Documents folder; it is fine to save it there.

You just used the Server app to remove the default self-signed SSL certificate and then create a self-signed certificate, which created the certificate and stored the public and private keys in your System keychain. You then created a CSR, which you would send to a CA.

Exercise 5.2
Import a Signed Certificate (Optional)

▶ **Prerequisites**

- ▶ Exercise 5.1, "Create a Certificate Signing Request"
- ▶ A certification authority must have signed your CSR.

In this exercise, you use the Server app to replace your self-signed SSL certificate with the signed SSL certificate you received from a certification authority.

Several certification authorities offer to sign your CSR on a trial basis for a limited amount of time; at the time of this writing, at least one CA will sign a CSR for a domain that you do not control, for testing purposes, with a CA that is not trusted. This is fine for the purposes of this exercise. Choosing the CA is outside the scope of this guide.

Even if you do not submit your CSR to a CA for a test signed certificate, you can follow along with these steps, but you will not have anything to import, and you will be instructed to skip the last step of the exercise.

> **NOTE** ▶ Once you send your CSR to a CA to sign, the CA sends you a signed certificate. The procedure varies between each certification authority, and is beyond the scope of this guide.

1   To import a signed certificate, in the Settings pane of the Server app, next to SSL Certificate, click Edit.

2   Click the Action (gear icon) pop-up menu and choose Manage Certificates.

3   Select the certificate with your server's host name.

4   Click the disclosure triangle for Details to display the details for the SSL certificate.

5   Confirm that you selected the self-signed certificate you just created. You should see additional information that the default self-signed certificate does not contain, such as Organization, Organizational Unit, and State/Province.

If you selected the default self-signed certificate, only the Common Name and Country fields are populated; select the other self-signed certificate instead.

6   Click the Action (gear icon) pop-up menu and choose Replace Certificate With Signed Or Renewed Certificate.

Note that the text "Private Key" is present; this indicates that the Server app is using the private key associated with your self-signed certificate; you do not need to provide the private key in this interface.

7   Drag the signed certificate (and any intermediate certificates that your CA instructs you to download and install) over the text "Drag a file containing the new certificate here."

If you did not submit your CSR to any CA, you will not have any signed certificates, so you can simply click Cancel and skip to the end of this exercise.

NOTE ▶ Some CAs also instruct you to download and install one or more intermediate certificates. If this is the case, follow their instructions.

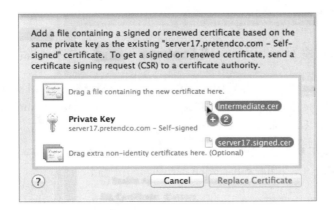

8   Click Replace Certificate.

You just used the Server app to replace your self-signed SSL certificate with the signed SSL certificate you received from a certification authority.

Exercise 5.3
Archive Your Certificate (Optional)

▶ **Prerequisite**

> ▶ Exercise 5.1, "Create a Certificate Signing Request"

In this exercise, you use Keychain Access to create a secure archive of your certificate, including your private key and learn to reimport it if needed later.

Archiving Your SSL Certificate

Making a backup of your SSL certificate and private key is a good idea. Luckily, Keychain Access makes it easy to archive your certificate and private key in a secure way.

1   On your server computer, open Keychain Access, select System in the Keychains column, select My Certificates in the Category column, and select the certificate with your server's host name.

> **NOTE** ▶ If you enabled Apple Push Notifications, you will also see certificates that start with the string "APSP" listed.

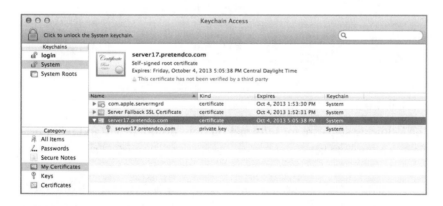

2   Choose File > Export Items.

3   Enter a name for the archive, such as your hostname, and specify a location, such as the desktop.

4   In the File Format pop-up menu, choose Personal Information Exchange (.p12).

5   Click Save. Provide your local administrator credentials and click OK.

6   Type **ladminpw** as the password to protect your private key, move into the Verify field, and then type **ladminpw** again to verify (because you cannot see the characters you enter), and click OK.

Note that Keychain Access evaluates the strength of the password you enter.

NOTE ▶ In a production environment, you should use a strong password.

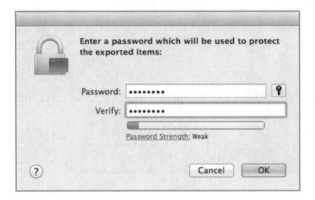

Reimporting the Exported Certificate

NOTE ▶ The following steps are for information only, do not delete and reimport your certificate and private key.

1   If you later need to reimport the certificate, choose "Import a Certificate Identity" in the Server app's Manage Certificates section and drag the .p12 file into the appropriate field.

2   Provide the passphrase you used when you exported the certificate and click Decrypt.

If the certificate is self-signed, the pane looks like the following figure:

If the certificate is signed by a CA, the pane looks like the following figure. Notice that the "Issued by" contains information about the CA's certificate that signed your CSR. Many CAs require you to also download and import an intermediate certificate, and in this example, the intermediate certificate was also dragged into the field, which is indicated in the figure by the text "1 non-identity certificate will be added."

3   In either case, click Import to import the items.

You used Keychain Access to create a secure archive of your certificate, including your private key. The archive is protected by a password, but it's recommended to keep this archive file in a secure location.

Exercise 5.4
Configure Your Server to Use Its New SSL Certificate

▶ **Prerequisite**

▶   Exercise 5.1, "Create a Certificate Signing Request"

Because you do not control the domain pretendco.com, you cannot get a CA to sign a CSR for your server's SSL certificate with a CA that is generally trusted, for production use. Because your server's SSL certificate is not in a certificate chain anchored by a CA that is configured in the System Roots keychain, computers and devices will not trust your server's SSL certificate; you can address this in Exercise 5.5, "Configure Your Administrator Computer to Trust an SSL Certificate."

Use the Server app to configure your server's Websites service to use the self-signed certificate you just created.

1 In the Server app, in your server's Settings section, next to the SSL Certificate field, click Edit.

2 Click the Certificate pop-up menu, and note that you see your newly created self-signed certificate as an option.

Choose Custom. This means that you can separately configure each service to use a different certificate, or no certificate at all.

3 For the Websites service, click the pop-up menu, and then choose your newly created self-signed certificate.

4 Click OK to save the change and dismiss the SSL Certificates pane.

Turn on the Websites service.

5 In the Server app sidebar, select the Websites service.

6 Click the On/Off switch to turn the service on.

You just configured an OS X Server service to use a self-signed certificate for the Websites service, and turned on the Websites service. The next step is to confirm that the service actually uses the self-signed certificate; this is covered in Exercise 5.5.

Exercise 5.5
Configure Your Administrator Computer to Trust an SSL Certificate

► **Prerequisites**

- ► Exercise 5.1, "Create a Certificate Signing Request"

- ► Exercise 5.4, "Configure Your Server to Use Its New SSL Certificate"

In a production environment, it is best to use a valid SSL certificate that's been signed by a trusted CA. If that isn't possible, you should configure your users' computers and devices to trust your server's self-signed SSL certificate, so that your users do not get into the habit of configuring their devices to trust unverified SSL certificates.

This lesson shows you how to configure an individual computer to trust your server's self-signed SSL certificate; it is beyond the scope of this lesson to show you how to replicate the end result on multiple computers and devices.

Verify That the Web Service Uses the New Certificate

On your administrator computer, confirm that you are using your server's DNS service, otherwise you will not be able to connect to its web service using its host name; then open Safari to your server's default HTTPS website. Finally, configure your administrator computer to trust the SSL certificate.

1   On your administrator computer, open System Preferences.

2   Open the Network pane.

3   Select the active network service, and confirm that your server's IP address is listed for the DNS Service value.

   If you are using Wi-Fi, you need to click Advanced, and then click the DNS tab to view the DNS Service value.

4   On your administrator computer, open Safari, press Command-L to set the cursor in the location field, enter **https://servern.pretendco.com** (where *n* is your student number), and press Return.

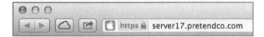

Your certificate is not signed by a trusted CA, and you'll see the message that Safari can't verify the identity of the website.

Configure your administrator computer to trust this SSL certificate.

1   Click Show Certificate.

2   Click the Details disclosure triangle and confirm that the Subject Name section contains the information you specified when you created the self-signed SSL certificate.

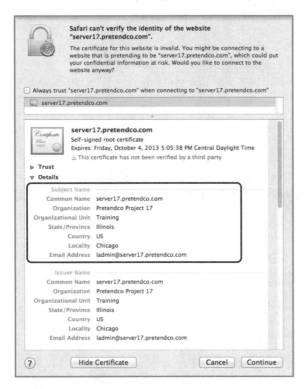

3   Click the Trust disclosure triangle.

Note that the pop-up menus for Secure Sockets Layer (SSL) and X.509 Basic Policy are set to "no value specified," which means that your administrator computer does not trust this certificate for SSL.

4   Select the checkbox "Always trust 'server*n*.pretendco.com' when connecting to 'server*n*.pretendco.com'" (where *n* is your student number).

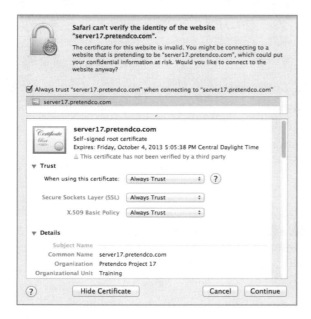

Note that this changes the pop-up menus in the Trust section to Always Trust.

5 Click Continue.

6 Provide your login credentials and click Update Settings.

This updates your settings for the currently logged in user; this does not affect any other user on this computer.

7 Confirm that Safari opens the page using SSL, with the Safari location field displaying an icon that contains the text "https" and a lock icon.

8 Keep Safari open for the next section of this exercise.

Confirm That You Trust the SSL Certificate

To view the SSL certificate the Websites service is using, perform the following steps.

1 In the Location field, click the "https" icon.

2 In the pane that informs you that Safari is using an encrypted connection, click Show Certificate.

3   Click the Details disclosure triangle to display the contents of the Details section.

4   Confirm that the Subject Name section contains the information you specified when you created the self-signed SSL certificate.

5   Click OK to close the pane.

6   Press Command-Q to quit Safari.

You confirmed that the Websites service actually uses the SSL certificate as you configured in the previous exercise.

You did not get a CA to sign your certificate for production use, so you needed to configure your administrator computer to trust the certificate.

Exercise 5.6
Clean Up

To ensure that the rest of the exercises are consistent, turn off the Websites service.

1 In the Server app sidebar, select the Websites service, and click the switch to turn the service off.

2 Confirm that no green status indicators appear next to the Websites service. This indicates that the service is off.

You are ready to complete the tasks of any other lesson's exercises.

Additional Resources

The following documents provide more information about using SSL.

Many other documents are available at www.apple.com/osx/server/resources/documentation.html.

Apple Root Certification Authority: www.apple.com/certificateauthority/

Apple Root Certificate Program: www.apple.com/certificateauthority/ca_program.html

Apple Certificate Policy: www.apple.com/certificateauthority/Apple_Certificate_Policy

Adding new trusted root certificates to System.keychain: http://derflounder.wordpress.com/2011/03/13/adding-new-trusted-root-certificates-to-system-keychain/

OS X Server Administration Guides
OS X Server: Advanced Administration
http://help.apple.com/advancedserveradmin/mac/10.8/

Apple Knowledge Base Documents
You can check for new and updated Knowledge Base documents at www.apple.com/support/.

Document HT4777, "OS X Server: Configuring WebDAV sharing for Active Directory accounts"

Document HT4813, "Mac OS X Server: Configuring clients to use SSL for Open Directory binding"

Document HT4837, "OS X Server: Using the Profile Manager or Wiki service with Active Directory or third-party LDAP services"

Document HT5300, "OS X Server: Steps to take before upgrading or migrating the Open Directory database"

Document HT5349, "OS X Server: How to reset Profile Manager to its original state"

Document HT5381, "OS X Server: Upgrade and migration"

Document HT5382, "OS X Server: Upgrading Websites service from previous versions"

Document HT5415, "OS X Server: About the RADIUS Service"

Document PH10949, "OS X Mountain Lion: Secure Sockets Layer (SSL)"

Lesson Review

1. What's the difference between a root CA and an intermediate CA?
2. What's the problem with just using a self-signed SSL certificate?
3. What tool do you use to create a new self-signed SSL certificate and a CSR?
4. What do you need before you can create a CSR?

Answers

1. An intermediate CA's public key certificate is signed by another CA. A root CA's public key certificate is signed by itself. Note that there is a set of root CAs and intermediate CAs that OS X trusts.
2. Computers and devices accessing services that use a self-signed SSL certificate will see a message that the SSL certificate is not trusted. It is a security risk to teach users to just trust any SSL certificate that causes a warning.
3. Use the Server app to create a new self-signed SSL certificate and a CSR.
4. You need a self-signed SSL certificate before you can use it to create a CSR.

Lesson 6
Using Status and Notifications

A server can only perform its functions when it is in good health and has the resources it needs. OS X Server, via its Server app, provides monitoring and issues notifications if something triggers a threshold or condition. Using the monitoring and notifications features can help keep the server running properly.

GOALS

▶ Monitoring OS X Server

▶ Setting up notifications

Reference 6.1
Monitoring and Status Concepts

As much as we would like, servers, even OS X server computers, need some attention from time to time and can't be left to their own devices. It is inefficient to regularly peruse all the operating parameters to make sure the server is healthy. We can utilize the built-in capabilities of the server to tell us when things go wrong or show us when certain trigger points are reached. When these points are reached, OS X Server can notify us via an email alert. This doesn't remove the need to look over the server once in a while, but it can help us recognize that a situation is happening or could happen shortly.

Four major sections in the Server app help you monitor the server:

▶ Alerts—Set up what is considered a trigger point and the email address(es) of who will get the alerts.

▶ Logs—Quickly access and search logs for the services provided by OS X Server.

▶ Stats—View graphs for processor and memory usage plus network traffic for time periods ranging from 1 hour to 7 days.

▶ Storage—See a list of all visible volumes available to the server and the amount of storage space left.

Reference 6.2
OS X Server Alerts

In the Status section of the Server app, the Alerts pane allows you to configure both the list of email addresses to receive alerts and what alerts will be sent. The Alerts pane has two tabs:

▶ Alerts—Where the messages are shown

▶ Delivery—Where the email recipients are listed and what will be delivered to them. There is also the choice for push notifications.

NOTE ▶ Push notification is available only once the Apple Push Notification service is configured and enabled on the server.

When choosing an email address for notifications, it is recommended to create a separate email account that can link to multiple people rather than sending it to specific users from the Server app. This prevents a situation where a person responsible for the server leaves the group and notifications go unnoticed. An account like alerts@pretendco.com could be used for multiple purposes and decouples the alerts from individuals.

After you use the Server app to enable Apple push notifications, and supply an Apple ID for push notifications, your server sends alerts to any Mac with Mountain Lion on which you use the Server app to manage your server. These alerts appear in the Server app and in the Notification Center of these computers. In the following figure, the server is configured to send alerts to the ladmin user on client17 and server17.

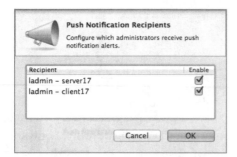

You can use the Notifications preference to configure how the notifications for the Server app appear.

Alert messages will be displayed with a brief description on what has occurred. You can filter the result by adding a term at the bottom of the pane. Double-click the alert, or click the Action (gear icon) menu and choose View Alert, to get additional information regarding the alert. In some cases a button is available to help rectify the error, but you must understand what caused the error and how clicking the button may help or hurt the server.

Reference 6.3
Logs in OS X Server

In the Status section of the Server app, the Logs pane allows quick access to the logs for the various services running on the server. A search box allows you to help track down specific items in the logs.

Certain logs will always be available, but others become available once the service has been turned on.

Additional logs are available using the Console app located at /Applications/Utilities.

Reference 6.4
Stats in OS X Server

In the Stats pane, three performance graphs are available:

▶ Processor Usage—Divided into System CPU and User CPU to help determine what is using the most CPU cycles.

▶ Memory Usage—Shows how much physical RAM is being used.

▶ Network Traffic—Shows outbound and inbound traffic.

All three graphs are adjustable to show time intervals from the past hour to the past 7 days.

When using the graphs, realize that the actual numbers reflected on the graph don't tell the whole story. Often, the shape of the graph is most important. Review the graphs once in a while to get used to what is normal and be able to identify when a change is happening.

A normal Processor Usage graph might show a certain percentage during the workday with spikes corresponding to heavy server utilization. It may indicate a problem when the graphs show a higher than usual percentage with no usage changes to account for it. This might indicate that it is time to do some more research.

Memory usage might creep up over time if an application isn't releasing RAM. The graph might also show that all available RAM is being used continuously, which may indicate that the server needs a RAM upgrade.

Network traffic should also follow the usage patterns. Heavy access will be shown in the graphs, but traffic at night or other times of low usage might indicate a backup process or access that isn't planned.

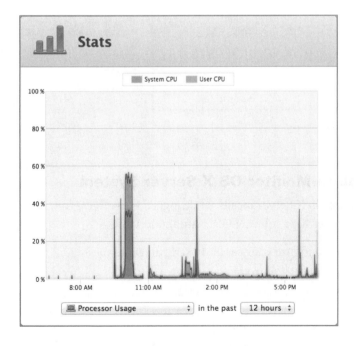

Reference 6.5
Storage

Storage is listed in the Hardware section of the Server app. Select the server in the sidebar and then click the Storage tab. Each volume attached to the server is listed, and the available amount of storage capacity is listed next to it with a bar graph for quick review. Each volume can be reviewed and permissions viewed and changed (covered further in Lessons 13 and 14).

Exercise 6.1
Use the Server App to Monitor OS X Server System

You use Server app to manage OS X Server locally while logged in on the server, or to manage it remotely from another Mac running OS X Mountain Lion.

You can use the Server app to configure your server to send an email message, a push notification, or both, when any of the following conditions occur:

▶ An SSL certificate is about to expire.

▶ A disk that OS X Server uses is unreachable.

▶ The S.M.A.R.T (Self-Monitoring, Analysis and Reporting Technology) status of a disk anticipates failure.

► A disk is low on available space.

► Mail storage quota has been exceeded.

► An email message has a virus.

► The network configuration has changed.

► Software updates for your OS X Server are available.

1 To allow push notifications, select the server in the sidebar. Click the Settings tab.

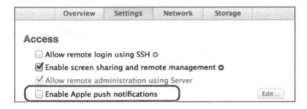

2 If the "Enable Apple push notifications" checkbox is not already selected, select it now.

3 If you haven't already configured an Apple ID to be used for push notifications, in the dialog, enter your Apple ID to obtain the push notification certificate. Click Ok when done.

To configure the email address that is the recipient of alerts from the Server app:

1 In the Server app sidebar, select Alerts.

2 Click the Delivery tab, and click the Email Addresses Edit button.

3 Click the Add (+) button.

4 Enter an email address (you can use your own) that will receive alerts, and click OK.

It's a good idea to use the Server app to proactively monitor your server, so you can address any issues that crop up, rather than reacting to an alert in a crisis situation.

Configure which alerts you want to be sent:

1   In the Server app sidebar, select Alerts.

2   Click the Delivery tab, and select the alert types you want to be sent out.

One of the alerts is for low disk space; instead of waiting for an alert, regularly use the Server app to display information about available disk space.

1   In the Server app sidebar, select your server.

2   Click the Storage tab and review the amount of available space.

Although no alert exists for an abnormally high amount of processor usage, memory usage, or network traffic, monitoring these occasionally is still a good idea. The Server app displays a graph of the following categories of information:

▶ Processor Usage (including System CPU and User CPU)

▶ Memory Usage

▶ Network Traffic (including Outbound Traffic and Inbound Traffic)

To use the Server app to display the available graphs:

1 In the Server app sidebar, select Stats.

2 Click the pop-up menu to choose Processor Usage, Memory Usage, or Network Traffic.

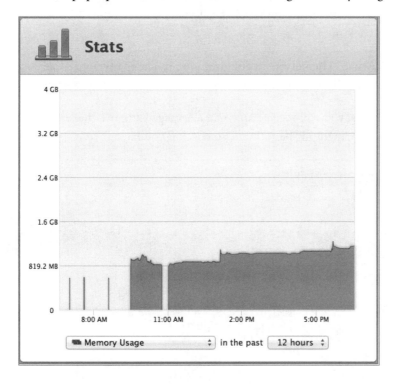

3 Click the menu on the right to choose the duration of time to include for the graph.

Trigger an Alert (Optional)

Use the following optional steps to temporarily change your server's network configuration. This causes the server to send you an alert. This requires a wireless network, your
server to connected to the Internet, and the server app to be configured with a valid email
address that you can access.

NOTE ▶ The resulting alert email will be sent from root@server*n*.pretendco.com
(where *n* is your student number) and might be considered spam by an email filter.
You may need to configure your spam filters to accept email from that address.

1   Unplug the Ethernet cable, enable wireless networking, and then connect the server
to a wireless network if possible. In a classroom training situation, your instructor
will tell you which wireless network to use. Leave the cable unplugged for at least one
minute and then disconnect from the wireless network by turning off AirPort. Plug
the Ethernet cable back in.

2   In the alerts, notice that "The network configuration has changed" notice has
appeared. Double-click the alert to read the details. Click Done when finished.

3   Within a few moments, you will receive an email alert regarding the change. It is possible for the email to be caught in spam filters, so check if you haven't received the alert.

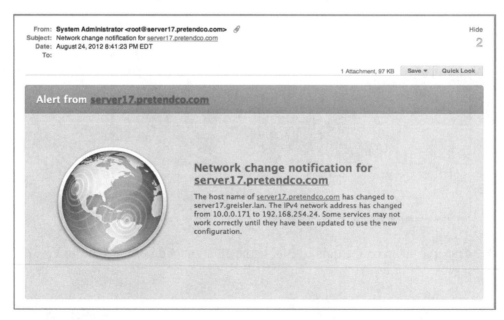

Additional Resources

The following documents provide more information about status and notifications in OS X Server.

Many other documents are available at www.apple.com/osx/server/resources/documentation.html.

OS X Server Administration Guides

OS X Server: Advanced Administration
http://help.apple.com/advancedserveradmin/mac/10.8/

Apple Knowledge Base Documents

You can check for new and updated Knowledge Base documents at www.apple.com/support/.

Document HT3947, "OS X Server: Push Notification Server and supported applications"

Lesson Review

1. What is the purpose of alerts?

2. What are the two ways alerts can be delivered?

3. If you wish to use push alerts, what is the first step you need to take?

4. If an alert details offers to update services, what is the correct action?

5. Which volumes are shown in the Storage tab in the Server app?

Answers

1. To provide a system of warning of various conditions.

2. Email and alerts pushed to the Server app.

3. Configure the Apple Push Notification service for the server you are using.

4. Understand the alert and rectify the situation before making any configuration changes, as they may be unneeded.

5. All that are visible and mounted on the server.

Lesson **7**

Backing Up OS X Server

As much as we might hope otherwise, problems do occur and sometimes that leads to the need to recover a server whose hardware or software has failed. To help protect against failures, a proven backup system needs to be utilized. Although there are many backup choices on the market, OS X since v10.5 has had Time Machine built in. When used with OS X Server, it can provide a functional, low-cost, and simple backup solution.

GOALS

▶ Back up OS X Server

▶ Restore OS X Server

Reference 7.1
Backup Concepts

There are a number of considerations when it comes to backing up computers. You need to decide when and how often it gets backed up, where it gets backed up, and how often the backup media is rotated.

The commercial products available to back up OS X Server offer a wide range of backup techniques and choice of media. With these products you can define exactly how often the server gets backed up and what gets backed up. You can decide if you are going to back up to tape, hard drives, or cloud storage. You get to decide what style of backup to use such as:

▶ Full image—The entire server's drive is replicated block by block, but it requires that the server be stopped and started from another volume.

▶ Full file level copy—The entire volume is copied file by file. This takes longer and doesn't require the server to be started from another volume, but unless certain services, especially ones that use a database, are stopped, the backup may not be totally valid.

▶ Incremental—Only the changes from the previous backup are copied. This takes less time and space, but can take longer to restore as it may need to read from multiple incremental copies to get that full amount of data.

▶ Continuous—Also known as continuous data protection (CDP), where changes are committed to the backup in short intervals rather than waiting for the end of the day. This allows for more granular backups.

When deciding on the media, consider capacity, lifespan, and portability. Some popular choices include:

▶ Tape—While tape's death has been reported on for years, it stays viable by offering large capacities, portability, and increasing speed. The downside is the tape drives and libraries tend to require care and effort to keep running.

▶ Disk—The cost of disk has decreased to the point where its capacity and speed are a balance to the concerns of lifespan and lack of portability when installed in a large array of drives. Individual drives are portable, of course.

▶ Cloud-based storage—Storing data on a remote host over the Internet is becoming extremely popular and viable with increasing bandwidth and the availability of inexpensive data storage plans. The downside is the reliance on a third party to keep your data safe and the length of time to restore data over the Internet. Some hosts will allow you to make a local backup and send it to them for "seeding," where they copy your data from disk to their infrastructure and send you a disk for restores.

Regardless of the choice of backup technique and media, testing the restores is immensely critical. Data has been lost because a trusted backup turned out to have a problem when a restore was needed. Backups should be tested on a regular basis and verified as valid.

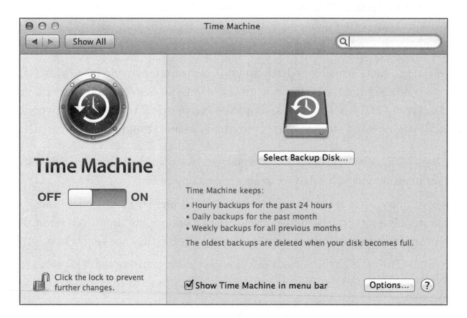

Reference 7.2
Time Machine

Apple has provided a simple to use and effective backup application in all versions of OS X since v10.5. Time Machine was originally conceived to make it easy to back up computers with little effort. The process of setting up Time Machine is simply to connect an external hard drive and turn on Time Machine.

Time Machine has grown in capability and is a viable choice to back up OS X Server. Time Machine can be considered a form of continuous data protection and also handles the databases OS X Server uses properly.

> **NOTE** ▶ If you have moved your service data off the startup volume, you need to refer to Knowledge Base document HT5139, "Restoring OS X Server from a Time Machine backup" for instructions on how to use command-line tools to restore the service data properly.

Backup targets for Time Machine are limited to hard drive volumes visible to the server and Time Machine–enabled network AFP sharepoints.

> **NOTE** ▶ For more information regarding Time Machine, refer to Lesson 18 in *Apple Pro Training Series: OS X Support Essentials*.

For OS X Server, Time Machine can back up service data, including the following:

▶ Contacts

▶ File Sharing

▶ Calendar

▶ Messages

▶ Mail

▶ Open Directory

▶ Profile Manager

▶ Time Machine (the service for providing a backup target across a network)

▶ VPN

▶ Web

▶ Wiki

Time Machine will not back up the following:

▶   /tmp/

▶   /Library/Logs/

▶   /Library/Caches/

▶   /Users/<username>/Library/Caches

One of the new features in Time Machine for OS X Mountain Lion is the ability to back up to more than one target. This makes it easy to connect a hard drive to the server for continuous protection and connect a second drive that is rotated offsite. With two or more hard drives being rotated offsite, a disaster recovery plan can be implemented while providing instant recovery of data from the local drive as needed.

Time Machine is capable of taking snapshots and backing up onto its own startup volume. The snapshots feature is a convenience designed for laptops but shouldn't be considered for production servers.

Time Machine makes a backup once an hour for 24 hours. Beyond 24 hours it saves a daily backup for a month, and then weekly backups from that point on until the target volume fills up. The oldest backups are deleted at that point. If you don't want to lose your backups, replace the backup targets as they get close to full.

Exercise 7.1
Use Time Machine to Back Up OS X Server

It is important to consider backup when planning your IT environment. With Time Machine, backup and restore becomes very easy. This exercise guides you through the basics of using Time Machine.

Prepare two temporary destinations for the Time Machine backup.

Option 1: Use Two External Disks As Time Machine Destinations

If you have two external HFS+ formatted disks that you can erase before and after you perform the exercises, follow these steps. Otherwise, skip to the next section, Option 2: Use Internal Volumes As Time Machine Destinations.

1   Physically connect both external disks to your server computer.

2   In the finder, choose Finder > Finder Preferences.

3   If necessary, click General in the toolbar, and select the checkbox to show Hard disks on the desktop.

4   Select one of your external disks, press Return to change the name, enter **BackupTarget** as the name, and press Return to finish changing the name.

5   Name the other disk **Backup2**.

Skip Option 2, and continue with the section "Configure Time Machine".

Option 2: Use Internal Volumes As Time Machine Destinations

Alternatively, considering that ACLs prevent you from removing backup files from a Time Machine destination, and that this is a test environment, you can use the following steps to use Disk Utility to create two new temporary volumes on your existing disk. In a production environment, a Time Machine destination should be a volume on a physically separate disk.

1   On your server computer, click LaunchPad in the Dock, click Other, and open Disk Utility.

2   In the Disk Utility sidebar, select the disk that contains your server's startup volume. Be sure to select the disk, and not the volume.

3   Click the Partition tab.

4   Click Add (+). If the disk with your startup volume already has multiple partitions, you may need to first select a volume with extra space, like your startup volume, before the Add button becomes available.

5   Select the new volume you just created. In the Name field, enter **BackupTarget**.

6   Create the second extra volume by clicking Add (+).

7   Select this second new volume, which should be automatically named BackupTarget.

8   In the Name field, enter **Backup2**.

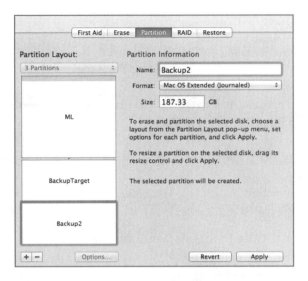

9 Click Apply, and in the dialog to confirm your action, click Partition.

Configure Time Machine

1 On your server computer, open System Preferences, and select the Time Machine preference pane.

2 In the Time Machine preference pane, click Select Backup Disk.

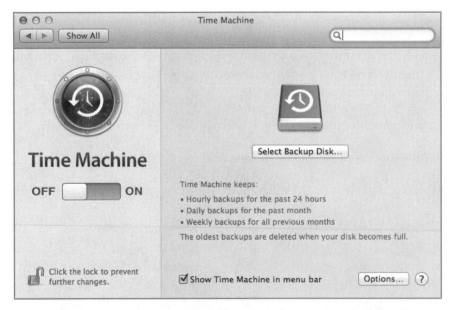

3 Select BackupTarget and click Use Disk. If you have partitioned the boot drive and are asked, "Are you sure you want to back up to the same device your original data is on?" then click "Use Selected Volume". If you are asked to erase the disk, click Erase.

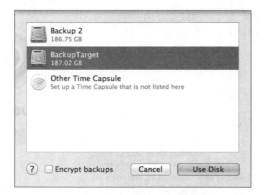

4 In the main Time Machine pane, click Options to review the list of items that you could select to exclude from backups. Review the options but leave everything as default for this exercise.

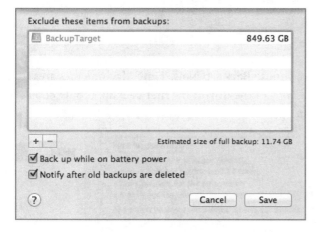

5 Click Cancel to return to close the exclusions sheet.

6 Click Select Disk to add the second destination.

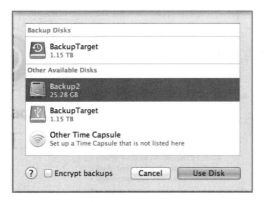

7 Select Backup2 and click Use Disk.

8 When you are asked if you want to replace your existing backup target or use both, click Use Both.

9 From the Time Machine menu, choose Back Up Now. Time Machine prepares for the backups and makes a complete copy of the disk at the first backup. It only copies what has changed from that point on.

Exercise 7.2
Restore from Time Machine Backup (Optional)

► **Prerequisite**

► Exercise 7.1, "Use Time Machine to Back Up OS X Server"

Because it takes a while to complete a backup, consider continuing with another lesson, then returning to this exercise after the backup has completed. Don't worry, you can work while a backup is being made, just be sure to follow the steps of this exercise to initiate one last backup before you restore.

In this exercise, you will restore a file from the Finder (since we know your Downloads folder has a default file named About Downloads, you will use that file as an example), then you will explore restoring the entire system from OS X Recovery.

1   On your server computer, click the Time Machine menu and confirm that it lists the time the latest backup completed. If the backup is still running, return to this exercise later.

2   Click the Time Machine menu and choose Back Up Now to do one last backup before you perform the restore. Wait until this backup is complete, which should only take a few moments.

3   On your server computer, from the Go menu, choose Downloads.

4   From the Time Machine menu, choose Enter Time Machine.

5   Navigate to an earlier time by clicking the up arrow. This arrow points back in time.

6   Select the About Downloads file.

7   Click Restore. When asked whether to keep the original file, replace the file, or keep both files, click Keep Both and compare the files.

8 The files in Time Machine's backup volume are also directly available simply by navigating to the backup volume, finding the backup time folder you want, and copying the file you need.

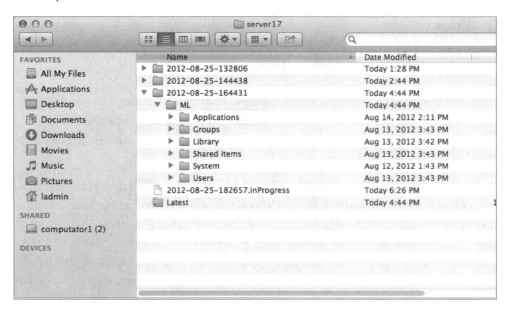

9 Restart your server and hold the Option key. Choose the Recovery volume and once started from it, choose Restore From Time Machine Backup from the OS X Utilities window. Follow the assistant but do not restore.

NOTE ▶ Using Time Machine is a handy way to restore your test server back to a known state. If during your testing you break the server or want to revert to a known good version, Time Machine can make it easy.

Additional Resources

The following documents provide more information about backup procedures in OS X Server.

Many other documents are available at www.apple.com/osx/server/resources/documentation.html.

OS X Server Administration Guides

OS X Server: Advanced Administration

http://help.apple.com/advancedserveradmin/mac/10.8/

Apple Knowledge Base Documents

You can check for new and updated Knowledge Base documents at www.apple.com/support/.

Document HT5139, "Restoring OS X Server from a Time Machine backups"

Document HT3275, "Time Machine: Troubleshooting backup issues"

Document TS2986, "OS X: Cannot install on a volume used by Time Machine for backups"

Document HT4878, "OS X Lion: About Time Machine's 'local snapshots' on portable Macs"

Document HT5096, "Time Machine: How to transfer backups from the current backup drive to a new backup drive"

Lesson Review

1. Why use Time Machine to back up OS X Server?
2. What files are not backed up by Time Machine that might be important in a server to a system administrator?
3. What kind of backup targets can be used for Time Machine?
4. If you don't want to drop the oldest backups, what should you do?
5. What are three ways of recovering data from a Time Machine backup?

Answers

1. To provide a simple backup system that is capable of backing up OS X Server and restoring its services.
2. /Library/Logs/.
3. Locally connected volumes and AFP file shares.
4. Don't let the backup target volumes fill up or the oldest backups will be dropped.
5. From the Time Machine graphical interface, directly from the backup volume, and via Restore from Time Machine Backup in the Recovery volume.

Configuring Accounts

Lesson **8**

Managing Local Users

Authentication is the process by which a person identifies which user account she wants to use on the system. This is similar to, but slightly different from, saying that authentication is how a person proves his or her identity to a system. The distinction is useful because multiple people may share the same user name and password, or one person may have multiple user accounts on the same system. In each case, the person supplies user account *credentials* (which usually consist of a name and a password) to identify the user account the person wants to use, and if the supplied credentials are valid, the person successfully authenticates. Although there are other methods of authenticating a user account, such as smart cards or voice print, the combination of name and password is the most common (and is assumed for this lesson).

GOALS

▶ Understand authentication and authorization

▶ Create and configure local user accounts

▶ Create and configure local group accounts

▶ Import local accounts

▶ Manage service access authorization

Authorization is the process that determines what an authenticated user account is allowed to do on the system. OS X Server can disallow authorization to use OS X Server services unless a user is explicitly granted authorization to use the service. In Lesson 13, "Providing File Sharing Services," you will learn more about authorization to access a particular file.

In this lesson you will use the Server app to:

▶ Configure local user and group accounts.

▶ Import local accounts.

▶ Configure access to services.

Reference 8.1
Understanding Authentication and Authorization

When configuring any server for access by users, you'll need to determine what services the server will provide and what levels of user access to assign. For many of the services this guide covers, such as file sharing, you'll need to create specific user accounts on your server.

When considering the creation of user accounts, you'll want to determine how to best set up your users, how to organize them into groups that match the needs of your organization, and how to best maintain this information over time. As with any service or information technology task, the best approach is to thoroughly plan your requirements and approach before starting to implement a solution.

Using Authentication and Authorization

Authentication occurs in many different contexts in OS X and OS X Server, but it most commonly involves using a login window. For example, when you start up an OS X computer, you may have to enter a user name and password in an initial login window before being allowed to use the system at all.

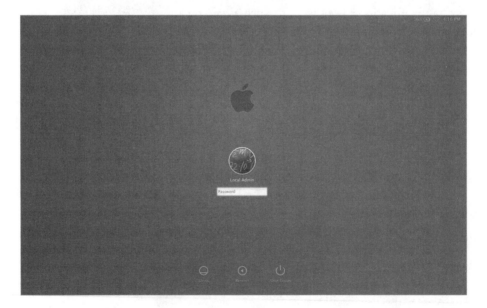

Authentication also occurs when you attempt to connect to a network file service, whether via AFP or SMB; in the following figure, you need to provide a name and a password to authenticate for the AFP service.

A user must authenticate before accessing these services, even if logging in just as a guest user. Depending on what he is trying to access, the user may or may not get feedback on whether he entered the wrong password (authentication) or is not allowed access to the service (authorization). For instance, if you enter a wrong password at the login window, the login window will simply shake and return you to the login window; this is the behavior for many authentication dialogs in OS X and OS X Server.

If you do not have authorization to log in at a computer, even if the user name and password are correct, the login window will again shake and return to the login window. The user experience is the same, despite the different reasons for the user not being able to access a service.

Reference 8.2
Creating and Administering User and Administrator Server Accounts

A number of tools are available to create and administer user and group accounts. You use the Users & Groups preferences on OS X to define local users and perform very basic administration of local groups. However, System Preferences does not have a remote mode; you have to use tools such as Screen Sharing or Apple Remote Desktop to remotely administer System Preferences on an OS X Server computer.

NOTE ▸ It is common to drop the word "account" from the term "user account."

This lesson focuses on using the Server app to remotely manage local user and group accounts, and to remotely manage access to the services OS X Server provides.

OS X stores local user and group accounts in the local directory domain (also known as local directory node). You will learn about managing local network accounts in Lesson 10, "Managing Local Network Accounts."

To administer a server with the Server app, you must authenticate as an administrator. This is required whether you use the Server app at the server locally or remotely from another computer.

Using the Server App for Configuring User Accounts

To grant a person specific permissions on OS X Server, you must set up a user account for that person. The Server app is the primary tool you will use in this lesson for creating and configuring user accounts on OS X Server. You'll use the Server app to create network user accounts in the next lesson.

Standard local user accounts on OS X enable a person to access files and applications local to that computer. After you install OS X Server, local user accounts continue to allow access to files and services, whether you use a local user account to log in on the OS X Server computer, or you use a local user account to access OS X Server services such as mail and file sharing services. When you use another computer, you can use a server's local user account to remotely access various services offered by that server. But you cannot use that local user account at another computer's login window to log in to that computer, unless that other computer also has a local user account with the same name and password defined in its local directory domain. This is a complication you should avoid by using a centralized directory, which is covered in the next lesson.

When you use the Server app to create a user, you can specify the following settings:

- ▶ Full name
- ▶ Account name
- ▶ Email address
- ▶ Password
- ▶ Whether or not the user can administer the server
- ▶ Home folder (appears if the File Sharing service has been started)
- ▶ Disk quota

A user account's full name is also known as a long name or name; it is common practice to use a person's full name, with the first letter of each name capitalized, and a space between each word in the name. The name can contain no more than 255 bytes, so character sets that occupy multiple bytes per character have a lower maximum number of characters.

The account name, also known as short name, is an abbreviated name, usually consisting of all lowercase characters. A user can authenticate using the full name or account name. OS X uses a user's account name when creating a home folder for that user. Carefully consider the account name before assigning it, because it is not a trivial task to change a user's account name. You are not permitted to use the space character in a user's account name; it must contain at least one letter, and can contain only the following characters:

► a through z

► A through Z

► 0 through 9

► _ (underscore)

► − (hyphen)

► . (period)

For a little more information about the user, select the user in the Users pane, secondary click, and choose Advanced Options from the shortcut menu.

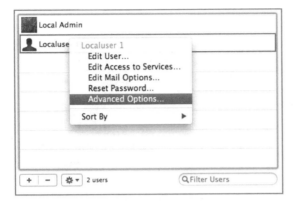

In the advanced settings pane, you can view and modify several attributes of a user account.

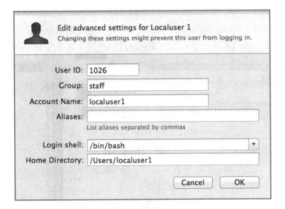

The full list of attributes listed in the advanced settings pane is:

▶   User ID

▶   Group

▶   Account Name

▶   Aliases

▶   Login shell

▶   Home Directory

You should not modify these attributes without completely understanding the ramifications of the change.

NOTE ▶ Invalid settings can prevent the user from logging in or accessing resources.

A full explanation of all of these attributes is outside the scope of this guide, but some are important enough that they are explained in the following sections.

The user ID (UID) is a numerical value that the system uses to differentiate one user from another. Though users gain access to the system with a name or short name, each name is associated with a UID, and the UID is used in making authorization decisions. In the unlikely event that two users are logged in with different names and passwords, but with the same UID, when they access documents and folders, the system will consider them to be the same owner. Because of this, the system will provide both users with the same access to documents and folders, a situation you should avoid.

> **NOTE ▸** The Server app allows you to configure multiple users with the same UID, but this is not recommended.

The group is the primary group the user is associated with, even though you can configure the user to be associated with multiple groups. You do not need to explicitly add a user to its primary group. Note that when you view a group's list of members, a user that is a member of a group because the group is the user's primary group will *not* be listed as a member of the group, even though it effectively is a member of that group.

It is recommended that you do not change the account name in the advanced settings pane, because this could prevent the user from accessing resources.

You can assign one or more aliases for a user account. An alias allows a user to access services by authenticating with one of her aliases and her password. An alias is sometimes a shorter or otherwise more convenient string of text than the account name.

Configuring Local User Accounts

OS X Server maintains a list of local user accounts for managing access to resources. In this section, you will learn how to use the Server app to:

▸ Create local users that can access services and files on your server.

▸ Give a local user the ability to administer your server.

▸ Create local groups.

▸ Assign local users to a local group.

▸ Assign local groups to a local user.

▸ Assign local groups to a local group.

Creating Local Users That Can Access Services and Files on Your Server

The Users pane of the Next Steps drawer offers some information as well as a link to the Users pane.

In the Users pane in the Server app, simply click the Add (+) button to create a new user.

Enter values for the new user's attributes, and then click Done.

Giving a Local User the Ability to Administer Your Server

An administrator account is a special type of user account on OS X Server that enables the user to administer the server. A user with an administrator account can create, edit, and delete user accounts, as well as modify the settings of various running services on the server where the administrator account exists. The administrator uses the Server app to perform basic account and service management.

It is simple to make a local user an administrator. Just select the checkbox for "Allow user to administer this server." You can enable this when you create the user, or at any time afterwards. You'll create a user and make it an administrator.

When you make a user account an administrator, the operating system makes that user account a member of the local group that has the full name of Administrators. Any member of the administrators group can use the Server app and can unlock all the preferences in System Preferences. Any member of the administrators group can also change file ownership and can run commands as the root user in the command-line environment, so consider carefully before enabling a user account to be a member of the administrators group.

NOTE ▶ You can also use the Users & Groups pane of System Preferences to specify that any user is an administrator.

NOTE ▶ When you select "Allow user to administer this server" for a user, you add him or her to the local group named admin. You can use the credentials for any user in the admin group to access secure system preferences like the Users & Groups and Security panes, among other privileges. Be careful about which users you assign as part of the local group admin.

In the list of users, there is no indication that any user is an administrator user.

To remove administrator status for a user, simply deselect the checkbox labeled "Allow user to administer this server," and click Done.

Creating Local Groups

Groups allow you to assign privileges to groups of users, so you don't have to modify each user individually. In the Server app sidebar, click Groups.

To create a group, click Add (+), enter information in the fields, and click Done.

Assigning Local Users to a Local Group

The most common approach for populating groups with users is to select a group and add one or more users to it. On your server, you will select a group, click Add (+), and then add users to the group. When you use the Server app to add a user to a group, you can't just enter the name; you have to actually choose a user from a list that appears when you start typing.

You could also choose Browse, and then select users and groups from the new window that appears, and drag them into the list of members.

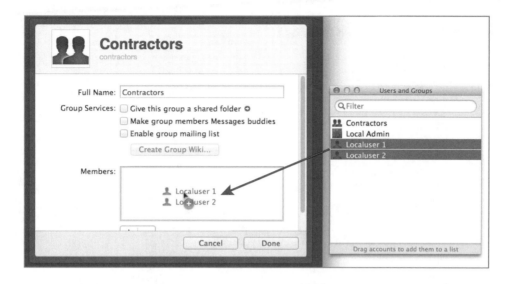

Assigning Local Groups to a Local User

Just as you can assign a user to a group, you can edit a user to add groups to that user. The effect is the same: You add a user as a member of a group.

After you add a group to a user, you can verify your action by looking at that group's list of members.

Assigning Local Groups to a Local Group

You can make a group a member of another group. This way, when you want to allow a group of groups to access the same resource, you can configure the parent group, instead of separately configuring each group.

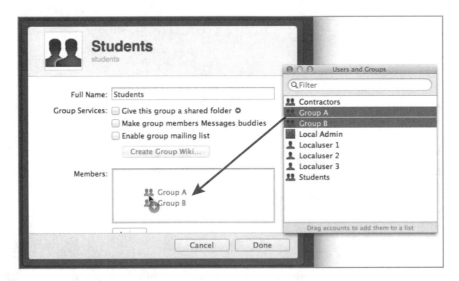

Importing Accounts

You can create accounts individually, or you can import them from a properly formatted file. The file could be created on your own, created with a third-party tool, or created with command-line tools.

Any time you import users from a file, and that file does not specify a password for a user, you will need to set their passwords after you import the users.

Importing a List of Users with the Server App

The Server app can import a list of users that contains user account data. The first line must be a header line that defines what kind of data is contained in the file and how the text is formatted. The user data must follow the header line. To import accounts, choose Manage > Import Accounts from File.

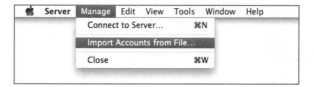

In the Import Users pane, navigate to select your input file. Be sure to provide administrator credentials, otherwise you'll get an error message.

If the import file does not contain plain text passwords, set the users passwords: Select the users you just imported, secondary click, and choose Reset Password from the shortcut menu.

Of course, you should always use secure passwords in a production environment.

Here's an example of an import file with an appropriate header line that describes the content of the file.

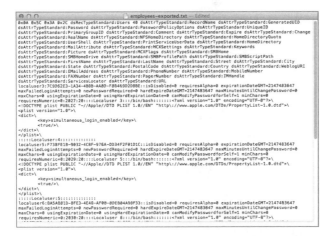

MORE INFO ▸ For more information about using Workgroup Manager to generate an appropriate header line for an import file, download and install Workgroup Manager, and see Workgroup Manager's Help.

Reference 8.3
Managing Access to Services

By default, if you have not configured your server to be an Open Directory server, it does not check for authorization before granting access to OS X Server services such as Mail, File Sharing, and Calendar services. In this state, if a given service is running, and someone can connect to it and successfully authenticate, OS X Server grants authorization to use the service.

However, you can choose to manage service access control manually. Once managed, after someone attempts to connect to a given service and successfully authenticates with a user account, OS X Server checks to see if that user is authorized to use the service before granting access to it. As you'll learn in the next lesson, managing access control is set up automatically after you configure your server as an Open Directory server.

Manually Managing Service Access

When you secondary click a user and choose "Edit Access to Services" from the shortcut menu, you see a list of services, and a few buttons. Each service's checkbox is unavailable, because at this point, you are not managing access to service yet; every authenticated user can access the service if the service is running.

When you click the Manage Service Access button, you are asked if you want to manually manage service access. Even after you click Manage, every user you create with the server automatically is granted authorization to each of your OS X Server services by default (of course, no user can access a given service if the service isn't running).

When you secondary click a user and choose "Edit Access to Services" from the shortcut menu, you see a list of services, and each service has a checkbox you can select or deselect. When you deselect a checkbox, you remove authorization for that user to access the service.

OS X Server grants authorization to a service for a user if the user, or any group that the user is a member of, has the access checkbox selected for that service. Therefore, when you edit a user's access to services and deselect a checkbox for a service, if the user is in a group for which access to that service is authorized, a message indicates that the user will still have access to the service.

> **MORE INFO ▶** If you create an account with Workgroup Manager, it does not config-ure the account to be able to access services; in fact, Workgroup Manager offers this warning when you create a new user account: "New users may not have access to ser-vices. If service access controls are enabled, you need to grant access to desired services for users created in Workgroup Manager." You can do this with the Server app.

Using Groups to Manage Access to Services

You may find that long-term administration will be easier if you manage access to services based on organizational roles assigned to groups rather than to individual people. This will make it much easier when changes occur within your organization, because you'll need to change only group membership rather than individual file and service permissions for each person.

When you enable File Sharing with the Server app, it automatically enables the AFP service for Apple file sharing (AFP is also used for the Time Machine backup service) and the SMB service for Windows clients. (You will learn more about these services in Lesson 13, "Providing File Sharing Services.")

> **MORE INFO ▶** Some system groups are normally hidden from view, with names like com.apple.access_afp and com.apple.access_backup, which contain the names of users and groups that have authorization to use a given service. You can view these groups by choosing View > Show System Accounts. You may see this referred to as Service Access Control Lists (SACLs) in other places. In most circumstances, it is best to not directly modify these system group files; instead, use the Server app to configure user or group access to services.

Reference 8.4
Troubleshooting

Keep the concepts of authentication and authorization separate in your head; just because you can authenticate doesn't mean that you're authorized for a given action.

Troubleshooting Importing Users

When you use the Server app to import users or groups, a log file is automatically created in a folder named ImportExport in your Library/Logs folder of your home folder. Since you imported users in earlier exercises, you can use the Console app to inspect the import log.

Note that this log file shows an example of successfully importing six user records, with an error importing one record. Some problems associated with importing accounts, if they occur, will appear in these log files.

Troubleshooting Accessing Services

It can be somewhat confusing if a user is trying to connect to a service for which she doesn't have authorization. Despite the fact that she has entered her password correctly, she may believe that she hasn't, because she sees the authentication window shake or sees an error message. It may be useful to have users try to authenticate to a service they do have access to, so you can confirm that their passwords aren't the problem.

Exercise 8.1
Create and Configure Local User Accounts

For any users to access your server, they need to have an account on the server. Use the Server app, the primary tool for creating and managing user accounts for OS X Server, to create users. You will eventually configure Localuser 1 as an administrator, and use Localuser 1 credentials to create a user named Localuser 2.

Start by connecting to your server.

1   On your administrator computer, in the Next Steps drawer, click Add Users.

2   Click the blue word "Users," which is a link to the Users pane; this produces the same result as clicking Users in the Server app sidebar.

Create a New User

After creating the user, you will edit this user's basic attributes again.

1   At the lower left of the Users pane, click the Add (+) button to add a new user.

2   Enter the following information:

  ▶   Full Name: Localuser 1

  ▶   Account Name: localuser1

  ▶   Email Address: Leave blank.

  ▶   Password: local

  ▶   Verify: local

3   For now, leave the checkbox for "Allow user to administer this server" deselected.

4   Review the settings for this new user.

5   Click Done to create the user.

Edit a User

Use the Server app to edit the basic attributes for this user: Change the picture for the user, and allow the user to administer the computer. Selecting the checkbox to allow the user to administer the computer automatically adds the user to the Administrators group.

1   In the list of users, double-click Localuser 1 to edit this user's basic attributes.

> **NOTE ▸** Additional methods of editing the user's basic attributes include clicking the Action (gear icon) pop-up menu and choosing Edit User; secondary clicking the user and choosing Edit User from the shortcut menu; and pressing Command-Down Arrow.

2   Click the silhouette for the user, and select a picture from the available pictures.

3   Select the checkbox labeled "Allow user to administer this server."

4   Click Done to save the changes you just made.

Use the Server app to inspect and edit additional attributes for this user. Add an alias (you can use an alias instead of your full name or account name for some kinds of authentication, and the Mail service accepts messages addressed using aliases).

5   In the list of users, secondary click Localuser 1 and choose Advanced Options from the shortcut menu.

6   In the Aliases field, enter localuserone.

WARNING! ▸ Even though you have the ability to change various options here, your user may have difficulty logging in or accessing files if you change the value for some attributes. Update only the Aliases field in this exercise.

7   Click OK to close the Advanced Settings pane.

Use a Different Account with the Server App

Next, use the Localuser 1 account to connect to your server and create another local user.

1   To close your connection to your server, click the Server app's close button (or press Command-W, or choose Manage > Close).

2   Choose Manage > Connect to Server (or press Command-N).

3   Select your server, and click Continue.

4   Deselect the checkbox to remember this password.

5   For Administrator Name enter localuser1, and for Administrator Password enter local. Click Connect.

6 At the lower left of the Users pane, click the Add (+) button to add a new user.

7 Click the silhouette for this new user, and choose Edit Picture.

8 If your administrator computer has a camera, you can click the Camera tab, take a photo of yourself to use for this user, and click Done to use that photo for this user.

If you do not want to use your photo, or if your administrator computer does not have a camera, click Cancel, and then click the silhouette for the user and select an existing picture.

9 Enter the following information for this new user:

▶ Full Name: **Localuser 2**

▶ Account Name: **localuser2**

▶ Email Address: Leave blank.

▶ Password: **local**

▶ Verify: **local**

10 Leave the checkbox "Allow user to administer this server" deselected.

11 Click Done to create the user.

Try to Use the Server App as a Nonadministrator User

You were able to create a new local user after you connected as Localuser 1 to your server with the Server app, because earlier you selected the checkbox to allow Localuser 1 to administer the server. Try to use Localuser 2's credentials to connect to your server with the Server app; you won't be able to, which will confirm that only users in the Administrators group have the ability to administer the server.

1   Press Command-W to close your connection to your server.

2   Open a new connection to a server (choose Manage > Connect to Server, or press Command-N).

3   Select your server, and click Continue.

4   Deselect the checkbox to remember this password.

5   For Administrator Name enter localuser2, and for Administrator Password enter local.

6   Click Connect.

Since the user Localuser 2 is not an administrator, you see a message requiring administrator login.

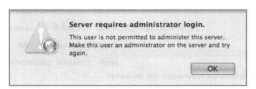

7   Click OK to dismiss the alert.

8   Click Cancel to return to the "Choose a Mac" window.

Connect as the regular local administrator account you've been using for most of this guide.

1   At the "Choose a Mac" window, select your server, and click Continue.

2   Deselect the checkbox to remember this password.

3   Enter your local administrator credentials and click Connect. (For Administrator Name enter ladmin, for Administrator Password enter ladminpw.)

You can leave the Server app open while you work on the next exercise.

In this exercise, you used the Server app to create and configure local user accounts, including a local administrator account. You demonstrated that you cannot use the Server app with an account that is not an administrator account.

Exercise 8.2
Import Local User Accounts

In this scenario, you have a tab-separated text file that was generated from the employee information database. It includes some information about each employee, including first name, last name, full name, a shortened name to use for the account name, and a password for the user. This file also has a properly formatted header line.

You also have a text file that was generated from another server (with Workgroup Manager). Because OS X Server cannot export user passwords, you have to reset user passwords after you import them.

Import User Accounts from a Delimited Text File

1   On your administrator computer, in the Server app choose Manage > Import Accounts From File.

2   In the open file dialog, click Documents in the sidebar, open StudentMaterials, and then open Lesson08.

3   Select the employees-tabdelimited.txt file.

4 If necessary, enter your local administrator credentials.

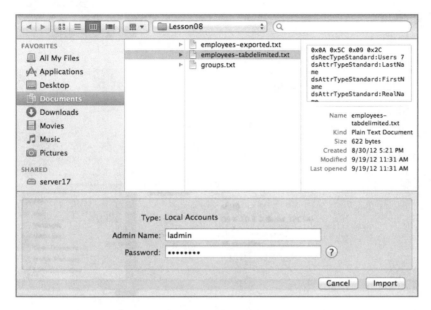

5 Click the right border of the import sheet, and drag the border to the right so that you can preview more contents of the file.

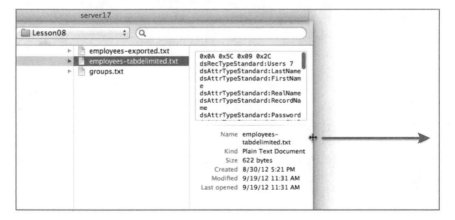

The header line (the first line) has the number seven, which indicates that each record contains seven attributes. In the right column of the Import window, you get a preview of the contents of the text file.

In this scenario, the text file contains the following 7 attributes:

► Last name

► First name

► Full name

► Account name

► Password

► User Shell

► Primary Group ID

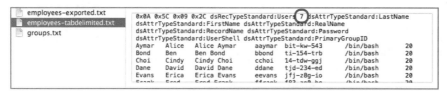

6 Click Import.

After the import has completed, Server app displays the Users pane.

You just imported seven user accounts.

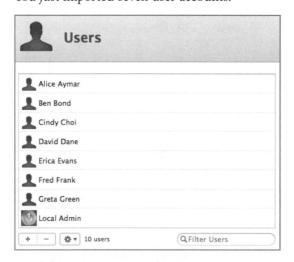

Import Users from an Exported Formatted File

You'll use the Server app to import users from a properly formatted file, such as one exported on another server with Workgroup Manager. This import file has more users with "Localuser" as the first name, to re-enforce the idea that you are still working in the server's local directory.

1   On your administrator computer, in the Server app choose Manage > Import Accounts From File.

2   Click your Documents icon in the sidebar, open the StudentMaterials folder, and then open the Lesson08 folder.

3   Select the employees-exported.txt file.

Note that in the right column, you see a preview of the contents of the text file. The first header line is much longer than the previous header line. This header line states that each user record contains 40 attributes (as opposed to the previous file, in which each user record contains 7 attributes).

4   If necessary, enter your local administrator credentials.

5   Click Import to import the file.

During the import, the status is displayed in the lower-right corner of the Server app window.

When the status in the lower-right corner of the Server app window disappears, an additional six users have been imported (Localuser 3 through Localuser 8).

6   Scroll down to the bottom of the list of users.

Because passwords are not included in this import file, you need to set a password for each of the new accounts. For now, you'll set each account to use the password "local".

7   Select all the newly imported accounts, Localuser 3 through Localuser 8, by selecting Localuser 3, holding down the Shift key, and then selecting Localuser 8.

8   Secondary click while your pointer is still over one of the selected users, to reveal the shortcut menu. Text indicates how many users are part of your selection.

9   Choose Reset Password.

10 In both the New Password and Verify fields, enter local.

11 Click Change Password.

You've imported users from two different types of files. The first was a simple text file, as if exported from some external list of employees, with attributes separated by the tab character. This file included passwords, so you did not need to reset these user passwords. This file included a header line that specified which characters were used as attribute and value delimiters, as well as which fields in the text file corresponded with which attributes.

The second import file was exported from another server, so it did not include passwords, so you had to set passwords for these users.

You will review the logs related to importing these users in Exercise 8.4, "Troubleshoot Problems with Importing Accounts."

Exercise 8.3
Create and Configure Local Groups

▶ **Prerequisites**

    ▶   Exercise 8.2, "Import Local User Accounts"

You can use the Server app to create and organize groups as well as users. You will create groups with the Server app, and associate users and groups with each other.

1   On your administrator computer, if you are not already connected to your server, open the Server app, connect to your server, and authenticate as a local administrator

2   In the Server app sidebar, select Groups.

Create a Group

1   In the Groups pane, click the Add (+) button.

2   Enter the following information for the first new group:

    ▶   Full Name: Engineering

    ▶   Group Name: engr

3   Click Done to create the group.

    NOTE ▶ If you try to create a group named "admin," you'll get a notice that a group with that name already exists.

Import Groups

Rather than spend a lot of time creating more groups, import some groups with a group import file. You will use these groups for the rest of the exercise.

1   Choose Manage > Import Accounts from File.

2   If the Lesson08 folder is not already displayed, click your Documents icon in the side-bar, and then open the StudentMaterials/Lesson08 folder.

3   Select the groups.txt file.

    Note in the file preview that this text file has a header line that defines the special characters, the account type (Groups), and the names of the attributes included.

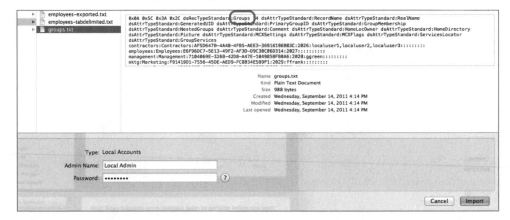

4   If necessary, enter your local administrator credentials.

5   Click Import.

The Server app displays the groups you just created and imported.

6   Double-click the Projects group.

The import file included a list of users that are members of the Projects group, so you'll see them listed as members of the group.

7   Click Done to go back to the list of groups.

Add Users to Groups

You'll use the Server app to add users to groups. Even though you used an import file that had a number of groups populated with users, you may need to update group membership at some point later.

In this scenario, in your organization, a few people were added to a new Engineering department, so you should add their user accounts to the Engineering group. Add Alice Aymar and Ben Bond to the Engineering group.

1   Double-click the Engineering group.

2   Click the silhouette for the Engineering group, and select a picture for the group.

3   Below the Members field, click the Add (+) button.

4   In the text field, press the Spacebar.

5   Choose Browse, which opens a new window that displays the local users and groups.

6   Drag the new window over to one side of the Server app window.

7   Drag Alice Aymar and Ben Bond to the Members list.

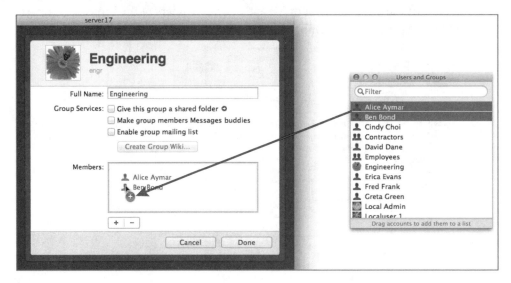

8   Click Done to save the changes to the list of groups.

9   Close the window that displays the list of local users and groups.

Add Group Membership to a User Account

While you could easily use the same process you used in the previous section to add users to the newly created groups, this time you'll try an alternate approach by adding groups to a user's account. In this scenario, Cindy Choi joined both the Marketing and the Engineering groups. Add these groups to that user's account.

1   Select Users in the Server app sidebar.

2   Double-click Cindy Choi.

3   Below the Groups list, click the Add (+) button to add a group.

4   Press the Spacebar and choose Browse.

5 Drag the window that displays local groups over to the side.

6 Select the Engineering group, hold down the Command key, and then select the Marketing group.

7 Drag the Marketing and Engineering groups to the Groups field.

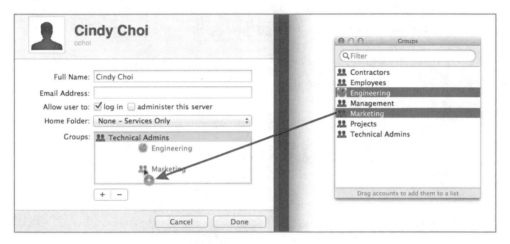

8 Click Done to save the changes to the user.

9 Close the window that displays the list of local groups.

Add Groups to Groups

Nesting groups, or adding groups to groups, is critical to simplifying user and group management. In this scenario, each Pretendco employee is a member of one of three departments: Marketing, Engineering, or Management. There is a group named Employees, and you plan to use this group to allow all employees access to resources. Although you could populate the Employees group with all the individual Marketing, Engineering, and Management user accounts, the easiest approach is to simply add the three groups to the Employees group. When the structure of your organization changes over time—for example, if a new department is created—you would need to use the Server app to create a new group for this department, and add its group to the Employees group.

When you are finished with this exercise, the Pretendco Employees group will consist of three groups: Marketing, Engineering, and Management.

1 Select Groups in the Server app sidebar.

2   Double-click the Employees group.

3   Click the Add (+) button below the Members list. If the Users & Groups window is
    not displayed next to the Server app window, enter some text in the text field and
    then choose Browse.

4   In the Users & Groups window, Command-click the Marketing, Engineering, and
    Management groups to select these groups.

5   Drag these three groups to the Members list of the Employees group.

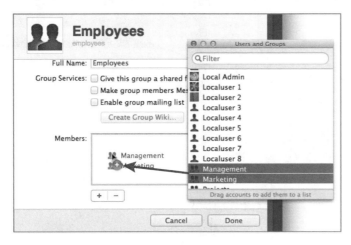

6   After dragging the groups into the Members list, confirm that there are now three
    groups listed.

7   Close the window that displays the list of users and groups.

8   Click Done.

All members of the Marketing, Engineering, and Management groups now have access to the resources the Employees group can access.

Exercise 8.4
Troubleshoot Problems with Importing Accounts

▶ **Prerequisites**

- ▶ Exercise 8.2, "Import Local User Accounts"
- ▶ Exercise 8.3, "Create and Configure Local Groups"

When you use the Server app to import users or groups, a log file is automatically created in a folder named ImportExport in the Library/Logs folder of your home folder. Since you imported users in an earlier exercise, you can use the Console app to inspect the import log.

On your administrator computer, open the Console app.

1   If the Console app is not already running, open Launchpad, open Other, and open Console.

2   If no sidebar is displayed for the Console window, click Show Log List in the toolbar.

The Console app displays logs from several locations on your computer. The tilde character (~) is a symbol for your home folder, so ~/Library/Logs is a folder in your home folder, and is for logs specifically related to your user account. The /var/log and /Library/Logs folders are for system logs. You will look for a log file in the ImportExport folder in your ~/Library/Logs folder.

3   Click the disclosure triangle for ~/Library/Logs to display the contents of that folder, and then click the disclosure triangle for ImportExport to display the contents of that folder.

4   Select a log file under ImportExport.

Note that this log file shows that you imported a number of records without error. Some problems associated with importing accounts, if they occur, will appear in these log files.

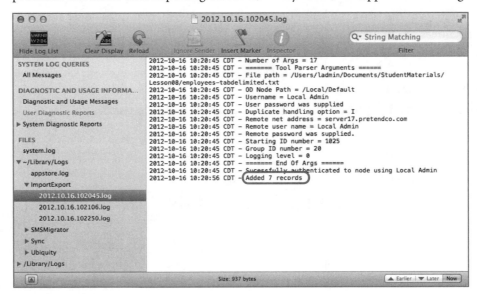

Exercise 8.5
Manage Service Access

▶ **Prerequisites**

- ▶ Exercise 8.1, "Create and Configure Local User Accounts"
- ▶ Exercise 8.2, "Import Local User Accounts"
- ▶ Exercise 8.3, "Create and Configure Local Groups"

Now that you have experience controlling authentication with users and groups, it's time to move on to authorization. You can limit access to services at the user and group level. Use the Server app to enable specific services from a user's perspective.

You may not want all users with accounts on your server to access all the services your server offers. In this exercise, you will configure access for the two services associated with the File Sharing service, AFP (Apple Filing Protocol, primarily for Mac computers) and SMB (Server Message Block, primarily for Windows). You will learn more about the File Sharing service in Lesson 13, "Providing File Sharing Services."

Use the Server app to disallow a particular user from accessing the File Sharing service.

Start out by restricting access to the File Sharing service.

1   If it is not already open, open the Server app, select your server, and authenticate as a local administrator.

2   In the Server app sidebar, select Users.

3   Select Localuser 1 and Localuser 2.

    At this point, Localuser 1 should be an administrator user, and Localuser 2 should be a regular user. If you don't have these users, go ahead and create them now with the Server app.

4   Secondary click the selected users and choose "Edit Access to Services" from the shortcut menu.

5   Click Manage Service Access.

6   In the dialog that appears, click Manage.

7   Deselect the checkbox for File Sharing.

    NOTE ▶ The Time Machine service relies on the File Sharing service; when you deselect the File Sharing service, you can no longer modify the Time Machine checkbox.

8   Click OK.

    You just removed authorization to use the File Sharing service for the two users. Other users are still authorized to use the File Sharing service.

Turn on File Sharing and Verify Authorization

Turn on File Sharing and use it to verify authorization and lack of authorization to use the service.

1   In the Server app sidebar, select File Sharing.

2   Click the On/Off switch to turn on the service.

From your administrator computer, attempt to connect to your server via AFP.

1   On your administrator computer, in the Finder choose Go > Connect to Server.

2   In the Server Address field, enter your server's complete host name servern.pretendco .com, where *n* is your student number), and click Connect.

In the connection dialog, attempt to authenticate with the following user account, which is not authorized to use the file sharing service.

3   In the Name field, enter localuser1, in the Password field enter local, and click Connect.

The window shakes, indicating a problem with either authentication or authorization. In this case, the user is not authorized to use the File Sharing service, even though it is a member of the Administrators group.

4   In the Name field, enter localuser2, in the Password field type local, and click Connect.

The window shakes, indicating a problem with either authentication or authorization. In this case, the user is not authorized to use the File Sharing service.

5   In the Name field, enter localuser3, in the Password field enter local, and click Connect.

A list of available volumes appears.

6   Select the Users volume and click OK.

7   Confirm that you can actually see files; you will see a home folder for each local user you have created, as well as the folder named Shared.

8   In the Finder window sidebar, click the Eject button next to your server's icon to disconnect.

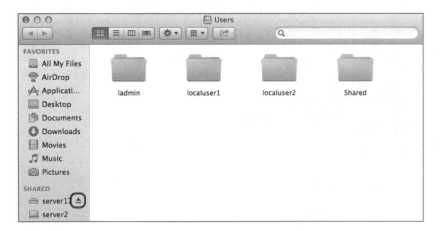

You just verified that when you remove authorization for a user to access a service, the user cannot access the service.

Exercise 8.6
Clean Up

► **Prerequisites**

- ► Exercise 8.1, "Create and Configure Local User Accounts"
- ► Exercise 8.2, "Import Local User Accounts"
- ► Exercise 8.3, "Create and Configure Local Groups"

In the next lesson, you will configure your server to manage network accounts. Your server will then have multiple directories: the local directory and the network directory. You'll have network users and groups to work with in the next lesson.

In order to prevent confusion, you will:

- ► Delete the local user and local group accounts you were just working with.
- ► Stop the File Sharing service.

Make sure that you connect to your server with the local administrator you had been using before you started the exercises in this lesson, rather than with the Localuser 1 account. Start by closing the active Server app window.

1   In the Server app, choose Manage > Close (or press Command-W) to close the Server app window.

Open the Server app again and connect with credentials for the local administrator that you have been using before you started the exercises in this lesson. Just to be sure that you do not delete system accounts (accounts that are normally hidden, and which are crucial to the normal operation of the system), confirm that the Server app is not displaying system accounts.

1   Open the Server app, select your server, and authenticate as the local administrator you have been using before you started the exercises in this lesson (for Administrator Name enter ladmin, and for Administrator Password enter ladminpw).

2   Click the View menu, but do not choose any options. Confirm that the second menu choice is Show System Accounts.

If the second menu choice is Hide System Accounts, choose Hide System Accounts, and then click the View menu again to confirm that Show System Accounts is the second menu choice.

Now that you are sure you will not accidentally delete system accounts, delete the other accounts you created in the exercises for this lesson.

1   For each user (except for the local administrator you had been using before you started the exercises in this lesson) select the user, click the Delete (–) button, and then at the dialog, click Delete.

TIP If you accidentally click Delete after you select the user you are currently using to authenticate to the Server app, you will see a dialog informing you that the Server app will not allow you to delete this user. If you have multiple users selected, it will offer to delete the other selected users.

Delete the groups you created and imported.

1   In the Server app sidebar, select Groups.

2   Select one group, and then press Command-A (or choose Edit > Select All).

3   Click the Delete (–) button.

4   At the confirmation pane, click Delete to delete the groups.

Stop the File Sharing service.

1   In the Server app sidebar, select File Sharing.

2   Click the On/Off switch to turn off the service.

You are ready to continue with the other exercises in this guide.

Additional Resources

The following documents provide more information about managing local accounts. Additional resources are available at www.apple.com/osx/server/resources/documentation.html.

OS X Server Administration Guides

OS X Server: Advanced Server Administration
http://help.apple.com/advancedserveradmin/mac/10.8/.

Apple Knowledge Base Documents

You can check for new and updated Knowledge Base documents at www.apple.com/support/.

Document HT5417, "OS X Server: Providing Service Access to Users in External Directories"

Document HT1822, "OS X Server: Admin tools compatibility information"

Download DL1567, "Workgroup Manager 10.8"

Lesson Review

1. Describe the difference between authentication and authorization, and give an example of each.
2. What is the difference between user and administrator accounts on OS X Server?
3. Which applications can you use to configure OS X Server local user and group settings?
4. What tool can you use to import and export user accounts?
5. Which two formats of files can you use to import users with the Server app?
6. If you decide to manually manage access to services, what are some services included in the list?
7. When you select the checkbox to grant authorization for a user to access File Sharing services, what file sharing protocols does this enable for the user?
8. When you click the Manage Service Access button, does this prevent users that you create in the future from being able to access your OS X Server services?

Answers

1. Authentication is the process by which the system requires you to provide information before it allows you to access a specific account. An example is entering a name and password while connecting to a the Apple Filing Protocol service. Authorization refers to the process by which permissions are used to regulate a user's access to specific resources, such as files and shared folders, once the user has been successfully authenticated.

2. User accounts provide basic access to a computer or server, whereas administrator accounts allow a person to administer the computer. On OS X Server, an administrator account is typically used for changing settings on the server computer itself, usually through the Server app.

3. You can use the Users & Groups preferences and the Server app to create and configure local users and groups.

4. You can use the Server app to import user accounts. Additionally, as you will see in the next lesson, you can use the Server app to import network users after you authenticate as a directory administrator.

5. You can use the Server app to import a character-delimited text file with user information, but you need a header line to define the characteristics of the information contained in the file. You can also import a text file that has a header line at the beginning of the file that defines the contents of the file.

6. Services include Calendar, Contacts, File Sharing, FTP, Mail, Messages, Profile Manager, Time Machine, and VPN.

7. Authorization to use File Sharing includes AFP and SMB protocols.

8. No, even after you choose to manage service access manually, new users that you create automatically get authorization to access services. Of course, you can edit a user and remove authorization for that user to access a service.

Lesson **9**

Configuring Open Directory Services

This lesson describes how using a directory service can help you manage users and resources on your network. You will learn about the features of Apple Open Directory services and how these services can be integrated with other directory services in a mixed environment. You will also learn how to set up and manage directories and user accounts with the Server app. Finally, you'll become familiar with common Open Directory services issues and learn how to resolve them.

Open Directory is extremely versatile when dealing with a variety of other directory services, such as Active Directory, eDirectory, and Network Information Service (NIS), but mixed platform directory service scenarios are outside the scope of this document.

If you are performing the exercises independently, and do not have an extra server computer, study and review, but do not perform, the tasks that involve the other directory server.

GOALS

▶ Understand the Open Directory server roles you can configure on OS X Server

▶ Configure OS X Server as an Open Directory server

▶ Bind OS X Server to another Open Directory server

▶ Locate and identify Open Directory–related log files

Reference 9.1
Introducing Directory Services Concepts

Giving a user multiple user accounts on different computers can cause problems. For instance, if each computer in a network has its own authentication database, a user might have to remember a different password for each computer. Even if you assign the user the same password on every computer, the information can become inconsistent over time, because the user may change a password in one location but forget to do so in another. You can solve this problem by using a single source of identification and authentication information.

Directory services provide this central repository for information about the computers, applications, and users in an organization. With directory services, you can maintain consistent information about all the users—such as their names and passwords—as well as about printers and other network resources. You can maintain this information in a single location rather than on individual computers. The result is that you can use directory services to:

▶ Provide a common user experience.

▶ Provide easier access to networked resources such as printers and servers.

▶ Allow users to log in on multiple computers using a single account.

For example, once you *bind* OS X computers to an Open Directory service (to bind is to configure one computer to use the directory services offered by another), users can freely log in to any bound OS X computer. They will have their session managed based on who they are, what group they belong to, what computer they logged in at, and what computer group the computer belongs to. Using a shared directory service also permits a user's home folder to be located on another server and to be mounted automatically on whatever computer the user logs in to, as long as that computer is bound to the shared directory.

What Is Open Directory?

Open Directory is the extensible directory-services architecture that is built into OS X. Open Directory acts as an intermediary between directories (which store information about users and resources) and the applications and system software processes that want to use the information.

In the context of OS X Server, the Open Directory service is actually a set of services that provide identification, authentication, and client management.

Many services on OS X require information from the Open Directory service to function. The Open Directory service can securely store and validate the passwords of users who want to log in to client computers on your network or use other network resources that require authentication. You can also use the Open Directory service to enforce global password policies, such as password expiration and minimum length.

You can use the Open Directory service to provide authentication to Windows users for file and print services, as well as other services that OS X Server provides.

Overview of Open Directory Service Components

Open Directory provides a centralized source for identification and authentication. For identification, Open Directory uses OpenLDAP, an open source implementation of the

Lightweight Directory Access Protocol (LDAP), a standard protocol used for accessing directory service data. Open Directory uses LDAPv3 to provide read-and-write access to the directory data.

The Open Directory service leverages other open source technologies, such as Kerberos, and combines them with powerful server-administration tools to deliver robust directory and authentication services that are easy to set up and manage. Because there are no per-seat or per-user license fees, Open Directory can scale to the needs of an organization without adding high costs to an IT budget.

After you bind an OS X computer to use an Open Directory server, that bound computer automatically gets access to network resources, including user authentication services, network home folders, and share points.

You can configure OS X Server in four basic Open Directory states:

▶   A standalone server

▶   An Open Directory master

▶   An Open Directory replica

▶   Connected to another directory service or multiple directory services (also referred to as a member server)

> **NOTE** ▶ You can configure your server to simultaneously connect to one or more other directory services, at the same time as serving as an Open Directory master or replica.

As you plan directory services for your network, consider the need to share user, resource, and management information among multiple computers and devices. If the need is low, little directory planning is necessary; everything can be accessed from a server's local directory. However, if you want to share information among computers, you need to set up at least one Open Directory server (an Open Directory master). Furthermore, if you want to provide high availability of directory services, you should set up at least one additional server to be an Open Directory replica.

Understanding the Standalone Server Role

The default state is for your server to host its local accounts. People must use accounts that are local users created on your server to access your server's services.

Understanding the Open Directory Master Role

When OS X Server is configured to manage network accounts and provide directory services, this is referred to as an Open Directory master. The action you will select to perform in the Server app is "Create a new Open Directory domain." A domain is an organizational boundary for a directory; you are creating a shared directory domain, also referred to as a node.

When you use the Server app to configure your server as an Open Directory master, it performs the following actions:

▶ Configures OpenLDAP, Kerberos, and Password Server databases

▶ Adds the new directory service to the authentication search path

▶ Creates a local network group named Workgroup

▶ Adds the local group Local Accounts to the network group Workgroup (hidden unless you choose View > Show System Accounts).

▶ Creates a new root SSL certification authority (CA) based on the organization name you provide at the time

▶ creates a new intermediate SSL certification authority, signed by the CA above

▶ Creates a new SSL certificate with your server's hostname, signed by the intermediate CA above (if you don't already have a signed SSL certificate with your server's hostname)

▶ Adds the CA, intermediate CA, and SSL certificate to the System keychain of your server

▶ Grants local accounts and local network accounts authorization to access OS X Server services

▶ Adds an access control entry (ACE) to the Public share point to allow Read & Write access for the local network group Workgroup (see Lesson 14, "Understanding File Access," for more information on ACEs)

This version of OS X Server has a new set of terms: local accounts and local network accounts. Local accounts are those accounts that are stored in your server's local node. Local network accounts are those accounts that are stored in your server's shared Open Directory node. The words "local network" differentiate the accounts from other nodes' directory accounts, as they are from the local network shared node.

Once you have set up your server to be an Open Directory master, you can configure other computers on your network to access the server's directory services.

To recap, your OS X computer has local user and group accounts; after configuring as an Open Directory master, this local database still exists. Creating an Open Directory master creates a secondary, shared LDAP database. The administrator of that database has the default short name of diradmin. Each database is separate, and managing either one requires different credentials. You have also created a Password Server database to store user passwords, as well as a Kerberos Key Distribution Center (KDC). You will learn about those later in this lesson.

Understanding the Open Directory Replica Role

Once you have a server configured as an Open Directory master, you can configure at least one more Mac with OS X Server as a directory replica to provide the same directory information and authentication information as the master. The replica server hosts a copy of the master's LDAP directory, its Password Server authentication database, and its Kerberos KDC. Open Directory servers notify each other whenever there is a change in directory information, so all Open Directory servers have a current store of information.

You can use replicas to scale your directory infrastructure, improve search-and-retrieval time on distributed networks, and to provide high availability of Open Directory services. Replication also protects against network outages, because client systems can use any replica in your organization.

When authentication data is transferred from the master to any replica, that data is encrypted as it is copied over.

> **TIP** Because replication and Kerberos use timestamps, it's best to synchronize the clocks on all Open Directory masters, replicas, and member servers. You can use the Date & Time system preference to specify the time server; you can use Apple time servers or an internal time service.

You can create nested replicas—that is, replicas of replicas. One master can have up to 32 replicas, and those replicas can have 32 replicas each; one master plus 32 replicas plus 32 × 32 replicas of those replicas totals 1,057 Open Directory servers for a single Open Directory domain. Nesting replicas is accomplished by joining one replica to your Open Directory master, and then joining other replicas to that first replica. You cannot have more than two layers of replicas.

The following figure has one Open Directory master and one replica that is also a relay, a replica that in turn has at least one replica.

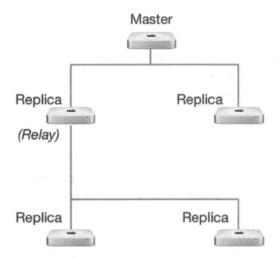

In the case of a disaster, you can promote an Open Directory replica to be the new master, but you must have either a Time Machine backup of your server that's configured as your Open Directory master, or an Open Directory archive. Search for "Archive and restore Open Directory data" in Help for more information.

Understanding Open Directory Locales

Open Directory locales is a feature that makes it easy for you to distribute the load among appropriate Open Directory servers. An Open Directory locale is a group of Open Directory servers that service a specified subnet; you use the Server app to define a locale, and then associate one or more Open Directory servers and one or more subnets with that locale. When a client computer (OS X v10.7 or later) is bound to any of your Open Directory servers, if that client computer is in a subnet associated with a locale, that client computer will prefer the Open Directory server(s) associated with that locale.

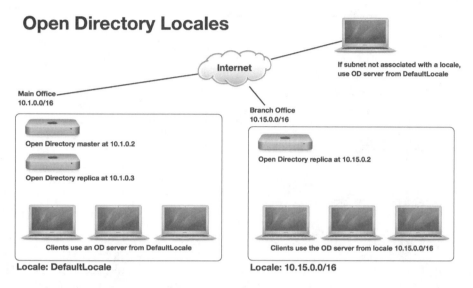

As soon as you configure your first Open Directory replica, OS X Server creates two locales.

▶ The first locale (Default Locale) is a failsafe, and includes the first replica you create, even if it not in the same subnet as your master; this is the locale that an OS X client uses if no locale is available for the client's subnet.

▶ The second locale is based on the subnet of the Open Directory master and includes the master only by default; Open Directory clients on the same subnet use this locale.

To create a new Open Directory locale, click the Locales tab, click Add (+), and specify information for the new locale.

Configuring Open Directory locales is outside the scope of this guide; see http://help. apple.com/advancedserveradmin/mac/10.8 for more information on configuring Open Directory locales.

Understanding the Role of Using Another Open Directory Server

If you intend to set up multiple servers, populating each server with the same user accounts would be extremely inefficient. Instead, you can bind your server to another directory system, in which case your server is referred to as a bound server or a member server. In this role, each server gets authentication, user information, and other directory information from some other server's directory service. This way, users can authenticate to your server with an account defined in your server's local directory, or with an account defined in any directory node that your server is bound to. The other directory node could be an Open Directory or an Active Directory system.

The Profile Manager service requires that your server be configured as an Open Directory master. That's fine, because it is possible for your server to both be an Open Directory master and be bound to another directory service. This is particularly useful for providing services to groups within a larger organization. If you are the administrator for a group of users within a larger organization, you can use OS X Server to provide additional services to existing groups defined in your larger organization, or to create additional groups of people for your smaller groups. You can achieve this without bothering the people who administer resources for the larger organization, regardless of what directory service your larger organization uses.

Understanding Access to Services

In the standalone state, your server by default does not check for authorization to access OS X Server services (except the SSH service); see Reference 8.3, "Managing Access to Services" for more information.

If you configure your server as an Open Directory master, the Server app configures your server to start checking for authorization to access OS X Server services. When you create new local accounts and new local network accounts with the Server app, the Server app grants the new accounts authorization to access OS X Server services.

If you configure your server as an Open Directory master and then bind to another directory server, you may need to grant authorization to use your server services to accounts from the other directory node. You may find it convenient to grant authorization to access OS X Server services to the other directory node's groups, so you do not need to configure individual user accounts from the other directory node.

Reference 9.2
Configuring Open Directory Services

In order to provide the full range of Open Directory services, each server participating in the Open Directory domain, whether a master, replica, or member server, needs to have consistent access to forward and reverse DNS records for all the other servers in the domain. You should use the Network Utility (or command-line tools) to confirm DNS records are available.

You use the Server app to configure your server as an Open Directory master or replica, and you use the Users & Groups preferences or Directory Utility to bind to another directory server.

Configuring OS X Server as an Open Directory Master

If your server is not already configured as an Open Directory master or connected to another directory service, you can turn on the Open Directory service, and the Server app walks you through configuring your server to be an Open Directory master or replica.

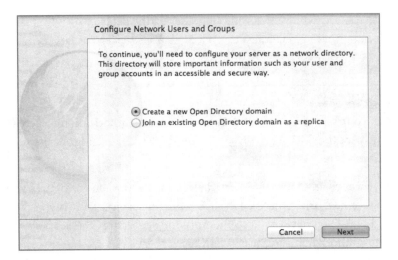

Start out by selecting "Create a new Open Directory domain" and clicking Next.

You are prompted to create a new user, with the default name of Directory Administrator, and short name of diradmin.

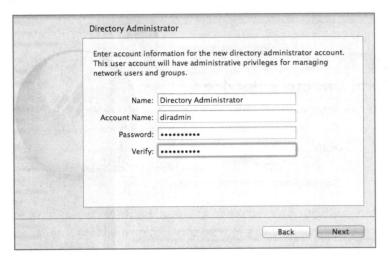

You are also prompted to provide an organization name and an admin email address.

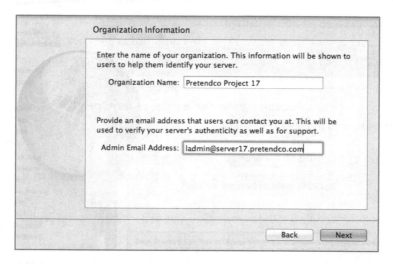

Once you confirm these settings, the Server app configures your server as an Open Directory master. Afterwards, the Open Directory pane displays your server, listed as master.

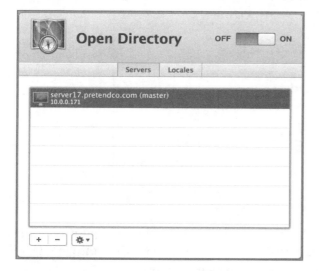

Configuring OS X Server as an Open Directory Replica

If you already have an Open Directory master on another Mac with OS X Server, you use the Server app to configure your server as a replica of another Open Directory master.

You can configure a server to be a replica, using the Server app on an existing master or replica, or using the Server app on a server you want to configure as a replica. The replica server you're adding must have remote administration access enabled before you can add it as a replica.

If you're using the Server app on an existing master or replica, in the Open Directory pane, click the Servers tab, and click Add (+). Then:

▶   Enter the host name (you could also enter an IP address or local host name, but this guide recommends using the host name to verify that the crucial DNS hostname records are available).

▶   Enter administrator credentials for the server you want to configure as the replica.

▶   Choose the parent server.

▶   Enter the directory administrator's credentials and click Next

If, instead, you're using the Server app on the server you want to configure as an Open Directory replica, select Open Directory in the Server app sidebar. Click the On/Off switch to On, select "Join an existing Open Directory domain as a replica," and click Next.

In the Parent Server field, enter another Open Directory server's host name (enter the master's host name to configure this server as a replica, or enter a replica's host name to configure this server as a replica of the replica), enter directory administrator credentials, and click Next.

Afterwards, the Server app displays your server as a replica of the master. In the Open Directory pane's Servers tab, you may need to click the disclosure triangle to view the master and its replica(s). In the following figure, server17 is the master, and server18 is the replica.

If you configure a replica of a replica, the Servers tab looks like the following figure, where server19 is a replica of server18, which is a replica of server17.

Configuring OS X Server to Use Another Open Directory Server

If you want your server to simply take advantage of a centralized directory service, and not offer directory services itself, you can bind your server to another directory service, so users can use credentials hosted by the centralized directory service to access services on your server.

Use the Users & Groups pane in System Preferences to bind your server to another directory. Open System Preferences, select Users & Groups, select Login Options, and click Join, or if the server is already an Open Directory server, click Edit instead of Join.

Enter the host name of an Open Directory server, or click the pop-up menu to browse for one.

When you see a message that "This server provides SSL certificates," click Trust. This adds the Open Directory's CA, intermediate CA, and SSL certificate to the System keychain so your Mac trusts services that use SSL certificates signed by the intermediate CA.

When you see the message that "This server does not provide a secure (SSL) connection," click Continue. By default, an Open Directory server does not provide LDAP services over SSL; for many organizations this is not a concern because the information stored in the LDAP directory is not considered sensitive. Configuring LDAP to use SSL is outside the scope of this guide.

When you see the Client Computer ID window, leave the Client Computer ID, which is generated from your host name, as it is.

You have the option to bind anonymously or set up authenticated binding.

Anonymous binding is appropriate when binding with OS X clients, but you should use authenticated binding, which mutually authenticates the member server and the Open Directory service, when binding OS X to an Open Directory server. An authenticated bind creates a computer record in the Open Directory service; this computer record is used to mutually authenticate the bind between the two servers.

NOTE ▸ Provide directory administrator credentials for the authenticated bind.

As an alternative, you can use Directory Utility, or the command-line environment, because they offer some advanced binding options, especially if you're binding to an Active Directory node.

Using Directory Utility Remotely

You can still use Directory Utility instead of System Preferences; in fact, the Users & Groups preferences offer a shortcut to Directory Utility, which is located in /System/ Library/CoreServices. Directory Utility offers a little more control than the Join button of the Users & Groups preferences, and it allows you to control a remote computer from OS X, so you don't need to rely on Screen Sharing being available.

Binding OS X to Your Open Directory Service

Once you have an Open Directory master (and perhaps one or more replicas) set up, you can also configure the client computers to bind to the directory service in order for your client computers to take advantage of Open Directory services. On each client computer, you use the Users & Groups preferences to specify a server that hosts an Open Directory service, or if you need more-advanced binding options, you use Directory Utility to create an LDAP configuration that has the address and search path for an Open Directory server.

Reference 9.3
Troubleshooting

Because Open Directory includes several services, several log files are used for tracking status and errors. You can use Server Admin to view status information and logs for Open Directory services. For example, you can use the password-service logs to monitor failed login attempts for suspicious activity, or use the Open Directory logs to see all failed authentication attempts, including the IP addresses that generated them. Review the logs periodically to determine whether there are numerous failed tries for the same password ID, which would indicate that somebody might be generating login guesses. It is imperative that you understand where to look first when troubleshooting Open Directory issues.

Accessing Open Directory Log Files

Generally, the first place to look when Open Directory issues arise is the log files. Recall that Open Directory comprises three main components: the LDAP database, the Password Server database, and the Kerberos Key Distribution Center. The Server app allows for easy viewing of many server-related Open Directory log files. The main log files are:

▶ Configuration log—Contains information about setting up and configuring Open Directory services (/Library/Logs/slapconfig.log)

▶ LDAP log—Contains information about providing LDAP services (/var/log/slapd.log)

▶ Open Directory log—Contains information about core Open Directory functionality (/var/log/opendirectoryd.log)

▶ Password Service Server log—Contains information about successes and failures authenticating with local network user credentials (/Library/Logs/PasswordService/ApplePasswordServer.Service.log)

▶ Password Service Error log—If it exists, contains information about errors in the Password Service (/Library/Logs/PasswordService/ApplePasswordServer.Error.log)

To view these log files, select Logs in the toolbar, click the pop-up menu, scroll to the Open Directory section of the pop-up menu, and choose one of the logs.

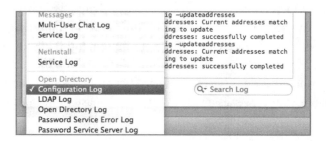

You can use the search field in the lower-right corner of the window. Keep in mind that you can resize the Server app window to view more log information in a single line, which can help you quickly read or skim the log files.

Interpreting log files can be a difficult task, and you may need the help of a more experienced system administrator. You can email the appropriate log file to the administrator.

Troubleshooting Directory Services

If a bound OS X computer experiences a startup delay, or the login window displays a red status indicator with the text "network accounts unavailable," the bound computer could be trying to access a directory node that is not available on your network.

There are several ways to begin troubleshooting when you are unable to connect to a directory service:

▶ Using Network Utility to confirm DNS records

▶ Using Login Options in the Users & Groups preferences to confirm that the network server is available

▶ Using Directory Utility to make sure the LDAP and other configurations are correct

▶ Using the Network preferences to make sure the computer's network location and other network settings are correct

▶ Inspecting the physical network connection for faults

▶ Using the Console app while logged in with a local user account to monitor the Directory Services login /var/log/opendirectoryd.log

> **MORE INFO** ▶ You can increase the level of logging detail for the Open Directory log; see the Knowledge Base document in the "Additional Resources" section at the end of this lesson.

Exercise 9.1
Configure Your Server to Manage Network Accounts

Now you're ready to configure the Open Directory service to create a shared directory and start authentication services for use by other computers on the network. In particular, three new network services will be running once Open Directory master configuration is complete: an LDAP (Lightweight Directory Access Protocol) service to provide access to shared directory data; and two authentication services, Password Server and Kerberos. In the following steps, you'll configure your server as an Open Directory master and verify the success of the configuration.

At this point, your server should have forward and reverse DNS records for itself, provided by either the classroom DNS service, or the DNS service on your server itself. Nevertheless, confirm the records with Network Utility.

1 On your server computer, open Launchpad, click Other, and then open Network Utility.

2 Click the Lookup tab.

3 Enter your server's host name in the field, and then click Lookup.

4 Confirm that your server's IP address is in the results field in the "Answer Section."

5 Enter your server's primary IPv4 address in the field, and then click Lookup.

6 Confirm that your server's host name is in the results field in the "Answer Section."

Once you've confirmed your DNS records, configure your server as an Open Directory master. You can do this from your administrator computer, or from your server computer.

1 If the Server app window does not display the Next Steps drawer, click the Next Steps button in the lower-left corner of the Server app window.

2 In the Next Steps drawer, click Add Users.

3 Click the phrase "Open Directory," which produces the same result as selecting Open Directory in the Server app sidebar.

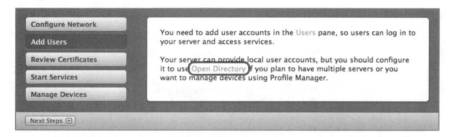

4 Click the On/Off switch to the On position.

5 Select "Create a new Open Directory domain" and click Next.

6 Configure a password.

If your server is not accessible from the Internet, in the Directory Administrator pane, enter diradminpw in the Password and Verify fields and click Next.

Of course, in a production environment, you should use a secure password.

7 In the Organization Information pane, enter appropriate information.

If the following fields do not already contain the information shown, enter it and click Next.

▶ Organization Name: **Pretendco Project** *n* (where *n* is your student number)

▶ Admin Email Address: **ladmin@server***n***.pretendco.com** (where *n* is your student number)

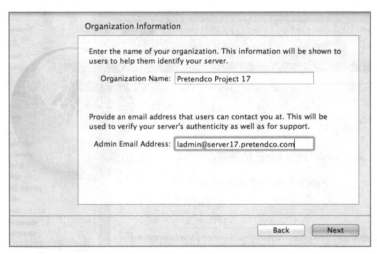

8 View the Confirm Settings pane, and click Set Up.

The Server app displays its progress in the lower-left corner of the Confirm Settings pane.

When it has completed the configuration, the Server app displays the Servers tab of the Open Directory pane, with your server listed as the master.

Now that your server is managing network accounts, also referred to as being configured as an Open Directory master, it has these three services running: LDAP, Password Server, and Kerberos.

Inspect the Group Workgroup

The Server app automatically created a group named Workgroup. When you create a new user with the Server app, the Server app automatically places the new user in the Workgroup group.

1   In the Server app sidebar, select Groups.

2   Click the pop-up menu and choose Local Network Groups.

3   Double-click the group Workgroup.

For now, the only entity listed as a member of the group named Workgroup is the group account named Local Accounts. This is a special system group account that doesn't actually have any members listed, but the operating system treats all local accounts as a member of this group, so all local accounts on the server computer are therefore treated as members of the group Workgroup.

4   Click Cancel to return to the list of groups.

In the exercise you configured your server to be an Open Directory master, and you inspected the new network group named Workgroup.

Exercise 9.2
Use Logs to Troubleshoot Using Open Directory

▶ **Prerequisites**

▶   Exercise 9.1, "Configure Your Server to Manage Network Accounts"

The logs on your server relating to being an Open Directory master are located in various folders, but you can access them all quickly with the Server app.

1   In the Server app sidebar, select Logs.

2   Scroll to the Open Directory section, and note the four logs related to Open Directory.

3   Choose Configuration Log.

4   In the search field, enter the word Intermediate, as an example.

Note that the first instance of this word is highlighted. Each time you press Return, the next instance of the search term flashes.

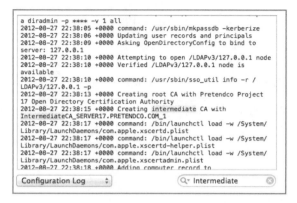

```
a diradmin -p **** -v 1 all
2012-08-27 22:38:05 +0000 command: /usr/sbin/mkpassdb -kerberize
2012-08-27 22:38:06 +0000 Updating user records and principals
2012-08-27 22:38:09 +0000 Asking OpenDirectoryConfig to bind to
server: 127.0.0.1
2012-08-27 22:38:10 +0000 Attempting to open /LDAPv3/127.0.0.1 node
2012-08-27 22:38:10 +0000 Verified /LDAPv3/127.0.0.1 node is
available
2012-08-27 22:38:10 +0000 command: /usr/sbin/sso_util info -r /
LDAPv3/127.0.0.1 -p
2012-08-27 22:38:13 +0000 Creating root CA with Pretendco Project
17 Open Directory Certification Authority
2012-08-27 22:38:15 +0000 Creating intermediate CA with
IntermediateCA_SERVER17.PRETENDCO.COM_1
2012-08-27 22:38:17 +0000 command: /bin/launchctl load -w /System/
Library/LaunchDaemons/com.apple.xscertd.plist
2012-08-27 22:38:17 +0000 command: /bin/launchctl load -w /System/
Library/LaunchDaemons/com.apple.xscertd-helper.plist
2012-08-27 22:38:17 +0000 command: /bin/launchctl load -w /System/
Library/LaunchDaemons/com.apple.xscertadmin.plist
2012-08-27 22:38:18 +0000 Adding computer record to
```

Configuration Log ⇕   Q⁻ Intermediate   ⊗

5   Click the pop-up menu that currently displays Configuration Log and choose LDAP Log, as another example.

6   Scroll through the LDAP log, and then inspect the other logs as well.

Additional Resources

The following documents provide more information about configuring Open Directory services for OS X Server. Additional resources are available at www.apple.com/osx/server/resources/documentation.html.

OS X Server Administration Guides

OS X Server: Advanced Administration
http://help.apple.com/advancedserveradmin/mac/10.8/

Apple Knowledge Base Documents

You can check for new and updated Knowledge Base documents at www.apple.com/osx/server/resources/documentation.html

Document HT1194, "Mac OS X Server: How to reset the Open Directory administrator password"

Document HT4696, "OS X Server: Changing opendirectoryd logging levels"

Document HT5300, "OS X Server: Steps to take before upgrading or migrating the Open Directory database"

Books

Carter, Gerald. *LDAP System Administration* (O'Reilly Media, Inc., 2003).

Garman, Jason. *Kerberos: The Definitive Guide* (O'Reilly Media, Inc., 2003).

URLs

OpenLDAP: Community developed LDAP software: www.openldap.org/

Lightweight Directory Access Protocol (v3): Technical Specification: www.rfc-editor.org/rfc/rfc3377.txt

Lesson Review

1. What is the main function of directory services?

2. What standard is used for data access with Open Directory? What version and level of support is provided for this standard?

3. In terms of Open Directory, what four roles can OS X Server play?

4. What criteria determines the Open Directory locale with which an OS X Open Directory client associates?

5. What log shows successful and failed attempts to authenticate against the password service?

Answers

1. Directory services provide a central repository for information about the computers, applications, and users in an organization.

2. Open Directory uses OpenLDAP and the Lightweight Directory Access Protocol (LDAP) standard to provide a common language for directory access. Open Directory uses LDAPv3 to provide read and write access to the directory data.

3. OS X Server Open Directory roles include Open Directory master, standalone server, connected to a directory system, and Open Directory replica.

4. If a Mountain Lion computer's IPv4 address is in the range of a subnet associated with an Open Directory locale, that computer should use any of the Open Directory servers associated with that locale. Otherwise, it will use the default locale.

5. Password Service Server Log, located at /Library/Logs/PasswordService/ApplePassword Server.Server.log shows successful and failed attempts to authenticate.

Lesson **10**

Managing Local Network Accounts

Once you have created shared LDAP directories, you need to populate them with information. User account information is probably the most important type of information you can store in a directory. User accounts stored in your server's shared directory are accessible to all the computers that search that directory; those accounts are now referred to as local network user accounts, though you may also see the terms network user accounts, or just network users.

GOALS

► Configure local network accounts

► Import local network accounts

► Describe authentication types

► Understand basic Kerberos infrastructure

► Configure global password policy

Reference 10.1
Using the Server App to Manage Network User Accounts

Use the Server app for basic and advanced management of users and services. The Server app automatically adds authorization for OS X Server services to local network users you create, and adds these users to the built-in group called Workgroup.

The Server app gives you the basic options for account management, including the account details, email address, services that a user is authorized to use, groups to which a user belongs, and global password policy.

To create a new user, select Users in the Server app sidebar, and then click the pop-up menu to choose the directory domain Local Network Users.

> **NOTE** ► This ability to choose the directory domain in the Server app is new with this version of OS X Server. If the pop-up menu is set to All Users, when you create a new user, the new user is created in the Local Network Users node.

Click Add (+) to create a new user, and then configure the user.

New User

Full Name:	
Account Name:	
Email Address:	
Password:	
Verify:	
	☐ Allow user to administer this server
Home Folder:	Local Only
Disk Quota:	☐ Limit usage to [ ] MB

Cancel   Done

TIP After you click Done to create the user, wait until the spinning gear in the lower-right corner of the Server app window disappears before clicking anything else in the Server app, otherwise you might interrupt the process of creating the user.

After you click Done, the Server app returns you to the list of users. When you double-click the user you just created to edit it, you'll see that when you create a user with the Server app, the user is automatically added to the local network group named Workgroup. You can modify the user's icon among other attributes.

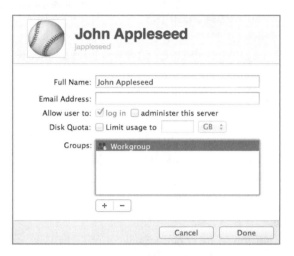

When you secondary click the user, and choose "Edit Access to Services" from the short-cut menu, you'll see that the user has authorization to access each of the listed services in the figure (these services are hosted on the server that's hosting the OD master).

MORE INFO ▶ When you create network user accounts outside the Server app, such as with Workgroup Manager or with command-line tools, those users are not auto-matically added to the group named Workgroup. Therefore, be careful when you use both the Server app and other methods to create network user accounts.

Using the Server App to Allow Access to Services for Accounts from Another Directory Node

If you configure your server to be an Open Directory server, after you bind to another directory service, users from the other directory service are not automatically authorized to use services on your server unless you explicitly give users or groups from the other directory node access to these services.

Simply select one or more external accounts, secondary click and choose "Edit Access to Services" from the shortcut menu, and then select the checkboxes for the services you want those users to be allowed to access.

Importing Local Network Accounts

Just like importing local accounts, you can import local network accounts. The import file must be a properly formatted file containing a header that defines the contents of the file.

> **MORE INFO ▸** For more information on creating a properly formatted file for importing accounts, see the section "Creating a Character-Delimited User Import File" in the document "User_Management_v10.6.pdf", which is included in the Additional Resources section at the end of this lesson.

Choose Manage > Import Accounts from File, select an import file, make sure the Type pop-up menu is set to Local Network Accounts, provide directory administrator credentials (as opposed to local administrator credentials), and click Import.

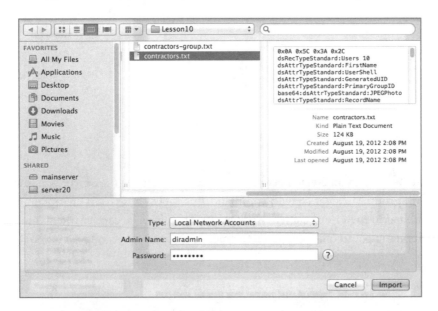

If your import file doesn't contain passwords, after you click Import, and after the Server app has completed importing the accounts, select your newly imported users, secondary click, and choose Reset Password.

You can also import local network groups. Note that the only thing that determines whether you are importing users or groups is the header of the import file. In the preceding figure, dsRecTypeStandard:Users specifies that the file contains user accounts. In the following figure, dsRecTypeStandard:Groups specifies that the file contains group accounts. You need to use the pop-up menu to specify into which directory node the Server app imports the accounts.

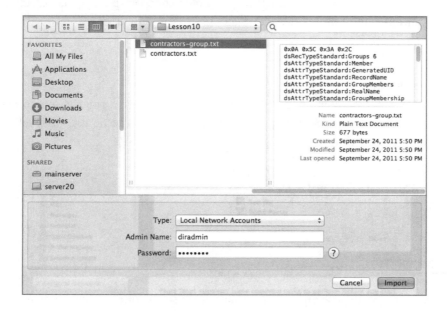

Reference 10.2
Configuring Authentication Methods on OS X Server

For authenticating users whose accounts are stored in shared directories on OS X Server, Open Directory offers a variety of options, including Kerberos and the many authentication methods that various network services require. Open Directory can authenticate users by using:

▶ Single sign-on with the Kerberos KDC built in to OS X Server

▶ A password stored securely in the Open Directory Password Server database

▶ A password stored as several hashes—including NTLMv1 and NTLMv2 (NT LAN Manager); and Microsoft Challenge Handshake Authentication Protocol (MS-CHAPv2), used for VPN—in a location that only the root user can access

▶ An older crypt password stored directly in the user's account (on the local file system or in the user's record stored in a third-party LDAP directory), for backward compatibility with legacy systems

▶ Local-only accounts, in which a shadow password is used, stored in a location accessible only by root

In addition, Open Directory lets you configure the "global password policy" that affects all users (except administrators) in the LDAP domain, such as automatic password expiration and minimum password length.

Disabling a User Account

To prevent a user from logging in or accessing services on your server, you can temporarily disable that user by using the Server app to remove access to his account. Simply edit the user and deselect the "Allow user to log in" checkbox.

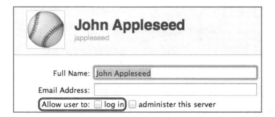

Doing so does not delete the user, nor does it change his user ID or any other information. It also doesn't delete any of the user's files. It simply prevents that user from authenticating and gaining access to the server via any method.

When a user account is disabled, you'll see the word "Disabled" next to the user in the list of users.

Setting Global Password Policies

Open Directory enforces global password policies. For example, a user's password policy can specify a password expiration interval. If the user is logging in and Open Directory discovers that the user's password has expired, the user must replace the expired password. Open Directory can then authenticate the user.

Password policies can disable a user account on a certain date, after a number of days, after a period of inactivity, or after a number of failed login attempts. Password policies can also require passwords to be a minimum length, contain at least one letter, contain at least one numeral, be mixed case, contain a character that is neither a number nor a letter, differ from the account name, differ from recent passwords, or be changed periodically.

Open Directory applies the same password policy rules to Password Server and Kerberos. Password policies do not affect administrator accounts. Administrators are exempt from password policies because they can change the policies at will; therefore, administrator accounts are not vulnerable to a troublemaker exploiting the "disable login after user makes n failed attempts" policy by performing repeated failed authentication attempts for an administrator account. However, this makes administrator accounts potentially more vulnerable to brute force attacks that attempt to guess the administrator password with repeated guesses of different passwords, so it is crucial that you choose a strong password for each account in the Administrators group.

Kerberos and Open Directory Password Server maintain password policies separately. OS X Server synchronizes the Kerberos password policy rules with Open Directory Password Server password policy rules.

After global password policies are put into effect, they are enforced only for users who change their passwords, or users you create or import. This is because the account's password was established prior to the establishment of the global policy.

> **MORE INFO** ▶ You can use Workgroup Manager to apply policies for individual user accounts, but this is outside the scope of this guide. User account settings may override global policies, and administrators are exempt from both types of policies.

To configure global password policy, select Users in the Server app sidebar, and confirm that the directory node pop-up menu displays Local Network Users. Click the action pop-up menu, and choose Edit Global Password Policy. Configure the options to match your organization's policy, and then click OK.

It is important to obtain your organization's password policies prior to setting these options. If you miss certain criteria required by your organization, and all users have been imported and have passwords set, changing these parameters may require users to change their passwords again to conform to the newer standards.

You can use either the Server app's Users pane or the Server app's Open Directory pane to configure global password policy; they have the same options and the same effects (although the Open Directory pane only offers global password policy for the local network users node).

Remember that the global password policy may not be applied when a user attempts to authenticate; it is applied only when:

▶   You create a new user.

▶   A user (with a password that was established before the password policy was established) changes her password.

   NOTE ▶ The "be reset on first user login" checkbox applies to users created after this option is selected.

Reference 10.3
Using Single Sign-On and Kerberos

Frequently, a user who is logged in on one computer needs to use resources located on another computer on the network. Users typically browse the network in the Finder and click to connect to the other computer. It would be a nuisance for users to have to enter a password for each connection. If you've deployed Open Directory, you've saved them that trouble. Open Directory provides a feature known as single sign-on, which relies on Kerberos. Single sign-on essentially means that when users log in, they automatically have access to other services they may need that day, such as Mail, file, Messages, and Calendar servers, and VPN connectivity, without again entering their user credentials; in this way, Kerberos provides both identification and authentication services.

Defining Kerberos Basics

A complete Kerberos transaction has three main players:

▶ The user

▶ The service the user is interested in accessing

▶ The KDC (Key Distribution Center), which is responsible for mediating between the user and the service, creating and routing secure tickets, and generally supplying the authentication mechanism

Within Kerberos there are different realms (specific databases or authentication domains). When you configure your server to be an Open Directory master, the realm name is the same as your server's host name, in all capital letters. Each realm contains the authentication information for users and services, called Kerberos principals. For example, for a user with a full name of Barbara Green and an account name of barbara on a KDC with the realm of SERVER17.PRETENDCO.COM, the user principal is barbara@SERVER17 .PRETENDCO.COM. By convention, realms use all uppercase characters.

For a service to take advantage of Kerberos, it must be Kerberized (modified to work with Kerberos), which means that it can defer authentication of its users to a KDC. Not only can OS X Server provide a KDC when configured to host a shared LDAP directory, but it can also provide several Kerberized services. An example of a service principal is afpserver/server17.pretendco.com@SERVER17.PRETENDCO.COM.

Finally, Kerberos enables you to keep a list of users in a single database called the KDC, which is configured on OS X Server once an Open Directory master has been created.

The process can be simplified into three major steps, which are illustrated in the following figure.

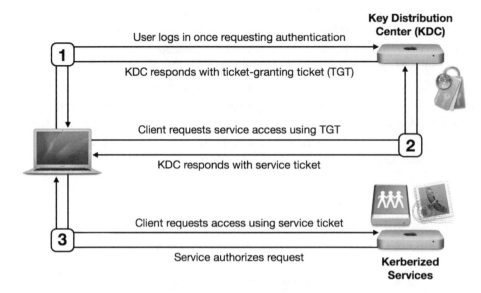

1. When a network user logs in on a Mac OS X v10.4 or later client computer, that computer negotiates with the KDC. If the user provides the correct user name and password, the KDC provides an initial ticket called a ticket-granting ticket (TGT). The TGT enables the user to subsequently ask for service tickets so she may connect to other servers and services on the network for the duration of the login session.

2. When the user on the client computer wants to access a Kerberized service, her computer presents her TGT to the KDC to obtain a service ticket.

3. The user's computer presents the service ticket to the Kerberized service to provide identification and authentication. The server that provides the Kerberized service grants the user access to the service (as long as the user is authorized to use the service).

When a user with a valid Kerberos TGT tries to access a Kerberized service, she does not need to provide her username, because the TGT contains her identity. Likewise, she does not need to provide a password, because the TGT provides authentication. In this way, Kerberos provides identification and authentication.

For example, when you have a TGT and attempt to access a Kerberized AFP or SMB service, you immediately see a list of shared folders to which you have access; because the service uses Kerberos to identify and authenticate you, you do not need to provide your username or password.

Kerberos is one of the components of Open Directory. The reason a user's password is stored in both the Password Server database and the Kerberos principal database is to allow users to authenticate to services that are not Kerberized. Users must enter a password every time they make a new connection to use those non-Kerberized services. Open Directory uses Password Server to provide support for those authentication protocols.

Because Kerberos is an open standard, Open Directory on OS X Server can be easily integrated into an existing Kerberos network. You can set up your OS X computers to use an existing KDC for authentication.

One security aspect to using Kerberos is that the tickets are time sensitive. Kerberos requires that the computers on your network be synchronized to within five minutes by default. Configure your OS X computers and your servers to use NTP, and synchronize to the same time server so this doesn't become an issue that prevents you from getting Kerberos tickets.

In order to obtain Kerberos tickets on a Mac, that Mac must be either of the following:

▶ Bound to a directory node that provides Kerberos services (such as an Active Directory domain or forest, or an Open Directory master or replica)

▶ An Open Directory master or replica

Examining Kerberos Tickets

The Ticket Viewer application allows you to confirm that you're able to obtain Kerberos tickets for a network user (you could also use command-line tools).

To use the Ticket Viewer, open it in /System/Library/CoreServices. Unless you've already used the Ticket Viewer as the currently logged-in user, the Ticket Viewer displays no identity by default; you must provide an identity by clicking Add Identity in the toolbar and entering a network user's principal, or account name, and password.

> **TIP** If you're using Ticket Viewer as a troubleshooting tool, deselecting the "Remember password in my keychain" checkbox is probably a good idea so that Ticket Viewer doesn't automatically use your keychain to obtain a ticket for you; leave the checkbox deselected so that you always have to enter an identity and a password.

After you click Continue, Ticket Viewer attempts to obtain a TGT. If Ticket Viewer successfully obtains a TGT, it displays the expiration date and time, which by default is ten hours from the time you obtain the ticket.

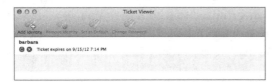

To see detailed information about the tickets associated with your identity, select the entry for your identity and choose Ticket > Diagnostic Information (or press Command-I). In the following figure, the first line includes the user account name (barbara), and the line that starts with "krbtgt" contains information about the TGT.

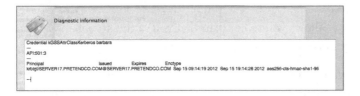

Once you have a TGT, you should be able to seamlessly access Kerberized services, as OS X automatically obtains a service ticket for each Kerberized service. In the following figure, the line that starts with "cifs" is for the service ticket OS X automatically obtained after the user attempted to access an SMB file sharing service.

NOTE ▶ The Ticket Viewer does not automatically update the diagnostic information pane, so you need to click the Close button in the bottom-right corner of the diagnostic information pane and then choose Ticket > Diagnostic Information again to refresh the information.

Once you've confirmed your ability to obtain tickets, you should relinquish the ticket so the ticket will not interfere with further investigation: click the X icon in your identity entry (next to the refresh icon).

Even though you may be logged in at the login window as a local user, you are able to get a Kerberos ticket as a network user. This is because, although you authenticated *locally* to your administrator computer, you authenticated against the Open Directory service for your network user account with Ticket Viewer.

Reference 10.4
Troubleshooting

See the "Troubleshooting" section of Lesson 8, "Managing Local Users," for troubleshooting importing local accounts and accessing services, and apply the same knowledge and procedures to troubleshoot problems importing network accounts and accessing services.

See the "Troubleshooting" section of Lesson 9, "Configuring Open Directory Services," for general troubleshooting of Open Directory services.

Troubleshooting Kerberos

When a user or service that uses Kerberos experiences authentication failures, try these techniques:

▶   Ensure that the DNS service you use is resolving addresses correctly. This is especially important at the time you are configuring a server to be an Open Directory master. If the DNS doesn't resolve addresses correctly, the incorrect address will be written to the Kerberos configuration files. Kerberos tickets won't be usable.

▶   Kerberos authentication is based on encrypted timestamps. If there's more than a five-minute difference between the KDC, client, and server computers, authentication may fail. Make sure that the clocks for all computers are synchronized using the NTP service of OS X Server or another network time server.

▶   Make sure that Kerberos authentication is enabled for the service in question.

▶ View the user's Kerberos ticket with the Ticket Viewer app.

▶ When you browse for services using the Finder window, OS X may not automatically use the expected Kerberos identity; use Go > Connect to Server and enter a URL instead.

MORE INFO ▶ You can use the klist command in the command-line environment to list information about your Kerberos credentials; see the man page for klist.

Exercise 10.1
Create and Import Network Accounts

▶ **Prerequisites**

  ▶ Exercise 9.1, "Configure Your Server to Manage Network Accounts"

  ▶ You need the text files from the student materials, which you obtained as part of Exercise 2.1 and Exercise 2.3.

You create local network user accounts and local network group accounts just like you create local user accounts and local group accounts, except that you specify the local network node in the pop-up menu.

In this scenario, within the greater Pretendco company, your group is working with some contractors. You need to give them access to your server's services, but these users shouldn't have access to the services outside your group. Therefore, you aren't going to ask the directory administrator of Pretendco's main directory server to create user accounts for these contractors.

Import Users into Your Server's Shared Directory Node
To expedite the exercise, in the student materials is a text file with more contractors your group is working with for the Pretendco scenario. This text file has a properly formatted header line. The import file defines these users with the password of "net". Of course, in a production environment, each user should have his own unique password or passphrase that is secret and secure.

1 In the Server app, choose Manage > Import Accounts from File.

2 In the sidebar, click Documents. Open StudentMaterials, and then open the Lesson10 folder.

3 Select the contractors-users.txt file.

4 Click the Type pop-up menu and choose Local Network Accounts.

5 Provide directory administrator credentials in the Admin Name and Password fields.

The suggested values from Lesson 9, "Configuring Open Directory Services" are Admin Name diradmin and Password diradminpw.

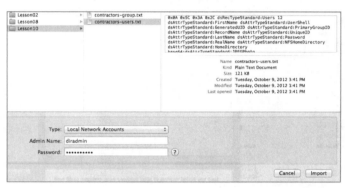

6 Click Import to start importing the file.

During the import, the status is displayed in the lower-right corner of the Server app window.

7 Select one of the newly imported users, secondary click, and choose "Edit Access to Services" from the shortcut menu.

Note that every service's checkbox is selected, meaning that the Server app has granted each imported local network user account the authorization to use each listed service.

8   Click Cancel to close the Service Access pane without making any changes.

You now have added eight local network user accounts.

On the computer you used to import the users, open the Console app and view the import log.

1   If the Console app is not already running, open Launchpad, open Other, and open Console.

2   If no sidebar is displayed for the Console window, click Show Log List in the toolbar.

The Console app displays logs from several locations on your computer. The tilde character (~) is a symbol for your home folder, so ~/Library/Logs is a folder in your home folder, and it is for logs specifically related to your user account. The /var/log and /Library/Logs folders are for system logs. You will look for a log file in the ImportExport folder in your ~/Library/Logs folder.

3   Click the disclosure triangle for ~/Library/Logs to display the contents of that folder, and then click the disclosure triangle for ImportExport to display its contents.

4   Select a log file under ImportExport.

Note that this log file shows that you imported a number of users without error. Some problems associated with importing accounts, if they occur, will appear in these log files.

Import a Group into Your Server's Shared Directory Node

To expedite the exercise, you have an import file with a properly formatted header line that defines all the imported users as members of the Contractors group (Account Name: contractors). You will confirm that this local network group has no explicit access to your server's services. However, local network user accounts you create with the Server app, or import with the Server app, automatically have access to all the services in this list, so this isn't a big concern.

1   In the Server app, choose Manage > Import Accounts from File.

2   In the sidebar, click Documents. Open StudentMaterials, and then open Lesson10.

3   Select the contractors-group.txt file.

4   Click the Type pop-up menu and choose Local Network Accounts.

5   Provide directory administrator credentials in the Admin Name and Password fields.

6 Click Import to start importing the file.

7 Select the Contractors group, secondary click, and choose "Edit Access to Services" from the shortcut menu.

Note that every service's checkbox is deselected.

8 Click Cancel to close the Service Access pane without making any changes.

You now have a new local network group populated with the local network users you previously imported.

Verify That Newly Imported Users Can Connect to Your Server's AFP Service

Turn on the File Sharing service if it isn't already on, and then use the Finder on your administrator computer to connect to your server's AFP service with a local network user account.

1 In the Server app, if the File Sharing service is not already on, with a green status indicator next to the service name in the sidebar, select File Sharing in the sidebar and click the On/Off switch to turn it on.

2 On your administrator computer, open the Finder.

3 If you don't already have a Finder window open, press Command-N to open a new one.

4 If an Eject button appears next to your server in the Finder sidebar, click the Eject button.

5 In the Finder sidebar, select your server.

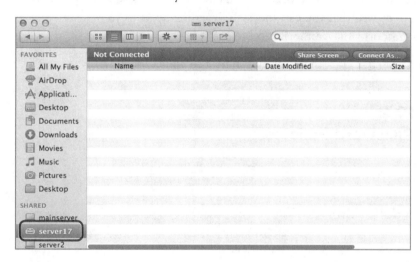

If your server does not appear in the Finder sidebar, click All under Shared, and then select your server.

6 Click Connect As.

7 Provide credentials for one of the users you imported:

▶ Name: **gary**

▶ Password: **net**

8   Click Connect.

The Finder displays the user account you are connected as, and displays the shared folders this user has access to.

9   Open the Public folder.

No files are in the Public folder, because you have not yet placed anything there. However, you have proved that you can successfully authenticate to your server, and that the user you imported has authorization to use the AFP service.

10   In the Finder sidebar, click the Eject button next to your server.

Exercise 10.2
Configure Password Policies

▶ **Prerequisite**

  ▶   Exercise 10.1, "Create and Import Network Accounts"

Configure Global Password Policy

It's easy to set up global password policies using the Server app. The settings you specify affect all network users, except for users in the Administrators group. The settings take effect only when a user changes her password. For this exercise, you'll configure the global password policy such that it requires:

▶   Users to become disabled after three failed attempts

▶   Passwords to contain at least one numeric character

▶   Passwords to contain at least eight characters

You'll also take advantage of the global password policy that requires newly created users to reset their passwords; you'll create a new local network user account, and then try to use its credentials to access the AFP service. You'll be prompted to change the password. Attempt to change it to something that does not match the policy you just configured, and then change it to a password that does conform to the policy.

1   In the Server app sidebar, select Users.

2   From the Action (gear icon) pop-up menu, choose Edit Global Password Policy.

3   Select the checkbox for "Disable login after user makes __ failed attempts" and enter 3 in the field.

4   Select the checkbox for "Passwords must contain at least one numeric character."

5   Select the checkbox for "Passwords must be reset on first user login."

6   Select the checkbox for "Passwords must contain at least __ characters" and enter 8 in the field.

Before you click OK, verify your settings against the settings in the following figure.

7   Click OK.

Create a new local network user for this exercise.

1   In the Users pane, set the pop-up menu to Local Network Accounts.

2   Click the Add (+) button.

3   Enter the following values:

▶   Full Name: Rick Reed

▶   Account Name: rick

▶   Password: net

▶   Leave the other fields at their defaults.

4   Click Done to save the changes.

Attempt to access your server's AFP service as this new user.

1   In the Server app, if the File Sharing service is not already on, with a green status indicator next to the service name in the sidebar, select File Sharing and click the On/Off switch to turn it on.

2   On your administrator computer, open the Finder.

3   If an Eject button appears next to your server in the Finder sidebar, click it.

4   In the Finder sidebar, select your server.

If your server does not appear in the Finder sidebar, click All under Shared, and then select your server.

5   Click Connect As.

6   Attempt to authenticate with the new user credentials. Enter the following and click Connect:

▶   Name: rick

▶   Password: net

Because you successfully provided Rick Reed's current password, but the password policy specifies that it must be changed at next login, you cannot gain access to the AFP service until you change the password.

Attempt to change the password to one that does not conform to the global password policy.

1   Enter the old password as well as a new password:

▶   Old Password: net

▶   New Password: new

▶   Verify: new

2 Click Change Password to confirm the new password.

You see a message that the password does not meet the policy. Click OK and try a different new password.

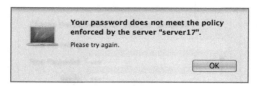

3 Enter the old password as well as a new password, following the global password policy that it must be at least eight characters and must include at least one number:

▶ Old Password: net

▶ New Password: rickpw88

▶ Verify: rickpw88

4 Click Change Password to confirm the new password.

Once you've successfully changed the password, you are authenticated and authorized to use the AFP service. You see a list of network volumes available to Rick Reed.

5 In the Finder sidebar, click Eject next to your server.

To prevent confusion in future exercises, remove the Rick Reed user, and remove your global password policy configuration.

1 In the Server app sidebar, select Users.

2 Select Rick Reed.

3   Click the Delete (–) button.

4   When asked to confirm that you want to permanently remove Rick Reed, click Delete.

Remove the global password policy configuration.

1   In the Server app sidebar, select Users.

2   From the Action (gear icon) pop-up menu, choose Edit Global Password Policy.

3   Deselect each checkbox, and then click OK.

Additional Resources

The following documents provide more information about managing local network accounts with OS X Server. Additional resources are available at www.apple.com/osx/server/resources/documentation.html.

OS X Server Administration Guides

OS X Server: Advanced Administration http://help.apple.com/advancedserveradmin/mac/10.8/

User_Management_v10.6.pdf http://manuals.info.apple.com/en_US/UserMgmt_v10.6.pdf

Apple Knowledge Base Documents

You can check for new and updated Knowledge Base documents at www.apple.com/support/.

Document HT4696, "OS X Server: Changing opendirectoryd logging levels"

Document HT5545, "OS X Server: Speeding up new account creation in Server.app"

Lesson Review

1. What tool can you use to check the ability to obtain a Kerberos ticket?
2. How do you import local network users from a text file with a properly formatted header line?
3. What are some reasons that a client computer might not be able to use Kerberos authentication to access a service?
4. In addition to authentication, what else can Kerberos provide?
5. How can you disable a local network user account so that it cannot be used to access services or log in on a bound Mac?
6. What are some examples of global password policies that you can apply to users that apply the next time they change their password?
7. What are some examples of global password policy you can configure to disable login after certain events occur?
8. How does a user obtain a Kerberos service ticket?

Answers

1. Ticket Viewer is in /System/Library/CoreServices, and you can use it to confirm the ability to obtain a Kerberos ticket.
2. Choose Manage > Import Accounts from File, select the text file, choose Local Network Accounts in the pop-up menu, provide directory administrator credentials, and click Import.
3. The client computer might not be bound to a directory service that provides Kerberos; the system time between the client computer and the server computer might be off by more than five minutes; there could be a DNS configuration issue; or the service might not be configured to use Kerberos.
4. Kerberos provides identification and authentication.

5. In the User pane of the Server app, double-click the user to edit the user, and deselect the checkbox "Allow user to log in."

6. Some examples include that passwords must differ from account name; contain at least one letter; contain both uppercase and lowercase letters; contain at least one numeric character; contain a character that isn't a letter or number; contain at least a given number of characters; or differ from the last given number of passwords used.

7. Some examples include that the login will be disabled on a specific date; after using it for a given number of times; after inactive for a given number of days; or after a user makes a given number of failed attempts.

8. Once a user has a ticket-granting ticket, OS X automatically attempts to obtain a service ticket when a user attempts to connect to a Kerberized service.

Managing Devices with
Configuration Profiles

Lesson **11**

Configuring OS X Server to Provide Device Management

OS X Server provides a service called Profile Manager that allows you, as the administrator, to assign certain behaviors to the client devices such as computers and mobile devices. Profile Manager also allows a user to perform basic management of her own devices.

GOALS

▸ Configure Profile Manager

▸ Understand the components of Profile Manager

Reference 11.1
Profile Manager

Profile Manager is an account management tool that allows the development and distribution of configurations and settings to control the experience on Lion and later computers and iOS 4 and later devices. The configurations and settings are contained in XML-based text files called profiles. Profile Manager has three parts:

▸ Profile Manager web tool

▸ User Portal website

▸ Mobile Device Management Server

Profile Manager Web App

The web tool allows easy access to the Profile Manager functionality from any browser that can connect to the OS X Server with the Profile Manager service turned on. An administrator can utilize the web interface to create profiles for use on client machines. It is also used to create and manage device accounts and device group accounts. Users and Groups are created in the Server app, but are displayed in the Profile Manager web app. The Profile Manager is reached at https://server.domain.com/profilemanager/.

User Portal

The User Portal is a simple way for users to enroll devices, obtain profiles, and wipe or lock their devices. The User Portal, accessed via a web browser at https://server.domain.com/mydevices/, lists the user's enrolled devices and available profiles.

Device Management

You can configure and enable the Mobile Device Management (MDM) functionality to allow you to create profiles for devices. When you or your users enroll Lion and later computers and iOS 4 or later devices, this allows over the air (OTA) management of devices, including remote wipe and lock.

> **NOTE** ▶ The usage of the Profile Manager, user portal, and device management will be covered in more detail in Lesson 12, "Managing with Profile Manager."

Reference 11.2
Configuring Profile Manager

To allow assigning profiles, the Profile Manager service must be enabled. Using profiles is significantly different than managing clients in earlier versions of OS X Server. Note that the older method of using Workgroup Manager, known as preferences management, is still valid in OS X Server v10.8, but this guide doesn't approach it. For information on OS X Managed Client, see Chapter 9, "Managing Accounts," in the book *Apple Training Series: Mac OS X Server Essentials v10.6.*

Terminology

In the context of device management, a profile is basically a collection of settings. Configuration profiles define settings such as Wi-Fi settings, email accounts, calendar accounts, and security policies. Enrollment profiles allow the server to manage your device. A payload is what's inside a profile.

Preparations for Profile Manager

Prior to configuring Profile Manager, you'll need to set up a few items to make the process more streamlined:

▶ Configure your server as a network directory server. This is also referred to as creating an Open Directory master.

▶ Obtain and install an SSL certificate. It is recommended to use one signed by a trusted certificate authority. You could use the certificate that is automatically generated when you configure your server as an Open Directory master, but if you use this certificate, you need to first configure devices to trust that certificate.

▶ Obtain an Apple ID for use when you request a push certificate from Apple through the http://appleid.apple.com website. Prior to using this ID, make sure you log in at that site and verify the email address. Otherwise, you might not have success requesting the push certificate.

Exercise 11.1
Enable Profile Manager

In this section, you'll go through the steps to enable Profile Manager, including the signing of a configuration profile.

1   Open Server app and select Profile Manager in the Server app sidebar.

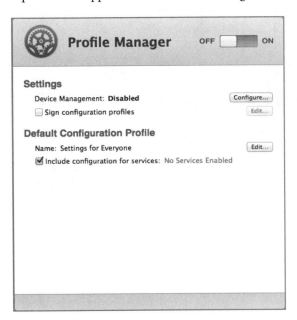

2   Click the Configure button, next to Device Management.

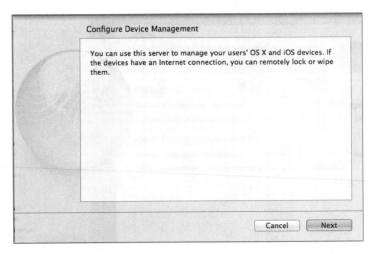

3   The service gathers some data and gives a description of its capabilities.

At the Configure Device Management pane, click Next.

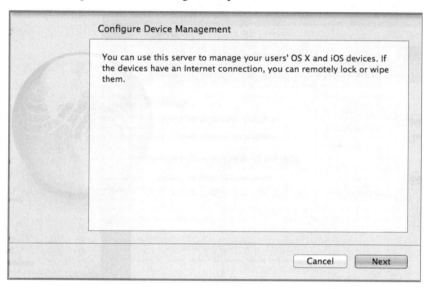

Configure Device Management

You can use this server to manage your users' OS X and iOS devices. If
the devices have an Internet connection, you can remotely lock or wipe
them.

Cancel   Next

4   If your server is already configured as an Open Directory master, skip to step 8.

5   If your server is not already configured as an Open Directory master, then at the Configure Network Users and Groups pane, select Create a new Open Directory domain, and click Next.

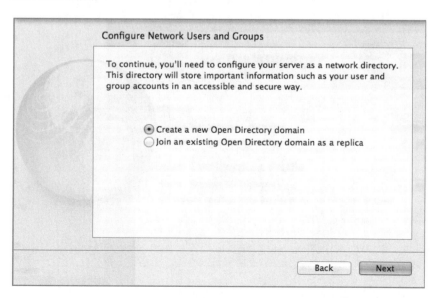

Configure Network Users and Groups

To continue, you'll need to configure your server as a network directory.
This directory will store important information such as your user and
group accounts in an accessible and secure way.

⦿ Create a new Open Directory domain
◯ Join an existing Open Directory domain as a replica

Back   Next

6 At the Directory Administrator pane, leave the Name and Account name fields at their default settings. Enter **diradminpw** in the Password and Verify fields (of course, in a production environment, you should always use a strong password).

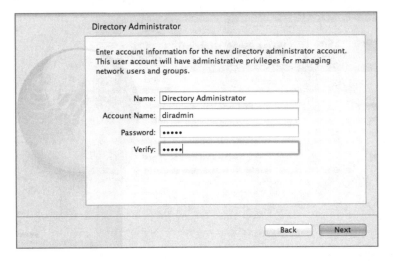

7 Click Next.

8 At the Organization Information pane, if necessary, in the Organization Name field, enter **Pretendco Project** *n* and in the Admin Email Address field, enter **ladmin@server***n***.pretendco.com** (where *n* is your student number).

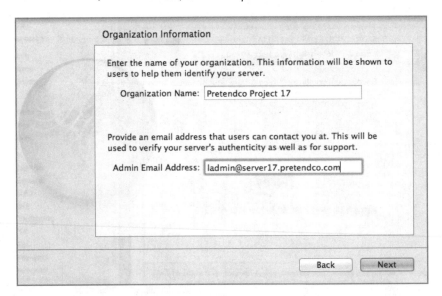

9 Click Next.

10 If your server is *not* already configured as an Open Directory master, then at the Confirm Settings pane, review the information, then click Set Up. It may take a few moments while the Server app configures your server as an Open Directory master. You can watch the status of the process in the lower-left corner of the pane.

11 At the Configure an SSL Certificate pane, click the Certificate pop-up menu, choose your SSL certificate, and click Next.

12 If you haven't already set up push notifications, you are prompted for an Apple ID, which the Server app uses to request Apple Push Notification certificates.

If you do not already have an Apple ID, click the link under the credential fields to create an Apple ID.

When you create an Apple ID, you need to click the verification link that Apple sends to the email address that you used when you created the new Apple ID.

NOTE ▸ It is possible to have been regularly using an Apple ID for other services, even if you have never verified it. If you have not yet verified your Apple ID, open http://appleid.apple.com in Safari, click Manage My ID, sign in with your Apple ID, click Send Verification Email to resend a verification email message to your email address, check your email, and finally, click the verification link.

Once you have an Apple ID which you've verified, enter your Apple ID credentials and click Next.

13 A green circle indicates that you've succeeded. Click Finish.

14 Select the "Sign configuration profiles" option, and then in the pop-up menu, choose the Code Signing certificate that was automatically created and signed by your Open Directory Intermediate CA.

By signing profiles with a certificate, you provide a way to validate that the profiles came from where they are supposed to and have not been tampered with.

15 Click the On/Off switch to turn on Profile Manager.

16 Monitor the status of starting the service: when the progress indicator in the lower-right corner of the Server app disappears, you're ready to start using the Profile Manager service.

Additional Resources

The following documents provide more information about using Profile Manager in OS X Server.

Many other documents are available at www.apple.com/osx/server/resources/documentation.html.

OS X Server Administration Guides

OS X Server: Advanced Administration
http://help.apple.com/advancedserveradmin/mac/10.8/

Apple Knowledge Base Documents

You can check for new and updated Knowledge Base documents at www.apple.com/support/.

Document HT4780, "Profile Manager 2: Scalability"

Document HT5349, "OS X Server: How to reset Profile Manager to its original state"

Document HT5302, "OS X Server: Ports used by Profile Manager"

Lesson Review

1. What tool is used to create profiles?

2. Why should a configuration profile be signed?

3. What is a configuration profile? An enrollment profile?

4. What steps are involved with turning on the Profile Manager service?

5. What steps are involved with specifying that you want to sign your configuration profiles?

6. What three components comprise Profile Manager?

Answers

1. The Profile Manager web app is used to create profiles.

2. A configuration profile should be signed to validate the contents of the profile.

3. A configuration profile contains settings and preferences to manage the user experience in a controlled device. An enrollment profile allows the device that it's installed on to be remotely controlled, performing such tasks as remote wipe and lock, and installation of other configuration profiles.

4. You can just click the On/Off switch in the Server app Profile Manager pane to turn on the Profile Manager service, but to enable device management (also known as Mobile Device Management), click the Configure button next to Device Management, select a valid SSL certificate, and specify a verified Apple ID to obtain an Apple Push Notification service certificate.

5. In the Server app Profile Manager pane, select the "Sign configuration profiles" option, and then choose a valid code signing certificate. Then when you create profiles with the Profile Manager web app, they are automatically signed.

6. The Profile Manager includes the Profile Manager web app, the user portal, and the optional device management (Mobile Device Management) service.

Lesson 12
Managing with Profile Manager

If you run an organization with several hundred users or even just a handful, how can you manage their experience with OS X and iOS? In previous lessons you learned management techniques involving the user name and password. There are many other aspects to user account management, and it is important to understand how these various aspects interact with each other.

OS X Server provides the Profile Manager service that allows you, as the administrator, to assign certain behaviors to the client devices such as computers and mobile devices.

Reference 12.1
Introducing Account Management

Account management was controlled by Workgroup Manager in Mac OS X 10.6 and earlier, but OS X Lion introduced the concept of profiles that contain configurations and settings. This continues in an expanded fashion with Mountain Lion. By assigning profiles to users, user groups, devices, or groups of devices you can achieve control over your systems.

With effective account management, you can achieve a range of results including but not limited to:

- Providing users with a consistent, controlled interface
- Controlling settings on mobile devices and computers
- Restricting certain resources for specific groups or individuals
- Securing computer use in key areas such as administrative offices, classrooms, or open labs
- Customizing the user experience
- Customizing Dock settings

GOALS

▶ Configure Profile Manager

▶ Construct management profiles

▶ Deliver profiles

▶ Install and delete profiles

▶ Manage users, groups of users, devices, and groups of devices using profiles

Levels of Management

You can create settings for four different types of accounts:

▶ User—Usually relates to a specific person. This is the account that the person identifies herself with when logging in to the machine. A user's short name or UID number uniquely identifies the user on a system.

▶ Group—Represents a group of users, a group of groups, or a mixture of both.

▶ Device—Similar to a user account, it's the singular entity that represents a given piece of hardware. This can be either a computer or iOS device. Device accounts are uniquely identified by their Ethernet ID, serial number, IMEI, or MEID.

▶ Device group—Represents a grouping of computers or iOS devices. Device groups can include other device groups nested in it, or a mixture of both individuals or nested groups.

Not all management levels make sense for all purposes, so when setting policy you have to decide what is appropriate. For example, you might want to define printers by device groups, because a typical situation has a group of computers located geographically close to a specific printer. You may want to set VPN access via a group of users such as remote salespeople. And individuals might have specific application access rights granted to them.

Each level can have a default group of settings and then custom settings. Mixing and layering profiles with conflicting settings is not recommended. The results may not be what were expected.

If a user or user group has an assigned profile, and the user logs into the user portal to enroll an OS X computer, the profiles assigned to that user will be applied to that computer regardless of who logs into that computer.

Managing Preferences for Users in a Group

Although you can set up preferences individually for users with network accounts, it's more efficient to manage preferences for the groups to which they belong. Using groups allows you to manage users regardless of which devices they use.

Managing Device Group Accounts

A device group account is set up for a group of computers or iOS devices that have the same preference settings and are available to the same set of users and groups. You create and modify these device groups in Profile Manager.

When you set up a device group, make sure you have already determined how the devices are identified. Use descriptions that are logical and easy to remember (for instance, the description might be the computer name). This also makes it easier to find the devices to add them to the correct device group.

Delivering Profiles

Once created, profiles can be delivered to users and computers or iOS devices in a number of ways:

▶ Via the User Portal—Where users log in to the portal with their account credentials and they are presented with the profiles assigned to them.

▶ Emailed to users—The profile is a simple text file, so it is easily transported.

▶ Web link—The profile can be published on a website for users to visit and download.

▶ Automatic push—The profile gets automatically pushed to the device with no user interaction (the device must be enrolled for this to work).

Automatic push relies on the Apple Push Notification service (APNs). This service is hosted by Apple and is provided to allow secure push notification to client devices. Once a server is configured to utilize APNs, client devices enrolled for management in Profile Manager check in with APNs waiting for notification signals to be sent by the Profile Manager via APNs. No data is included in the notification beyond informing the client that the Profile Manager has something for it. This keeps data secure between the Profile Manager and the client.

A list of installed profiles is available in OS X in the Profile preferences. An equivalent list is available in iOS by going to Profiles in Settings.

Remotely Locking or Wiping a Device

Once enrolled, a device or group of devices can be remotely locked or wiped. In this example, a remote lock will be performed. A remote wipe can be attempted, but only do it on a device you don't mind reconfiguring. The device can be locked via Profile Manager by an administrator or via the User Portal by the users themselves.

Upon requesting a lock, a confirmation pane will appear, a passcode will be requested, and the lock command will be sent. On Lion and Mountain Lion computers, the machine is shut down and an EFI passcode is set, so it needs to be entered to use the machine again. For iOS devices, the screen is locked and the passcode enforced.

▶ Profile Manager—Log in to the Profile Manager web app and select the device or group of devices to be locked. In the Action (gear icon) pop-up menu, choose Lock.

▶ User Portal—Once users log in, each device they enrolled will be displayed in the Devices pane.

Which Preferences Can Be Managed?

In addition to various other settings for user, group, devices, and device group accounts, Profile Manager provides control over the preferences listed in Table 12.1. Table 12.2 describes the manageable preferences payloads for devices and device groups.

Table 12.1 Manageable Preferences Payloads for Users and Groups

Preference	OS X	iOS	Description
General	•	•	Profile distribution type, how the profile can be removed, organization, and description
Passcode	•	•	Define passcode requirements such as length, complexity, reuse, and so on
Email	•	•	Configure email settings such as servers, account name, and so on
Exchange	•	•	Configure Exchange ActiveSync settings
LDAP	•	•	Configure connection to LDAP server
CardDAV	•	•	Configure access to CardDAV server
CalDAV	•	•	Configure access to CalDAV server
Network	•	•	Configure network setting on the device, including wireless and wired

Table 12.1 Manageable Preferences Payloads for Users and Groups

Preference	OS X	iOS	Description
VPN	•	•	Configure VPN settings: L2TP, PPTP, IPSec (Cisco), CiscoAnyConnect, Juniper SSL, F5 SSL, SonicWALL Mobile Connect, and Aruba VIA
Certificate	•	•	Allows the installation of PKCS1 and PKCS12 certificates
SCEP	•	•	Define connection to Simple Certificate Enrollment Protocol (SCEP) server
Web Clips	•	•	Display defined Web Clips as application icons
Security and Privacy	•	•	Control if diagnostic and usage data gets sent to Apple and whether user can override Gatekeeper (OS X only)
Identification	•		Configures identification information of user
Restrictions	•	•	Define application and content restrictions (separate OS X and iOS versions)
Subscribed Calendars		•	Configure calendar subscriptions
APN		•	Configure carrier settings such as the Access Point Name (Advanced use only)
Messages	•		Configure connection to Jabber or AIM chat servers
AD Certificate	•		Specify the settings for retrieving a certificate for your computer from Active Directory
Login Items	•		Specify applications, items and network mounts to launch at login
Mobility	•		Define mobility settings for OS X clients to allow cached credentials and portable home directories
Dock	•		Configure Dock behavior
Printing	•		Configure printing settings and access to printers or print queues
Parental Controls	•		Define settings for Parental Controls such as content filtering and time limits
Custom Settings	•		Apply custom preferences for items not defined in other payloads; similar to applying preference manifests in WGM

Table 12.2 Manageable Preferences Payloads for Devices and Device Groups

Preference	OS X	iOS	Description
General	•	•	Profile distribution type, how the profile can be removed, organization, and description
Passcode	•	•	Define passcode requirements such as length, complexity, reuse, and so on
Email		•	Configure email settings such as servers, account name, and so on
Exchange		•	Configure Exchange ActiveSync settings
LDAP		•	Configure connection to LDAP server
CardDAV		•	Configure access to CardDAV server
CalDAV		•	Configure access to CalDAV server
Network	•	•	Configure network setting on the device including wireless and wired
VPN	•	•	Configure VPN settings: L2TP, PPTP, IPSec (Cisco), CiscoAnyConnect, Juniper SSL, F5 SSL, SonicWALL Mobile Connect, and Aruba VIA
Certificate	•	•	Allows the installation of PKCS1 and PKCS12 certificates
SCEP	•	•	Define connection to Simple Certificate Enrollment Protocol (SCEP) server
Web Clips		•	Display defined Web Clips as application icons
AD Certificate	•		Specify AD certificate settings
Directory	•		Specify OD server settings
Restrictions	•	•	Define application and content restrictions (separate OS X and iOS versions)
Subscribed Calendars		•	Configure calendar subscriptions
APN		•	Configure carrier settings such as the Access Point Name (Advanced use only)
Login Items	•		Specify applications, items, and network mounts to launch at login
Mobility	•		Define mobility settings for OS X clients to allow cached credentials and portable home directories

Table 12.2 Manageable Preferences Payloads for Devices and Device Groups

Preference	OS X	iOS	Description
Dock	•		Configure Dock behavior
Printing	•		Configure printing settings and access to printers or print queues
Parental Controls	•		Define settings for Parental Controls such as content filtering and time limits
Security and Privacy	•		Define whether or not to send diagnostic and usage data to Apple (might change in the future)
Custom Settings	•		Apply custom preferences for items not defined in other payloads (similar to applying preference manifests in WGM)
Directory	•		Configure binding to directory services
Login Window	•		Configure Login window options, such as messages, appearance, access, and Login/LogoutHooks
Software Update	•		Define an Apple Software Update server to be used by the computer
Energy Saver	•		Define Energy Saver policy such as sleeping, timed actions, and wake settings

Reference 12.2
Troubleshooting

Occasionally things won't work the way you expect, and you'll have to troubleshoot the situation. Even a robust service like Profile Manager can have an occasional issue.

Viewing Logs

The Profile Manager–related logs are located at /Library/Logs/ProfileManager/ and can be viewed with Console by double-clicking. Errors may be reported and listed in the logs.

Viewing Profiles

If a device is not behaving as expected, look at the list of installed profiles on the device and see if the proper profiles have been installed. The solution may be as simple as applying the expected profile to the device.

Installing Profiles

If you're having problems installing a profile, you may have improper certificates. Review your SSL certificates for validity and make sure the trust profile has been installed on the device.

Problems Enrolling a Device

A trust profile must be installed prior to enrolling a device, unless you are using a certificate signed by a trusted certificate authority.

Pushing Profiles

If you're having problems pushing a profile, you may not have appropriate outbound ports open. Ports 2195, 2196, and 5223 are APNS related.

Exercise 12.1
Use Profile Manager

▶ **Prerequisites**

- ▶ Exercise 9.1, "Configure Your Server to Manage Network Accounts"

- ▶ Exercise 10.1, "Create and Import Network Accounts", or use the Server app to create network user Carl Dunn with an account name of carl, and a password of net.

- ▶ Exercise 11.1, "Enable Profile Manager"

This exercise utilizes Profile Manager to enroll and control devices using the various pieces that it comprises.

User Profile Portal

The User Profile Portal provides simple access for users to log in, apply profiles, and manage their devices. The portal is accessed via a web browser; by simply publishing the website, users anywhere in the world can enroll their devices—whether they be computers, iPhones, or other iOS-based mobile devices. Through the portal users can lock or wipe their enrolled devices.

NOTE ▶ The following example is for OS X, but the iOS version is conceptually and visually similar. Screenshots show the process in both OS X and iOS.

1   On your administration computer, navigate to the site https://server*n*.pretendco.com/ mydevices (where *n* is your student number).

2   Through a series of redirects the user is prompted for credentials to log in. Use Carl Dunn's user name (**carl**) and password (**net**).

The window has two tabs: Devices, where the user can enroll the device; and Profiles, where the various profiles made available will be displayed. Click the Profiles tab.

3 In the Profiles pane, click Install for the Trust Profile.

The profile downloads, and the Profiles preferences appear.

4 Click the Show Profile button to view the contents of the profile, review, and then click Continue.

5   In the next window, click Show Details to view more information regarding the certificates involved, and then click Install. Enter an administrator's credentials when prompted.

6 Back in the web browser, in the Devices pane, click Enroll.

You are asked if you want to enroll. View the profile and then click Install.

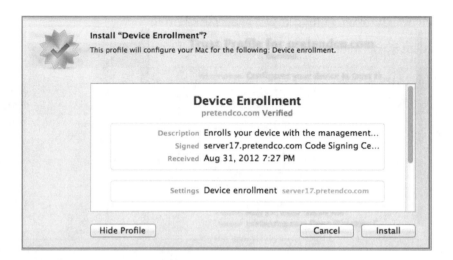

7   In the next screen, you are asked to install Remote Management, which allows the server to manage that machine. View the profile and click Continue. Enter an administrator's credentials when prompted.

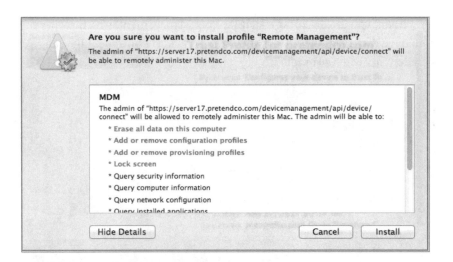

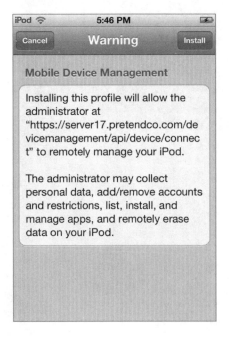

8   Now that the profile has been installed on the computer, refresh the view in the browser and notice that the computer is now listed on the Devices pane.

The user can now utilize any modern web browser to lock or wipe the computer remotely, if the machine were to get lost or stolen.

9   To lock the remote device, navigate to the site https://server*n*.pretendco.com/
mydevices (where *n* is your student number) on a different computer and log in
as Carl.

10 Select your administrator computer and lock it by clicking the Lock button and entering a six-digit passcode. For this exercise use something simple like 123456. Click the
Lock button again, and a confirmation box appears.

After confirmation, the remote computer reboots and then offers a dialog to unlock
the machine via the passcode. Enter the passcode (123456) and log in as ladmin.

Using Profile Manager

Once Profile Manager has been turned on, you access the actual management interface via a web application. The web application can be reached via web browser on any machine.

1   Navigate to the site https://server*n*.pretendco.com/profilemanager (where *n* is your student number) from your administrator computer.

2   Log in to the Profile Manager web app with an administrator's credentials.

3   The layout is a column view where the selection made in the left column defines the content of the column to the right. Select Devices and then click an enrolled computer.

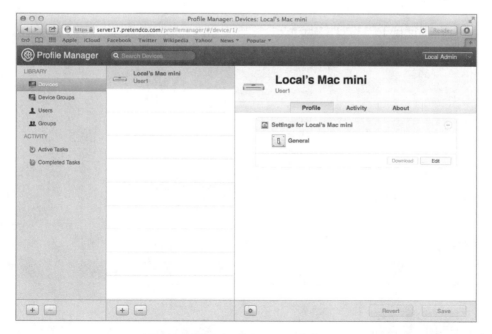

4   In the information pane, click the Profile tab and then click the Edit button.

5   Scroll down the list in the OS X section, noting that there are sections for iOS, OS X, and combined OS X and iOS. Select Dock and then click Configure.

6   Change the Position to Left and select the "Automatically hide and show the Dock" option.

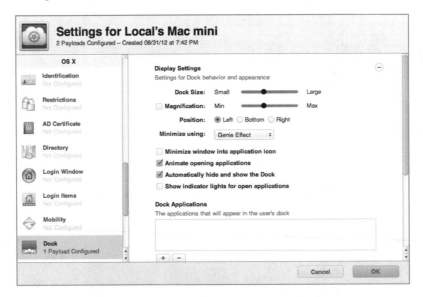

7   Scroll back to the top of the list in the left column and select General. Select Manual Download for the Profile Distribution Type. Click OK.

If Profile Distribution Type was left on Automatic Push, once the profile was saved, the Apple Push Notification service would have notified the client device and installed the profile automatically.

8   Note that the Dock preference is indicated in the settings for the computer.

9 In the warning dialog stating that new settings might be pushed to the managed devices, click Save.

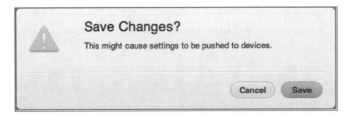

10 Click the Download button.

A copy of the preferences is stored in the profile downloaded to the machine on which Profile Manager is running. It is located in the Downloads folder of the currently running user. Secondary-click the .mobileconfig file, choose Open With, choose TextEdit, and view the contents. The profile is simply an XML text file with some binary due to it being signed. Quit TextEdit without making any changes to the file.

11 Double-click the profile to install it. Click Show Profile to view the contents of the profile.

12 Click Install and enter the local administrator's password.

13 Log out and log back in. Notice the Dock is now hidden on the left side.

14 Open the Profiles preferences and view the new profile.

15 Remove the Settings profile by highlighting it and clicking the Delete (–) button at the bottom of the left column. Acknowledge the removal and enter a local administrator's credentials. Upon logging out and back in, the original Dock location and behavior will be restored. Log out when done.

16 In Profile Manager, change the Dock preferences by setting the Position to Right and deselecting the "Automatically hide and show the Dock" option.

17 In the General payload, change the Profile Distribution Type to Automatic Push.

18 Click OK to save the preferences, and then click Save and Save again in the confirmation dialog to push the profile to the managed computer.

19 Look in the Activity list under Active Tasks to watch the push occur. Once finished, look in the Completed Tasks and find the push.

20 Log into the administrator account on the administration computer and check that the Dock is now on the right side.

Creating a Device Account Placeholder

There are two ways to set up a device account:

▶ During device enrollment the device account is created automatically.

▶ You can create a placeholder in Profile Manager, so when the user logs into the User Portal, predefined profiles are assigned to the device.

To manually create a placeholder in Profile Manager:

1   In the Profile Manager Library, select Devices.

2   Click the Add (+) button below the list of devices, and choose Add Placeholder.

3   Give the placeholder a name and choose how to identify the device by Ethernet ID, serial number, IMEI, or MEID.

4   Click Add.

5   From the placeholder entry, you can add profiles and management that will be applied automatically once the device is enrolled.

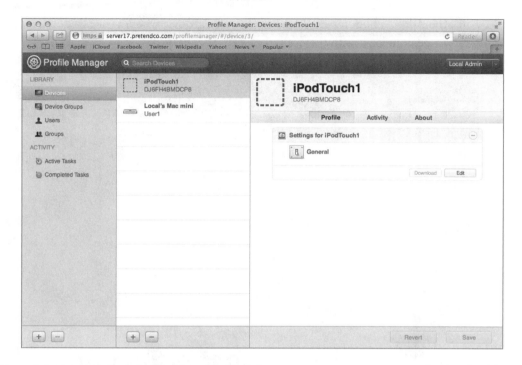

Lists of devices can be imported into Profile Manager via a comma-separated value (CSV) file. The file needs to be structured like this:

name, serial number, UDID, IMEI, MEID

Leave a field empty if you're not using that value.

This exercise is optional. To do the exercise you will need to create a CSV file with the appropriate information in it.

1   In the Profile Manager Library, select Devices.

2   Click the Add (+) button below the list of devices, and choose Import Placeholders.

3   Select the import file and upload.

Creating and Populating a Device Group

To create and populate a device group, use Profile Manager:

1   In the Profile Manager Library, select Device Groups.

2 Click the Add (+) button below the list of device groups, which creates a new group that can be populated with the desired name.

3 To add devices to the device group, click the Add (+) button under the device group pane, and choose Add Devices.

4 Click the device to add to the device group and then click Done.

5   To add device groups to the device group, click the Add (+) button under the device group pane, and choose Add Device Groups.

6   Click the device group to add to the device group and then click Done.

7   Click Save.

Managing Profiles Locally

Occasionally a profile will need to be viewed, added, or removed to make way for an updated profile or to simply stop management of the device. Managing the profiles local to a computer is done via the Profiles preferences. You added a profile to the computer in the previous exercise, and now you will remove one.

To remove a profile local to an OS X computer:

1   Open the Profiles preferences.

The various profiles installed on the computer are listed along with their contents and purposes.

2   Select the remote management profile, and click the Remove (–) button.

3   In the confirmation dialog box, click Remove. Enter a local administrator's credentials, if prompted, and click OK.

To remove a profile local to an iOS device:

1   Navigate to Settings/General/Profiles.

2   Tap the profile to show the details.

3   Tap the Remove button.

4   In the confirmation box, confirm the removal by tapping Remove.

5   Exit Settings.

Additional Resources

The following documents provide more information about managing with Profile Manager in OS X Server.

Many other documents are available at www.apple.com/osx/server/resources/documentation.html.

OS X Server Administration Guides

OS X Server: Advanced Administration
http://help.apple.com/advancedserveradmin/mac/10.8/

Apple Knowledge Base Documents

You can check for new and updated Knowledge Base documents at www.apple.com/support/.

Document TS1629, "Well known TCP and UDP ports used by Apple software products"

Lesson Review

1. At what levels can clients be managed?
2. Name at least three ways a profile can be delivered.
3. What service does push notification rely on?
4. How is a profile removed from an OS X computer? From an iOS device?
5. How can you view the content of a profile?

Answers

1. Users, user groups, devices, and device groups.
2. User portal, email, web page, or manual delivery. The mobile device management capabilities of Profile Manager can also push profiles to enrolled devices.
3. Apple Push Notification service (APNs).
4. In OS X 10.7 Lion and later, the profiles are managed in the Profiles preferences. On an iOS device, navigate to Settings/General/Profiles to view and remove installed profiles.
5. Any text editor. The text contained in the profile will be either straight XML or XML with some binary data if signed.

Providing File Services

Lesson **13**

Providing File Sharing Services

It is quite simple to use OS X Server to share files across a network for your users, whether they are using OS X, Windows, or iOS. The four basic steps are:

GOALS

▶ Configure OS X Server to share files with iOS, OS X, and Windows clients over the network

▶ Troubleshoot file services on OS X Server

▶ Plan.

▶ Configure accounts.

▶ Configure the File Sharing service.

▶ Monitor the server.

In this lesson you will explore the challenges associated with file sharing and the issues to consider when setting up file sharing. The main focus of the lesson is on setting up shared folders, also called share points, with appropriate access settings based on standard POSIX permissions and access control lists (ACLs). This lesson also addresses automatic network mounts, which provide a network destination for Time Machine backups, and general file sharing troubleshooting issues to consider when enabling file services on OS X Server.

You will learn how to use the Server app to add and configure individual share points, and you'll use the Console application while logged in to the server to monitor logs.

Reference 13.1
Addressing the Challenges of File Sharing

When planning to offer file services, there are a number of issues to consider. The obvious questions are:

▶ What content will you will share?

▶ What types of clients will be accessing your file server?

▶ What protocols will the client computers or devices use?

▶ What levels of access do your various users and groups require?

At first glance, these questions might seem relatively easy to answer, but in practice, especially in dynamic organizations, requirements can get very complex, and it can be difficult to facilitate your users' access to the things necessary to remain productive, without constant intervention from an administrator.

When accessing a file server, you typically have to authenticate, and then you see a choice of valid share points (also known as shares) available to mount. Here's an example dialog in which you must select one or more share points (which appear as network volumes) to use.

When you navigate inside a mounted share point, folder badges (small icons displayed on the lower-right corner of the folder icon) indicate the access rights for the user account whose credentials you used when you connected to the file service. Folders display a red do-not-enter sign for folders that you are not authorized to access, and a blue arrow for folders for which you have write-only access. In the following figure, you do not have access to most of the folders in the ladmin user's home folder, and you have write-only access to the Drop Box folder in ladmin's Public folder.

This is a combination of authorization for accessing the file sharing service, as well as authorization for accessing individual files and folders.

Authorization is a constant occurrence; every time a user accesses a file, the computer checks file permissions against the user's account information to see if the user is authorized to use the file.

After completing this lesson, you will be in a good position to carefully consider your file sharing needs before you implement file sharing on your server.

Understanding File Sharing Protocols

OS X Server includes a number of ways to share files. The method you select depends largely on the clients you expect to serve (although security is another factor to consider). You can use the Server app to enable the following file sharing services:

▶ Apple Filing Protocol (AFP)—This protocol is the native file sharing protocol for OS X.

▶ Windows file service—Server Message Block (SMB) is the native file sharing protocol for Windows, but is also used in UNIX environments.

▶ Web-based Distributed Authoring and Versioning (WebDAV)—This protocol is an extension to the web service protocol (HTTP), and enables various clients, including iOS applications, to access files hosted by your server.

▶ File Transfer Protocol (FTP)—This protocol is compatible with many devices and is still widely used, but in most common uses, it does not protect the authentication traffic. This file sharing protocol is lightweight in the sense that it is simple and does not have all the features available in the other file sharing services. FTP allows you to transfer files back and forth between client and server, but you cannot, for example, open a document over an FTP connection. The primary benefit of FTP is that it is ubiquitous: It is hard to find a Transfer Control Protocol (TCP)–capable computer that does not support FTP.

NOTE ▶ The FTP service is separated from the File Sharing service and has its own pane in the Server app.

When Windows clients use NetBIOS to browse for network file servers, a computer running OS X Server with file sharing enabled appears just like a Windows server with file sharing enabled.

NOTE ▶ OS X Server works with SMB clients that use UNICODE and extended security, including Mac OS X v10.6 Snow Leopard or later and Windows XP or later. Mac OS X v10.5 or earlier clients should use AFP instead of SMB.

A user with an iOS device can use a share point on your server, but only with apps that support WebDAV, and only to share points for which you enable WebDAV by selecting the appropriate checkbox.

If you do not provide a specific share point in the URL, all WebDAV-enabled share points will appear. Even without the benefit of SSL, the traffic for authentication is encrypted via WebDAV digest.

You can share a folder over several different protocols simultaneously. When you create a share point in the Server app:

▶   The share point is automatically enabled to be shared over AFP.

▶   The share point is automatically enabled to be shared over SMB.

▶   The share point is not automatically enabled for guest users.

If you want to share it over WebDAV, you must explicitly enable that service for that share point by selecting the "Share with iOS devices (WebDAV)" option. In order to access the WebDAV service protected with SSL, users should supply "https://" instead of "http://" as part of the URL.

Here is an example of using Keynote on an iPhone to open a connection to a WebDAV share point:

MORE INFO ▶ After signing in to your server's WebDAV service with an app like Keynote on iOS, the app displays the share points available via WebDAV; the user can navigate to a folder in which to open or save a document.

OS X Server also provides file service via Network File System (NFS). NFS is the traditional method of file sharing for UNIX-based computers. NFS has its heritage in research facilities and academia in the 1980s. Although it can be very convenient and flexible, and can be used with Kerberos to provide robust security, when used with legacy clients it can suffer from some security issues that do not affect the other protocols. The primary use for NFS is to provide files to NetInstall clients and UNIX or Linux computers. Although OS X can use NFS, you should normally use AFP for OS X clients.

> **MORE INFO** ▶ When you start the NetInstall service, OS X Server automatically creates the NetBootClients0 share point and makes it available to guest users over NFS. The "Allow guest users to access this share" checkbox for NetBootClients0 share point has a dash to indicate that the value varies; in this case, guest access is enabled for NFS and AFP but not for SMB.

The configuration and management for NFS are outside the scope of this guide; see the "Additional Resources" section at the end of this lesson for a Knowledge Base document regarding NFS.

Comparing File Sharing Protocols

This table provides a short comparison of file sharing protocols. There really isn't one best protocol. Instead, think of the protocols as different tools at your disposal to give different types of access.

	AFP	**SMB**	**WebDAV**
Native platform	OS X	Windows	Multi-platform
Security	Authentication is normally encrypted	Authentication is normally encrypted	Authentication via HTTP Digest is encrypted
Browsable	Bonjour	Bonjour and NetBIOS	Not browsable
Example URL	afp://server17. pretendco.com/ Users	smb://server17. pretendco.com/ Users	https://server17. pretendco.com/ Users

AFP and SMB are both full-featured file sharing protocols with reasonably good security.

> **TIP** ▶ If you use "https://" instead of "http://" in a WebDAV URL, both the authentication and the payload (the files transferred) are protected from snooping. However, if the SSL certificate your server is using is not valid, your WebDAV client may not allow you to access a WebDAV resource via HTTPS.

WebDAV uses HTTP Digest to encrypt authentication.

> **MORE INFO** ▶ In order to provide WebDAV service to Active Directory accounts, you must configure the WebDAV service to use Basic authentication instead of Digest authentication. In this scenario, it is recommended that you also require SSL for the WebDAV service, in order to protect the authentication. See the Knowledge Base document in the "Additional Resources" section at the end of this lesson.

When authenticating for FTP access, the username and password is not encrypted at all.

> **MORE INFO** ▶ SFTP (Secure FTP) uses the SSH service to securely transfer files using the SSH protocol. SFTP does not use the FTP service, and you must enable the SSH service in order for your users to use SFTP.

Planning File Services

When setting up file services on OS X Server, proper initial planning can save you time in the long run. Follow these guidelines when you first start planning to implement file services.

Plan Your File-Server Requirements

Determine your organizational requirements:

▶ How are your users organized?

▶ Is there a logical structure to follow for assigning users to groups that best addresses workflow needs?

▶ What types of computers will be used to access your file server?

▶ What share points and folder structures will be needed?

▶ Who needs what access to various files?

▶ How will users interact with one another when accessing these share points?

▶ How much storage space do you currently have, how much storage space do your users currently need, and at what rate will their need for storage grow?

▶ How will you back up and archive your storage?

These answers will dictate the file services you configure, as well as how you might organize groups and share points.

Use the Server App to Configure Users and Groups

The main goal is to end up with a group structure that best matches your organizational needs and allows easy maintenance over time. Setting up users and groups at the beginning is trivial. But, setting up users and groups that continue to work as the organization goes through natural changes over time is not as simple as it first appears. Nevertheless, having a logical group structure that can be used to allow and deny access to your server file system will save you from continually adjusting file-service access later on. OS X Server supports groups within groups and setting access control lists on folders.

> **TIP** For testing of groups, share points, and ACLs, you do not need to have all users entered. You may decide to test with a skeletal set of users and groups that meet the requirements of your organization. After verifying the groups and share points, you can then enter or import the full set of users.

Use the Server App to Start and Configure the File Sharing Service

The Server app is the main application you use to do the following:

▶ Start and stop the file sharing service.

▶ Add new share points.

▶ Remove share points.

For each share point, you can:

▶ Configure ownership, permissions, and the ACL for the share point.

▶ Enable or disable AFP for the share point.

▶ Enable or disable SMB for the share point.

▶ Enable or disable WebDAV for the share point.

▶ Allow or disallow guest access to the share point.

▶ Make the share point available for network home folders.

Perform Regular Maintenance

After you start the file sharing service, you'll need to perform regular maintenance. You will probably use the Server app to perform the following maintenance tasks as your needs change:

▶   Use the Users pane to add users to groups, groups to users, and groups to groups.

▶   Use the Users pane to modify the allowed services for each user.

▶   Use the File Sharing pane to add and remove share points.

▶   Use the File Sharing pane to modify ownership, permissions, and ACLs for share points.

▶   Use the Storage pane to modify ownership, permissions, and ACLs for folders and files.

Monitor Your Server for Problems

Monitoring server usage is a valuable method to keep track of workflow. You can view graphs and watch for usual traffic patterns, usage spikes, and low-usage periods that you could use to plan backups or perform server maintenance.

There are several ways to monitor your server:

▶   Use the Server app's Stats pane to monitor processor usage, memory usage, and network traffic.

▶   Use the Server app's Storage pane to check available disk space.

▶   Use the Server app's Connected Users tab in the File Sharing pane to monitor the number of connected users (this displays information about users connected via AFP and via SMB).

Be aware that if your server offers services other than file sharing, those other services could also affect resources such as network throughput, so you need to be careful interpreting the graphs.

Review Logs

If you log in at the server, you can use the Console app to view logs, including the following:

▶ /Library/Logs/AppleFileService/AppleFileServerError.log

▶ /Library/Logs/WebDAVSharing.log

▶ /var/log/apache2/access_log

▶ /var/log/apache2/error_log

From a remote computer (or on the server computer), you can use the Server app Logs pane to view logs related to file sharing, including the AFP Error log, and for WebDAV, the error and access logs associated with the default and secure websites.

The AFP Error log displays events such as the AFP service stopping. In the websites logs, you can use the search term "WebDAV" to separate log entries that relate to WebDAV from the log entries that relate to the Websites service in general.

You might use additional software, such as Terminal, or third-party software, to monitor your server.

Reference 13.2
Creating Share Points

After determining server and user requirements and entering at least a sample set of users and groups that represents the organizational structure, the next step in sharing files is to configure your share points. A share point can be any folder, disk, or volume mounted on the server. When you create a share point, you make that item and its contents available to network clients via the specified protocols. This includes deciding what items you want to give access to and organizing the items logically. It requires using your initial planning and knowledge of your users and their needs. You might decide that everything belongs in a single share point and use permissions to control access within that share point, or you might set up a more complex workflow. For example, you could have one share point for your copywriters and a separate share point for the copy editors. Perhaps you would also have a third share point where both groups could access common items or share files. Setting up effective share points requires as much knowledge of your users and how they work together as it does the technology of share points.

It is also important to keep in mind that different protocols handle issues like filename case-sensitivity differently. For this reason, it's usually best to limit your file sharing protocols to those needed by the clients connecting to your file sharing service. For example, if you have only OS X clients connecting to a share point, it will simplify things to use only the AFP service and disable SMB sharing for that share point.

Explore File Sharing

The On/Off switch turns the File Service on or off. The lower-right corner of the Server app window indicates the status of starting or stopping the File Sharing service. A service status indicator dot to the left of the service in the Server app sidebar appears when the service is on, and disappears when the service is off.

The Share Points pane is displayed by default, showing the following:

▶   The share points

▶   Buttons to Add (+) and Delete (–) share points

▶   The Action (gear icon) pop-up menu with choices to edit a selected share point, or to edit a greeting (which specifies a message to send to OS X users the first time they connect to the AFP service)

▶   A text filter field to limit the share points displayed

Understand the Default Share Points

If you enabled File Sharing on OS X before you installed OS X Server, you will have the same share points your OS X computer had. If you had not created any share points in

OS X before installing OS X Server, after installing OS X Server your server automatically shares the following folders:

► Groups (/Groups)

► Public (/Shared Items/Public)

► Users (/Users)

If you edit a group and select the checkbox "Give this group a shared folder," the Server app creates a folder for that group in the /Groups folder of your startup volume, whether or not Groups is a share point, and creates an access control entry (ACE) that gives the members of the group full access over their group folder.

Although these default share points are convenient, you are free to remove them.

> **MORE INFO** ► If you have configured and started the NetInstall service, you will see the additional share points named NetBootClients0 and NetBootSP0, which are used for NetInstall. There is more information about NetInstall in Lesson 15, "Leveraging NetInstall."

Add and Remove Share Points

It's pretty simple to add a shared folder that allows your users to access the files in the folder using any combination of AFP, SMB, and WebDAV. You can use the Server app to select an existing folder, or even to create a new folder to share.

To create a new shared folder, click Add (+) to open a pane that contains your startup volume and any other attached volumes.

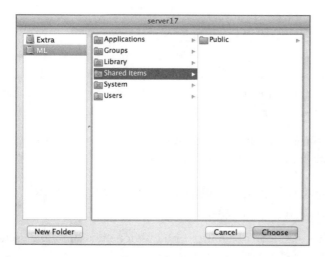

You have two options:

▸ Select an existing folder and click Choose.

▸ Create a new folder, select the new folder, and click Choose.

If you click New Folder, you'll be asked for the name of the new folder. Assign the folder a name, and click Create.

After you create a folder, you must remember to select the newly created folder before you click Choose, otherwise you will share the parent folder.

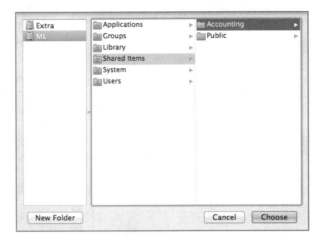

TIP ▸ Sometimes, administrators forget to select the folder they just created, and share the parent folder instead. Don't worry, you can always remove the shared folder and then add the newly created folder.

The newly shared folder appears in Share Points pane's list of share points. Each share point is listed. Note that there are some special icons to represent certain share points:

▸ The default Users share point has an icon of a folder with single user silhouette.

▸ The default Public share point has a plain folder icon.

▸ The default Groups folder has a an icon of a folder with a silhouette of multiple users.

Additionally, when you use the Server app from a remote administrator computer, the Server app displays any nondefault share point with an icon of a network disk with figures of multiple users (as in the Accounting share point in the following figure). If you are using the Server app on the server computer itself, the Server app displays any nondefault share point with an icon of a simple folder.

Removing a share point is just as easy. Select a share point and click Remove (–). When you remove a share point, you don't remove the folder or its contents from the file system, you just stop sharing it.

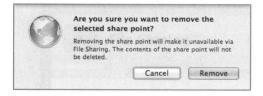

If someone using OS X has a share point from OS X Server mounted, and you stop the file sharing or remove that share point, the user will see a message indicating that the share point is no longer available:

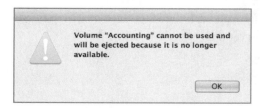

Configure Individual Share Points

In the next section, you will look at what kinds of changes you can make to a share point.

To edit a share point's configuration you could select a share point and do any of the following:

▶ Double-click the share point.

▶ Choose Edit Share Point from the Action (gear icon) pop-up menu.

▶ Press Command-Down Arrow.

> **TIP** In order to view all the options available without scrolling, you can resize the Server app window.

The editing pane includes the following:

▶ The full path to the shared folder (like /Shared Items/Public).

▶ The name of the shared folder (which by default is the name of the folder, but you can change it).

▶ An arrow icon next to "View Files"; when you click the icon, the Server app opens to that folder in the Storage pane of the Server app.

▶ The Access pane, which includes standard UNIX ownership and permissions, and can also include access control list (ACL) information.

▶ Checkboxes to enable and disable sharing over various protocols.

▶ A checkbox to enable or disable guest access.

▶ A checkbox to "Make available for home directories over" (AFP or SMB).

The guest access checkbox affects both AFP and SMB services, so when you use the Server app to enable guest access for AFP, you also enable guest access for SMB. Users from OS X or Windows client computers can access guest-enabled share points without providing any authentication. When users on OS X select your server's computer name in their Finder window sidebar's Shared section, they automatically connect as Guest. In the following figure, notice that the Finder displays the text "Connected as: Guest" below the toolbar, and displays the folders accessible to the Guest user.

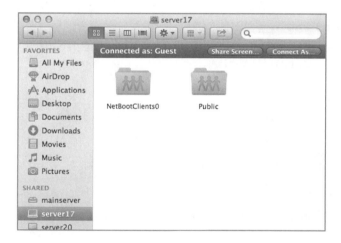

Configuring a Group Folder

When you edit a group and select the checkbox "Give this group a shared folder," the Server app creates a folder for that group in the Groups folder of your startup volume, whether or not Groups is a share point. If you want group members to be able to access the group folder via File Sharing services, be sure to make the Groups folder in the root of the startup volume a shared folder (this is how it is configured by default).

The Server app also creates an ACE in the folder's ACL that gives the members of the group full access over their group folder, so they can use their group folder for collaboration.

NOTE ▶ The behavior of the arrow icon next to the "Give this group a shared folder" checkbox depends on where you are running the server app. If you click the icon while logged in on your server, the Finder will open to the Groups folder. If you click the icon while using the Server app on an administrator computer, it attempts to open an AFP connection for the Groups folder on your server. If the group folder does not yet exist, be sure to select the checkbox "Give this group a shared folder," and then click Done, before you click the arrow icon.

Using the Connected Users Pane

The Connected Users pane displays information about the users who are currently connected via AFP or SMB (it does not include WebDAV and FTP connections).

The tab itself displays the number of connected users.

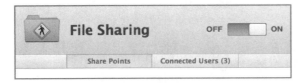

After you click the Connected Users tab, you see a list of connected users, including the following information:

▶ User name

▶ Address

▶ Idle time

▶ Type (AFP or SMB)

You can press Command-R (or choose View > Refresh) to refresh the list of currently connected users.

NOTE ▶ You may notice two entries for users that connect using SMB; this is expected.

If you select a user currently connected via AFP, the Send Message and Disconnect buttons become available. One example scenario would be to let people know that you're going to turn off the File Sharing service for maintenance; you could start by sending connected users a message to wrap up their work:

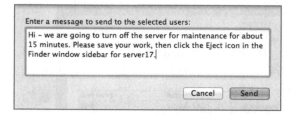

Or you could use the Disconnect button to send them a message and specify how much time will elapse before the Server app forcibly disconnects them.

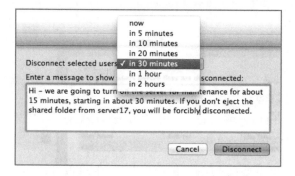

NOTE ▶ You can send messages to, and disconnect, only AFP users, not SMB users.

Understanding Case-Sensitivity Issues in File Sharing

Case sensitivity becomes an issue if you are copying files between two computers and only one of them has a case-sensitive file system. You can use Disk Utility to format a volume with a case-sensitive format, to handle legacy web content, for example. Suppose you have two files, Makefile and makefile, in the same folder on a case-sensitive volume shared by OS X Server. If an OS X user mounts the share point via AFP and then tries to copy both files to her desktop, she would see the following warning, because the default volume format for OS X is case insensitive.

If the user copies one file (makefile) to her desktop, and then attempts to copy the other file (Makefile) to her desktop, the Finder would display the warning message.

The Apple implementation of SMB in OS X has a distinct preference for lowercase filenames. For example, if your share point contains the files Makefile and makefile, and you mount that share point from an OS X client over SMB, you will see makefile but not Makefile in the Finder on the client computer.

If, at the server, you remove the file with the lowercase name, afterwards the client viewing the folder in the Finder via SMB will see only the file with the uppercase name. Likewise, if another file with the same name, but lowercase, appears, the client will see the uppercase filename disappear and the lowercase filename appear instead.

Not much can be done to synchronize case-sensitive and case-insensitive systems; you and your users need to work around the incompatibility. Given that AFP is a case-sensitive protocol, mounting a share point using AFP enables you to see the different case-sensitive files and use whichever one you'd like.

Reference 13.3
Troubleshooting File Services

Whether you're using AFP, SMB, or WebDAV, troubleshooting file services on OS X Server typically involves the following considerations:

▶   Service availability—Is the service turned on? For Time Machine, the File Sharing service must be turned on.

▶ User access—What users or groups should have access to the specific files and folders on the server, and are their appropriate permissions set correctly?

▶ Platform and protocol access—From which clients, such as Mac computers, Windows computers, or iOS devices, are users trying to access the server? What protocols are they using when accessing the server?

▶ Special needs—Are there any special circumstances, such as users needing access to files in a format not native to the system they are using?

▶ Concurrent access—Is there a possibility that in your users' workflow, there could be multiple clients simultaneously accessing the same files, regardless of the file sharing protocol(s) being used?

While the different sharing protocols (AFP, SMB, WebDAV) support multiple platforms, it can be tricky to provide concurrent access to the same files, especially with the Auto Save and Versions document management features in OS X. Concurrent access means that multiple users are trying to access or modify the same files at the same time. Many times this is dependent on the specific cross-platform applications knowing how to allow multiple users to access the same file. Because OS X Server includes support for ACLs, and these ACLs are compatible with those from the Windows platform, permissions mapping between Windows clients will be in line with what Windows users expect to see.

Reference 13.4
Providing FTP Service (Optional)

You use the File Sharing service to serve files via AFP, SMB, and WebDAV (and NFS, but you don't use the Server app to configure NFS), and you use the FTP service to serve files via FTP. As stated earlier, in most cases, the FTP service leaves everything in clear text: username, password, and the data in the files being transferred, so the FTP service might not be appropriate except for certain circumstances.

The FTP pane offers the On/Off switch, the Share pop-up menu to choose the parent folder (the folder that contains the files you make available via FTP), a basic access pane, and a View Files link to open the parent folder in the Storage pane.

By default, if you simply turn on the FTP service, users who successfully authenticate see contents of the default Websites folder (see Lesson 20, "Managing Web Services," for more information). However, you can click the Share pop-up menu to change the parent folder.

You can choose any share point configured on your server, or configure another folder to be the parent folder and then choose it. If you configure a custom parent folder, the FTP pane offers the View Files link to open the folder in the Storage pane, and the Server app displays the Access section (you'll learn more about controlling access to files in Lesson 14, "Understanding File Access").

In the following figure, the parent folder is a folder named FTPStuff at the root of the startup volume.

> **NOTE** ▶ Do not choose a parent folder with a space character in the full path to the folder (for example /Shared Items/Software Repository), otherwise the FTP service will not be able to serve files from that location.

If, instead, you choose a parent folder that's configured as a File Sharing share point (regardless of whether or not your File Sharing service is started), the FTP pane does not display access information; instead, it offers the Edit Share Point link to open the share point in the File Sharing pane.

You can use the OS X command-line environment or third-party software to access the FTP service with read and write capabilities. In the Finder, you can connect to the FTP service by choosing Go > Connect to Server, entering ftp://<your server's host name>, providing credentials, and clicking Connect, but the Finder is a read-only FTP client. Here's an example of how the Finder displays files available via FTP.

MORE INFO ▶ If someone attempts to try to connect anonymously, he will appear to make a successful connection but will see no files or folders available.

Because the FTP service normally does not encrypt the user name or password, it's recommended to leave the FTP service off unless there is no other alternative to meet your organization's needs to provide file service.

Exercise 13.1
Explore the File Sharing Service

> **Prerequisites**

> ▶ Exercise 9.1, "Configure Your Server to Manage Network Accounts" and Exercise 10.1, "Create and Import Network Accounts"; or use the Server app to create users Barbara Green and Todd Porter, each with an account name that is the same as their first name in lowercase, and a password of net, and each a member of a group named Contractors.

If you don't already have a Contractors group and the user accounts mentioned in this exercise, you can use the Users pane to create the users, use the Groups pane to create the Contractors group, and add the Barbara Green and Todd Porter users to the group.

You'll use the Server app to view the default shared folders, their respective protocols, and the available free space on your server's storage devices. Then you will create a new folder and make it available for file sharing.

1   On your administrator computer, if you are not already connected to your server with the Server app, open the Server app, press Command-N to connect to a server, and select your server.

2   If necessary, authenticate to your server with local administrator credentials.

3   In the Server app sidebar, select your server, and then click the Storage tab.

    The Storage pane displays your server's storage devices, including the startup volume. Using the disclosure triangles, you can navigate the hierarchy of the storage devices. The lower portion of the pane has a Column View button and a List View button.

4   Click the List View button, and then click the Column View button. Note the change.

5   Click the Action (gear icon) pop-up menu, but do not choose any item in the menu at this time.

    Note that you can use this menu to create a new folder, edit permissions, and propagate permissions. You will explore permissions in Exercise 14.1, "Configure Access Control."

6   In the Server app sidebar, click File Sharing.

7   In the Share Points pane, double-click Public to edit that share point.

8   If it is not already selected, select the "Allow guest users to access this share" option.

> **NOTE ▶** When you enable guest access, you enable it for both AFP and SMB protocols.

9   Click Done to return from the Public folder detail view to the File Sharing overview.

Stop and Start the File Sharing Service

Use the Server app to stop and start the File Sharing service and to verify that it is working properly. Regardless of how your File Sharing service is currently configured, start this exercise by making sure that "Enable screen sharing and remote management" is enabled, and File Sharing service is off.

1   In the Server app, select your server in the sidebar, and then click Settings.

2   Ensure that the checkbox is selected for "Enable screen sharing and remote management."

3   In the Server app sidebar, select the File Sharing service.

4   Click the On/Off switch to turn off the service.

On your administrator computer, observe how browsing for services with the Finder behaves before and after File Sharing services are started.

1   On your administrator computer, in the Finder, press Command-N to open a new Finder window.

2   If your server appears in the Finder window sidebar, select your server.

Otherwise, if there are enough computers on your network that your server does not appear in the Shared section of the Finder sidebar, click All, and then select your server.

Because your server's file sharing service is off, the Finder displays only the Share Screen button, and not the Connect As button.

3   In the Server app, in the File Sharing pane, click the On/Off switch to turn on the service.

The lower-right corner of the Server app window indicates the status of starting the File Sharing service. Once the File Sharing service has started, its service status indicator dot in the Server app sidebar reappears.

4   In the Finder, observe the change in your administrator computer's Finder: You are automatically connected as the Guest user, a Connect As button appears, and the shared folders identified as "guest accessible" in the Server app list of Share Points are listed in the Finder window.

When you turned on File Sharing, OS X Server used Bonjour to broadcast the availability of file sharing service to the local subnet. Your administrator computer's Finder received the broadcast and updated the Finder window sidebar accordingly.

Create a New Shared Folder

A folder has to exist on the server to be used as a file share. One way to create a new folder is to log in on the server and create a new folder with the Finder. However, you can also use the Server app to make new folders on your server.

1   In the Server app File Sharing pane, click the Add (+) button to add a new shared folder.

The Server app displays a list of volumes on the left, and a column view of folders for the selected volume on the right.

While the contents look similar to that of the Finder, there is a significant difference: You are looking at the file system of the server, not the local file system of your administrator computer. Any folders you create or choose are ones that exist on your server's storage devices.

2   Select your server's startup volume, and then select the Shared Items folder.

3   Click the New Folder button to create a new folder on the server.

The Server app prompts you for the folder name.

4   Enter the name Software Repository and click Create.

In this example, Software Repository could be a folder in which you place installation images of software you make available to individuals at your organization.

5   Select the new Software Repository folder, and then click Choose.

The new shared folder appears in the list of shared folders and is immediately available for file sharing clients to use.

On your administrator computer, you're currently connected via AFP as the Guest user. Connect to the new folder as the user Barbara Green.

1   On your administrator computer, click Connect As in the upper-right corner of the Finder window.

If you don't have a Finder window open to the Public folder on your server, press Command-N to open a new Finder window, and then select your server in the Finder window sidebar (or click All and select your server).

2   Provide Barbara Green's credentials (Name **barbara** and Password **net**) and click Connect.

You see a list of shared folders you can access.

3   Open the Software Repository folder.

4   Choose View > Show Status Bar.

Note the icon of a pencil with a slash through it in the lower-left corner of the Finder window, indicating that you do not have write access to this folder. You will learn more about this in Lesson 14, "Understanding File Access."

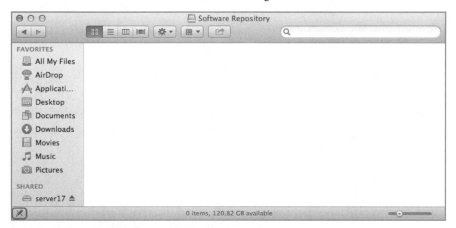

It is easy to use the Server app to create a new shared folder, but you need to update the permissions in order to allow users to create files and folders in that folder. One big timesaver is the feature in the Server app to create a shared folder for a group, which you will use next.

Give a Group a Shared Folder

Use the Server app to give the Contractors group a shared folder. One of the great things about this feature is that you do not need to perform any additional configuration to give users shared read and write access to the resources they create in this shared folder.

You'll give the Contractors group a shared folder, and then confirm that members of the group have read and write access to resources in the folder.

1   In the Server app sidebar, select Groups.

2   Double-click the Contractors group to edit that group.

3   Select the checkbox labeled "Give this group a shared folder."

4   Click Done to create the shared folder in the Groups folder.

5   In the Server app sidebar, select File Sharing to return to that pane.

Confirm that a member of the Contractors group can edit files in the Contractors group folder. You should still be connected to the server as the user Barbara Green, who is a member of the Contractors group.

Confirm that you are still connected as Barbara Green.

1   On your administrator computer, in the Finder, press Command-N to open a new Finder window.

2   In the Finder window sidebar, select your server, or click All and select your server.

3   If you do not see "Connected as: barbara" under the Finder window toolbar, click Connect As, and then provide barbara's credentials (Name **barbara** and Password **net**) and click Connect.

4   Open the Groups folder.

Note that because Barbara Green is not a member of the localaccounts and workgroup groups, those folders display a red icon. Additionally, the read-only icon in the lower-left corner of the Finder window indicates that Barbara Green does not have permission to create files in this folder (the Groups folder).

5   Open the contractors folder.

Note that the folder's name is based on the short name of the group.

6   Create a new folder by pressing Command-Shift-N, enter Barbara Created This as the folder name, and press Return to save the name change.

Note that when you view the contractors folder in the Finder, no icon appears in the lower-left corner of the Finder window. This means that you have read and write access to this folder (because the Server app automatically configures read and write access for members of the group).

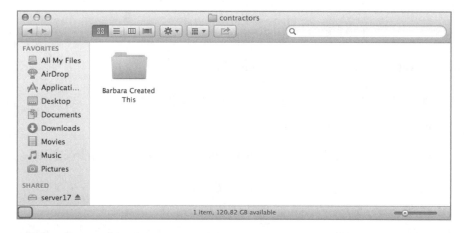

Connect as Todd Porter, another member of the Contractors group, and confirm that you can edit the resources Barbara Green placed into the folder.

1   In the Finder window, click the Eject icon next to your server sidebar to eject the volume.

2   Click Connect As and provide user credentials for a different user in the group (such as Name todd and Password net) and click Connect.

3   Open the Groups folder, and then open the contractors folder.

4   Press Command-Shift-N to create a new folder, enter Todd Created This as the folder name, and press Return to save the name change.

5   Drag the folder the other user created to the Trash, to demonstrate that you can modify a resource a different user created.

Clean Up

Remove the Software Repository folder, since you will not use it for any other exercise. Eject any network volumes if you still have them mounted.

1   On your administrator computer, open the Server app. Choose Manage > Connect to Server, select your server, and click Continue.

2   Provide administrator credentials (Administrator Name ladmin and Administrator Password ladminpw).

3   Click Connect.

4   In the Server app sidebar, select File Sharing.

5   Select the Software Repository share point.

6   Click Remove (–), and at the confirmation dialog, click Remove.

    Note that the contents of the share point will not be deleted.

7   Next to your server in the Finder window sidebar, click the Eject icon to eject the volume.

You used the Server app to view the default shared folders, their respective protocols, and the available free space on your server's storage devices. Then you created a new folder and made it available for file sharing. You created a group folder and saw that you do not need to take any extra steps to grant write access to this folder for members of the group.

You will learn more about how OS X Server controls access to files, so you have the ability to modify resources other users create, in Lesson 14, "Understanding File Access."

Exercise 13.2
Use Logs to Troubleshoot Problems with File Sharing Services

▶ **Prerequisites**

  ▶   Exercise 13.1, "Explore the File Sharing Service"

Given the classroom nature of the course, there may be few or no error messages within the logs. However, you should practice locating the logs and viewing their contents.

1   In the Server app sidebar, select Logs.

2   Click the pop-up menu and choose AFP Error Log.

    There shouldn't be much here under normal operation.

3   Click the pop-up menu and choose one of the logs in the Websites section.

    If you haven't accessed the File Sharing service via WebDAV, there will not be any WebDAV information in any of the Websites' logs.

Additional Resources

The following documents provide more information about providing File Sharing services. Additional resources are available at www.apple.com/osx/server/resources/documentation.html.

OS X Server Administration Guides

OS X Server: Advanced Server Administration
http://help.apple.com/advancedserveradmin/mac/10.8/

Apple Knowledge Base Documents

You can check for new and updated Knowledge Base documents at www.apple.com/support.

Document HT4283, "iWork for iOS: Using a WebDAV service"

Document HT4695, "OS X Server: How to configure NFS exports"

Document HT4700, "Connecting to legacy AFP services"

Document HT4777, "OS X Server: Configuring WebDAV sharing for Active Directory accounts"

Document HT5374, "OS X Server: Creating drop box folders for use with WebDAV file sharing"

Document PH3407, "Numbers for iOS (iPad): Share spreadsheets using a WebDAV server"

Document PH3457, "Numbers for iOS (iPhone, iPod touch): Share spreadsheets using a WebDAV server"

Document PH3496, "Keynote for iOS (iPad): Share presentations using a WebDAV server"

Document PH3535, "Keynote for iOS (iPhone, iPod touch): Share presentations using a WebDAV server"

Document PH3566, "Pages for iOS (iPad): Share documents using a WebDAV server"

Document PH3597, "Pages for iOS (iPhone, iPod touch): Share documents using a WebDAV server"

Document PH10917, "OS X Mountain Lion: How many computers can connect to your computer?"

Document PH11090, "OS X Mountain Lion: Servers and shared computers that you can connect to"

Document TS4149, "OS X Server: When saving files on SMB shares, the permissions may be changed so only the owner can read or write"

Document TS4354, "OS X Server: Shared folders on external storage no longer available after logging out locally from the server"

URLs

Welcome to WebDAV Resources: www.webdav.org/

Microsoft Open Specifications: Workgroup Server Protocol Program: www.microsoft.com/openspecifications/en/us/programs/wspp/default.aspx

Lesson Review

1. Name three file sharing protocols supported by the OS X Server File Sharing pane and their principal target clients.
2. What's one concern with using the FTP service?
3. How does OS X Server support browsing for Windows clients?
4. How do you enable guest access to a share point?
5. Where can you quickly view how many AFP and SMB connections there currently are to your server?
6. How can you configure a share point to be accessible to an app on an iOS device?
7. Where would you find information about AFP service errors?
8. How can you create a new share point?
9. What file sharing protocols are enabled by default for a share point you just created?
10. Do you need to start the Websites service in order to provide WebDAV service?

Answers

1. AFP for OS X clients, SMB for Windows clients, and WebDAV for iOS devices are three file sharing protocols supported by OS X Server.
2. Normally the network traffic is not encrypted for authenticating to the FTP service with username and password.
3. OS X Server uses NetBIOS to advertise its presence to Windows clients; Windows users see the server in their Network Neighborhood or Network Places.
4. Edit a share point and select the "Allow guest users to access this share" checkbox.
5. The Connected Users tab displays the number of AFP and SMB connections; you may need to choose View > Refresh (or press Command-R) to refresh the number.
6. Edit a share point and select the "Share with iOS devices (WebDAV)" checkbox.

7.   The Logs pane of the Console app displays the AFP Error log, which displays the contents of the log file: /Library/Logs/AppleFileService/AppleFileServiceError.Log.

8.   In the File Sharing list of share points, click Add (+) and either select an existing folder, or create a new folder and select the new folder.

9.   AFP and SMB are enabled by default for a new share point.

10. No, the Websites service does not need to be running in order for you to offer File Sharing services via WebDAV (of course, the File Sharing service must be running).

Lesson 14
Understanding File Access

Now that Lesson 13 has familiarized you with the file sharing protocols you can enable, and the basics of creating, removing, and editing share points, it's time to configure access to files. For access to files and folders, OS X Server uses basic file permissions in addition to optional access control lists (ACLs) to make authorization decisions about access to files and folders. In OS X, every file and every folder has a single user account assigned as its "owner," a single group associated with it, and an optional ACL. Access permissions are assigned for the owner, for the group, and for everyone else, and the optional ACL adds additional permissions information.

When a file sharing client uses the file sharing service, she must authenticate as a user (or as a guest if you enabled guest access for the share point). A remote user has the same access to files over file sharing that she would have if she logged in locally with the same user credentials she provided to mount the share point.

This lesson covers how to use the Server app to configure access to files.

Reference 14.1
Configuring Access to Share Points and Folders

Once you've created a share point and determined the protocols you will use, you can begin to address levels of access within that share point. You need to consider POSIX privileges (UNIX-based ownership and permissions) as well as file system ACLs. Using this very flexible system, you can apply complex access settings to any folder or file.

You can configure access for your shared folders with the Server app File Sharing pane, and you can configure access for any folder or file with the Server app Storage pane. Be aware that these two panes behave differently, and they display information differently. This guide first addresses the File Sharing pane; then it addresses the Storage pane.

Configuring Basic Access with the Server App File Sharing Pane

To configure access settings for a share point, use the Access pane when viewing that share point. The standard POSIX settings are listed with the owner's full name, followed by the word "owner" in parentheses; the full name of the group associated with the folder, followed by the words "primary group" in parentheses; and Everyone Else.

In the following figure, the local user System Administrator (the root user, who has access to every file on the system) is the owner, and the local group named Administrators is the primary group associated with the Users share point.

If there are any ACEs in that folder's ACL, these ACEs will appear above the POSIX entries. In the following figure, the first entry in the Access field is an ACE for the local network group Workgroup (the Server app automatically adds this ACE after configuring this server as an Open Directory master).

To change the standard POSIX owner of a share point, double-click the name of the current owner; to change the group, double-click the name of the current primary group. Once you start typing, a menu with names that match what you have typed appears. The following figure illustrates the process of changing the POSIX owner.

From there, you can either choose a name, or click Browse. If you click Browse, a sheet of users or groups (as appropriate) appears; choose an account and then click OK. The Server app then displays the account's full name in the owner or primary group field.

To change permissions, click the pop-up menu on the right, and choose any of the four options:

► Read & Write

► Read Only

► Write Only

► No Access

After making permissions changes, be sure to click Done to save your changes. If you select a different pane in the Server app, or quit the Server app, your changes might not get saved.

Once the user is authenticated, file permissions control access to the files and folders on your server. One setting should be called out with respect to permissions: the Others permissions, which is displayed as Everyone Else when editing permissions with the File

Sharing pane. When you set Others permissions, those permissions apply to everyone who can see the item (either a file or folder) who is neither the owner nor a member of the group assigned to the item.

Allowing Guest Access

You enable guest access for a share point by enabling the checkbox for "Allow guest users to access this share."

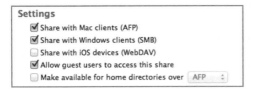

Guest access can be very useful, but before you enable it, be sure you understand its implications in your permissions scheme. As the name implies, guest access lets anyone who can connect to your server use its share points. A user who authenticates as Guest is given Others permissions for file and folder access. If you give read-only access to Others on a share point that allows guest access, everyone on your network (and, if your server has a public IP address and is not protected by a firewall, the entire Internet) can see and mount that share point, a situation you might not intend to allow.

If a user creates an item on an AFP share point while connected as Guest, the AFP client sets the owner of that item to "nobody."

If a folder is buried deep within a file hierarchy where guests can't go (because the enclosing folders don't grant access to Others), guests can't use the Finder to browse to that folder.

> **TIP** The best way to validate permissions is by connecting to the file sharing service from a client computer, providing valid credentials (or connecting as Guest), and testing access.

Configure Access with the Server App Storage Pane

In contrast to the File Sharing pane, where you can configure access to share points, you can use the Server app Storage pane to configure permissions for individual files and folders; additionally, you have more granular control.

One way to get to the Storage pane is by selecting your server in the Server app sidebar, and then clicking the Storage pane. You can then navigate to a specific file or folder.

The other way to get to the Storage pane is via this shortcut: in the File Sharing pane, when you edit a share point and click the arrow next to the words "View Files," the Server app opens the share point's folder in the Storage pane.

In the Storage pane, when you select a file or folder and click the Action (gear icon) pop-up menu, you see three choices:

▶ New Folder

▶ Edit Permissions

▶ Propagate Permissions

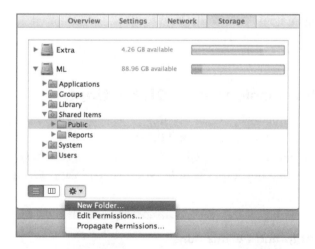

You'll learn more about Propagate Permissions later in this lesson. If you choose Edit Permissions, the Server app opens a permissions sheet that's similar to File Sharing pane's permissions field, but the Storage pane's permissions sheet offers you more configuration options.

Using the Storage Pane's Permissions Sheet

In the Storage pane's permissions sheet in the following figure, each ACE has a disclosure triangle to hide or reveal more information about the ACE; additionally, some information, like the Spotlight ACE, which is hidden in the File Sharing pane, is displayed in the permissions sheet.

NOTE ▶ The inherited ACE for Spotlight allows Spotlight to maintain an index of the files on your server. Do not modify or remove this ACE or you may experience unexpected behavior.

You'll learn more about modifying an item's ACL in the next section.

Reference 14.2
Understanding POSIX Permissions vs. ACL Settings

The Server app is a powerful tool with many options to configure file access. It is important to understand how the POSIX permissions model and the file system ACLs behave, and how they behave together, in order to accurately configure share points to behave as you intend. This section starts out with a quick review of POSIX ownership and permissions, and then considers ACLs.

Understanding POSIX Ownership and Permissions

The OS X standard file system permissions structure is based on decades-old UNIX-style permissions. This system is also sometimes referred to as POSIX-style permissions. In the POSIX permissions model, which OS X and OS X Server use, every file and every folder is associated with exactly one "owner" and exactly one "group." As an administrator, you can change the POSIX owner and the POSIX group, but keep in mind that every file must have one and only one owner, and one and only one group as part of the POSIX ownership. This limits your flexibility, so you may choose to use ACLs to add flexibility in managing access to files, but it is important for you to understand the basics of POSIX ownership and permissions. For more information, see "File System Permissions" in Lesson 12, "Permissions and Sharing" in the guide *Apple Pro Training Series: OS X Support Essentials.*

When you move an item from one folder to another *within* a single volume, that item always retains its original ownership and permissions. In contrast, when you create a new item on a network volume via AFP, SMB, or WebDAV, or copy an item from one volume to another volume, OS X uses the following rules for ownership and permissions for the new file or folder:

▶ The owner of the new item is the user who created or copied the item.

▶ The group is the group associated with the enclosing folder; in other words, the newly copied item inherits its group from the enclosing folder.

▶ The owner is assigned read and write permissions.

▶ The group is assigned read-only permissions.

▶ Others (also displayed as Everyone Else) is assigned read-only permissions.

Under this model, if you create an item in a folder in which the group has read/write permission, the new item will not inherit that group permission, so other users are not able to edit that item (but because they have read/write permission to the folder, they can remove the item from the folder).

Without using ACLs, if a user wants to grant other group members write access to the new item, she must modify its permissions manually, using the Finder's Get Info command, chmod in the command line, or some third-party tool. This would be required for every new item; instead, you can use ACLs to prevent the need for users to add this step of manually modifying permissions to their workflow.

> **MORE INFO** ▶ The variable that controls the POSIX permissions for newly created files is called the umask. Changing the umask from the default value is not recommended, and is outside the scope of this guide. When a user creates files on the server via AFP or SMB, the user's umask on the client computer affects the permissions for the newly created items, however, the umask on the server computer affects the permissions for files created via WebDAV.

Understanding Access Control Lists

Because of the limitations of the POSIX permissions model, consider using ACLs to help control access to folders and files. The Apple ACL model maps to the Windows ACL model, so Windows users experience the same permissions for folders and files that OS X users do.

In this section you'll learn about applying ACLs with the Server app, with the File Sharing pane, which presents a simplified interface, and also with the Storage pane's permissions sheet, which offers more flexibility. You'll learn how ACL inheritance works, and why it is so powerful.

> **NOTE** ▸ You can apply ACLs on only Mac OS Extended volumes, which is the default format for OS X.

In OS X Server, you use the Server app to configure ACLs. An ACL is made up of one or more ACEs. Each ACE includes the following:

▸ The globally unique ID (GUID) of the one user or group for which this ACE applies

▸ Whether the ACE allows access or denies access (you can use the Server app to create only Allow entries; and though you cannot use the Server app to create Deny entries, it displays a checkbox as selected in order to indicate that a rule specifies *either* Allow or Deny)

▸ The permission the ACE allows or denies (see the section "Configuring Complex Permissions for an ACE")

▸ The inheritance rules for the ACE (see the section "Understanding ACL Inheritance")

▸ The folder or file to which the ACE applies

> **NOTE** ▸ The Server app does not visually distinguish between Allow and Deny. You simply see a checkbox. When you assign a new ACE, it is assumed that you are assigning an Allow rule. However, when you look at an ACE that has Deny, such as the ACE for a user home folder for Everyone to Deny Delete, you can't tell whether this rule is an Allow or a Deny rule.

You can add as many ACEs for an item as you like, and you have a much larger range of permission types available than with standard POSIX permissions, which you'll learn about in the section ahead, "Configuring Complex Permissions for an ACE."

Understanding How File System ACLs Work

When you use the Server app to define ACLs, you are creating individual ACEs. These entries and lists are specific to a file system location.

The order of entries is important because lists are evaluated top to bottom by OS X.

Allow and deny matches work differently for ACLs. When evaluating ACLs, the operating system starts with the first ACE and moves downward, stopping at the ACE that applies to the user and matches the operation, such as reading, being performed. The permission (either to allow or to deny) for the ACE is then applied. Any ACEs further down in the list are then ignored. Any matching Allow or Deny ACE overrides standard POSIX permissions.

Configuring ACLs with the Server App File Sharing Pane

In the Server app File Sharing pane, when editing a share point, you add a new ACE for a share point with the following general steps:

NOTE ▶ This is an example workflow, and not part of this lesson's exercise.

1   Click Add (+).

2   Specify the user or group. You must choose the account from the list, or choose Browse and choose the account from the list.

3   Specify the access to allow. Note that you can specify Read & Write, Read, or Write.

4   Repeat steps 1 through 3 for additional ACEs, and then click Done to save the changes.

Configuring ACLs with the Server App Storage Pane

The Storage pane of the Server app offers a little more flexibility than the File Sharing pane for configuring ACLs, particularly the ability to:

▶ Configure complex permissions for an ACE, more than just Read & Write, Read, or Write.

▶ Configure the inheritance for ACLs.

▶ Configure POSIX ownership and permissions and the ACL for an individual file, not just for folders.

▶ Configure POSIX ownership and permissions for files that are not shared (the File Sharing pane allows you to configure share points only).

To access the Storage pane, select your server in the Server app sidebar, and click the Storage tab. You can select an existing folder, or create a new folder. To access the permissions sheet for a file or folder, select a file or folder, click the Action (gear icon) pop-up menu and choose Edit Permissions.

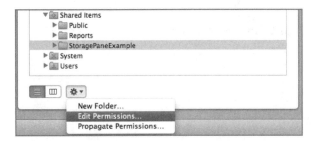

Once you are viewing the permissions sheet, you can click Add (+) to create a new ACE. Unlike in the File Sharing pane, there is no Browse option; you need to start typing and choose a user or group that matches what you have entered from the list.

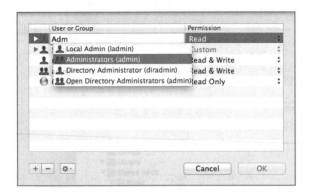

After you specify the user or group for the ACE, you can click the permissions pop-up menu and choose Full Control, Read & Write, Read, or Write.

Of course, your permissions choice is just a starting point; you can fine-tune the permissions, as you'll see in the next section.

Configuring Complex Permissions for an ACE

When you edit an ACE with the Storage pane's permissions sheet, you can use the disclosure triangles to show the details for the ACE. You have four broad categories for which you can apply Allow rules:

▶ Administration

▶ Read

▶ Write

▶ Inheritance

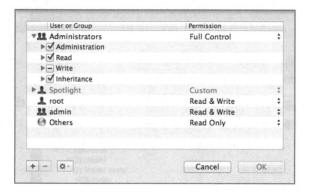

For the first three (Administration, Read, and Write), selecting a checkbox allows access for the user in the ACE. Deselecting a checkbox does not deny access, it just doesn't explicitly allow access.

For the Administration set of permissions, you can select or deselect to allow permissions for:

▶   Change Permissions—User can change standard permissions.

▶   Change Owner—User can change the item's ownership to himself or herself.

For the Read set of permissions, you can select or deselect to allow permissions for:

▶   Read Attributes—User can view the item's attributes, such as name, size, and date modified.

▶   Read Extended Attributes—User can view additional attributes, including ACL and attributes added by third-party software.

▶   List Folder Contents (Read Data)—User can read files and see the contents of a folder.

▶   Traverse Folder (Execute File)—User can open files, or traverse a folder.

▶   Read Permissions—User can read the POSIX permissions.

For the Write set of permissions, you can select or deselect to allow permissions for:

▶   Write Attributes—User can change POSIX permissions.

▶   Write Extended Attributes—User can change ACL or other extended attributes.

▶   Create Files (Write Data)—User can create files, including changing files for most applications.

▶   Create Folder (Append Data)—User can create new folders and append data to files.

▶   Delete—User can delete files or folders.

▶   Delete Subfolders and Files—User can delete subfolders and files.

With just these 13 checkboxes, you have a large amount of flexibility to allow additional permissions beyond what you can configure with just POSIX permissions.

Because the Server app does not allow you to create Deny rules, if you need to deny access, a good strategy is to set the standard POSIX permissions for Others to No Access, and then configure an ACL to build up rules to allow appropriate access for various groups.

Understanding ACL Inheritance

One powerful feature of ACLs is inheritance: When you create an ACE for a folder, from that point on, when a user creates a new item in that folder, the operating system assigns that same ACE to the new item. In other words, the ACE is inherited. For each ACE in the folder's ACL, you can control how that ACE is inherited; when you edit an ACE, you can select or deselect each of the following checkboxes (by default, all four "Apply to" check-boxes are selected):

▶ Apply to this folder—This ACE applies to this folder.

▶ Apply to child folders—This ACE will be assigned to new folders inside this folder, but not necessarily to new folders that are created inside the child folders of this folder, unless "Apply to all descendants" is also selected.

▶ Apply to child files—This ACE will be assigned to new files inside this folder, but not necessarily to files that are inside the child folders of this folder, unless "Apply to all descendants" is also selected.

▶ Apply to all descendants—This makes the two preceding options apply to items in an infinite level of nested folders in this folder.

When an ACE is inherited from a folder, it appears dimmed as in the following figure (you can inspect an inherited ACE but not edit it):

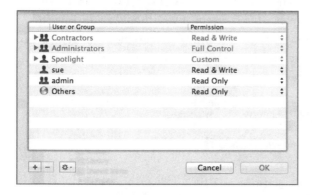

If an inherited ACL doesn't meet your needs, first consider why the ACL model didn't work in this case: Do you need a different share point, a different group, or maybe a different set of ACEs in the ACL? In any event, you can click the Action (gear icon) pop-up menu and choose one of these two actions to change the inherited entries:

▶ Remove Inherited Entries

▶ Make Inherited Entries Explicit

Remove Inherited Entries removes all the inherited ACEs, not just one ACE that you might have selected. The inherited ACL could be an aggregation of inherited ACEs from more than one parent folder.

Make Inherited Entries Explicit applies all the inherited ACEs as if they were applied directly to the ACL on the current file or folder. Once you perform this action, you can edit the ACEs, including editing or removing individual ACEs that were previously dimmed. The following figure illustrates what happens if you choose Make Inherited Entries Explicit: The ACEs are no longer dimmed, and you can remove them or modify them. The ACE for Spotlight is automatically created—do not modify that ACE.

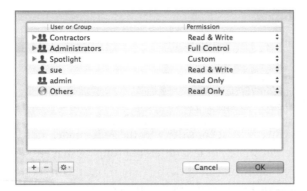

When you use the Server app's File Sharing pane to update a folder's ACL that has inheritance rules, the Server app automatically updates the ACL for items in the folder that have already inherited the ACL (this is not the case if you update the ACL using the Storage pane).

Understanding Sorting ACLs Canonically

The order in which each ACE is listed in an ACL is important, and can possibly change the behavior of an ACL, especially if a Deny rule is involved. Although the Server app does *not* allow you to create ACEs to deny access, some ACLs do contain one or more Deny ACEs. In the Storage pane's permissions sheet, you can click the Action (gear icon) pop-up menu and choose Sort Access Control List Canonically. This reorders the ACEs into a standard order for applying ACLs. If you don't have Deny rules in your ACL, it isn't crucial to use this command.

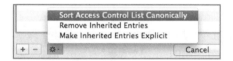

Understanding ACL Portability

Because ACLs are applied when a file or folder is created:

▶ If you move an item from one location to another on the same volume, the ACL for that item (if one exists) does not change, and is still associated with the item.

▶ If you copy an item from one location to another, the item's ACL does not get copied; the copied item will inherit, from its enclosing folder, any ACEs that are appropriately configured to be inherited.

However, what happens if you update an existing ACL, or create a new ACL, *after* files have already been created? You'll need to propagate the ACL.

Understanding Propagating Permissions

When you use the File Sharing pane to update a share point's ACLs or POSIX permissions, the Server app automatically propagates the ACL. When you propagate the ACL, the Server app adds each ACE of the current folder to the ACL of each child object (folders and files inside the parent folder), as an inherited ACE. Don't worry about overwriting explicitly defined ACEs for child objects, because propagating an ACL does not remove any explicitly defined ACEs.

In contrast, when you use the Storage pane's permissions sheet to create or update an ACL for an item, your actions affect only that item, and do not affect existing child objects. In the Storage permissions sheet, to propagate the ACL changes to existing child objects, you must do so manually. Click the Action (gear icon) pop-up menu and choose Propagate Permissions. The following figure illustrates that by default, the Access Control List checkbox is selected, but you can select additional checkboxes to also update different combinations of standard POSIX ownership and permissions to existing child objects.

Understanding Features Common to POSIX and ACLs

Now that you have a better understanding of POSIX ownership and permissions, as well as ACLs and ACEs, this section covers how the two models work together to affect access to files.

Distinguishing Between the Uses of UID, GID, and GUID

You have learned that POSIX owners and groups are determined by user and group IDs (UIDs and GIDs). Because UIDs and GIDs are simple integers, it is possible (but not recommended) for users to have duplicate user IDs. Usually this is an error, but sometimes an administrator will want the POSIX UID to be identical on two separate users. From a permissions perspective, this will grant these users identical access rights.

ACLs are much more complex and require a unique identification of a user or group. For this purpose, every user and group has a globally unique ID (GUID). This is not exposed in the Server app because there should be no reason to change it. Every time a user or group is created, a new 128-bit string (as shown in the following figure) is randomly generated for that user or group. In this way, users and groups are virtually guaranteed unique identification in ACLs.

When you create an ACE for a user or group, the ACE uses the GUID of that user or group, rather than the user name, user ID, group name, or group ID. When displaying an ACL, if the server computer cannot match an ACE's GUID to an account, the Server app displays the GUID instead of the account name in the ACL. Some reasons for this include that the account associated with the ACE:

▶ Has been deleted

▶ Belongs to a directory node that the server is bound to but is unavailable

▶ Belongs to a directory node that is unavailable, because the volume was connected to a different server when the ACE was created

Here's an example of an exposed GUID in the Server app. In the following figure, an ACE was created for a local network user, and then an administrator deleted the local network user with the Server app; the ACE was not automatically removed.

If you see this, without knowing what account corresponds to the GUID, you could either leave the entry in place or remove the entry. If you happen to import the account in a way that also imports its GUID, that entry will be associated with the user or group again. However, if the account associated with the GUID is truly gone forever, you can remove the ACE; highlight the ACE and click the Delete (–) button.

Understanding Group Membership and ACLs

When working with ACLs, it is important that you plan your setup properly to avoid conflicting permissions settings, such as having a user be a member of two groups, one with read permissions on a folder and one with no access permissions on the same folder. These types of conflicts can occur if you do not plan your ACL permissions models well.

Using ACLs to control access to server resources can be extremely valuable, as long as you take care up front to organize your user and group accounts appropriately. The recommended way to approach this management is to take advantage of using smaller groups to correctly reflect the needs of your organization, including nesting groups within groups. Use these group accounts to manage access on a more granular basis.

Understanding Multiple Groups

The standard POSIX permissions work well in a single desktop model such as OS X. Yet when the system becomes more complex, the standard POSIX permissions model does not scale well.

Complex workflows might require more than just the User, Group, and Others classes available with the standard POSIX permissions model. In particular, having a single group is very limiting. The POSIX owner must be an individual user account (it can't be a group), and granting permission to Others (Everyone Else) usually opens up the files to a wider audience than you want. Adding an ACL permits you to assign multiple groups to a folder, and assign each a unique permissions setting. Because ACLs can assign different permissions to multiple groups, you must carefully plan what your group structure is going to look like to avoid any confusion. This is a common requirement in any environment that has multiple groups collaborating on a single project.

Understanding Nested Groups

In addition to assigning multiple groups to a single folder, OS X Server allows groups to contain other groups. Breaking groups down into subgroups can make your access easier to understand as an administrator. You can use nested groups to reflect the structure of your organization.

While nested groups are powerful, they should be used with care. If you build a deep, complex hierarchy, you may find that access is harder—rather than easier—to understand. Mirroring your organizational structure is usually safe and useful. However, be wary of ad hoc groups that don't relate to any external structure. They may be a quick way to give access to some users, but later on may make it more difficult to understand your access.

Understanding POSIX and ACL Rules of Precedence

When a user attempts to perform an action that requires authorization (read a file, or create a folder), OS X will allow this action only if the user has permission for that action. Here is how OS X combines POSIX and ACLs when there is a request for a specific action:

1. If there is no ACL, POSIX rules apply.

2. If there is an ACL, the order of the ACEs matters. You can sort the ACEs in an ACL in a consistent and predictable way: In the Server app Storage pane, select an ACL, and then from the Action (gear icon) pop-up menu choose Sort Access Control List Canonically. This is especially important if you add an ACE to an ACL containing an ACE that denies access.

3. When evaluating an ACL, OS X evaluates the first ACE in the list and continues on to the next ACE until it finds an ACE that matches the permission required for the requested action, whether that permission is Allow or Deny. Even if a Deny ACE exists in an ACL, if a similar Allow ACE is listed first, the Allow ACE is the one that is used, because it is listed first. This is why it is so important to use the Sort Access Control List Canonically command.

4. A POSIX permission that is restrictive does not override an ACE that specifically allows a permission.

5. If no ACE applies to the permission required for the requested action, the POSIX permissions apply.

For example, if Barbara Green attempts to create a folder, the requested permission is Create Folder. Each ACE is evaluated until there is an ACE that either allows or denies Create Folder for Barbara Green or a group that Barbara Green belongs to.

Even though this is an unlikely scenario, it illustrates the combination of an ACL and POSIX permissions: If a folder has an ACE that allows Barbara Green (short name: barbara) full control, but the POSIX permission defines Barbara Green as the owner with access set to None, Barbara Green effectively has full control. The ACE is evaluated before the POSIX permissions.

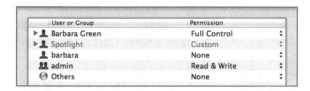

As another example, consider a folder with an ACL that has a single ACE that allows Carl Dunn to have Read permission, and the folder's POSIX permission defines Carl Dunn as the owner with Read & Write permission. When Carl Dunn attempts to create a file in that folder, there is no ACE that specifically addresses the Create Files (Write Data) request, so no ACE applies to that request. Therefore, the POSIX permissions apply, and Carl Dunn can create the file.

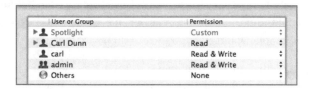

In this lesson you learned about POSIX ownership and permissions, file ACLs, and how you can configure share points and files to control access to files.

Exercise 14.1
Configure Access Control

In this exercise you will create a folder hierarchy and a means of controlling access to facilitate the workflow of the users and groups on your server, using standard POSIX permissions and file system ACLs. You will discover that the ability to manipulate a file can be determined by where the file is located in the system, rather than by who created or owns the specific file.

To properly configure your server, you will need to understand the intended workflow of your users. Here is the scenario: Your group needs a share point for a secret project, ProjectZ. The two people in the project, Maria Miller and Gary Pine, need to be able to read and write documents in the share point, including documents that the other person created. It is expected that more people will be added to the project later. No one else in the organization should see the folder for the project, except the Vice President (VP) of Sales, Lucy Sanchez, who needs only Read access to the files.

You can't just use the Server app to create the folder for the group in the Groups folder, because this folder would be visible to other people, and even though other people would not be able to browse the contents of the folder, other people would start asking questions about it.

You could start out by creating a group, configuring that group as the primary group for a folder, and assigning read-write permissions for the group to the folder, but that's not enough, because any new items created will automatically have a permission of read-only for the primary group. In addition, you need to create an ACE for the ProjectZ group to allow them read-write access. You will also need to create an ACE for Lucy Sanchez, the VP of Sales, to allow read access.

As part of this scenario, after you get the users, groups, and share points configured, be prepared for management to assign another request, which you will cheerfully fulfill.

Create the ProjectZ group and add the two users to the group.

1 On your administrator computer, if you are not already connected to your server, open the Server app and connect to your server.

2 In the Server app sidebar, select Groups.

3 If a pop-up menu is visible, set the pop-up menu to Local Network Groups.

4 Click Add (+) to create a new group, and enter the following information:

▶ Full Name: ProjectZ

▶ Group Name: projectz

5 Click Done to create the group.

6 Double-click the ProjectZ group and click Add (+). Press the Spacebar, choose Browse, and drag Maria Miller and Gary Pine to the Members list.

7 Click Done to save the changes.

8 If necessary, close the Users & Groups window.

Next, create a shared folder for the ProjectZ group, and configure its permissions so that:

▶ No one else can see the share point or its contents.

▶ Members of the ProjectZ group have Read & Write access to all items.

▶ Lucy Sanchez, the Sales VP, has Read-Only access to all items.

Start by creating the share point.

1 In the Server app sidebar, select File Sharing.

2 Click Add (+).

3 Navigate to the Shared Items folder on your server's startup volume.

4 Click New Folder.

5 Name the folder **ProjectZ**, and then click Create.

6 Select the new ProjectZ folder you just created, and then click Choose.

Configure access to the share point.

1 In the File Sharing pane, double-click the ProjectZ share point.

2 Make sure the checkbox is deselected for "Allow guest users to access this share."

3 Click the pop-up menu for permissions for the Everyone Else entry, and choose No Access.

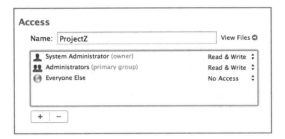

Note that the owner and primary group are inherited from the enclosing folder (Shared Items). Don't worry about that; the owner of new items will be the user that creates the item, and remember that over AFP and SMB, newly created items will get read-only access applied to the primary group, so you need to use an ACL to provide Read & Write access to the ProjectZ group.

4 Click Add (+).

5 Start typing **ProjectZ**, and then choose ProjectZ.

Confirm that the permission is automatically set to Read & Write for the ProjectZ group.

Create an ACE that allows Lucy Sanchez, the Sales VP, read-only access.

1 Click Add (+), start typing **Lucy**, and choose Lucy Sanchez.

2 Set the permissions for Lucy Sanchez to Read.

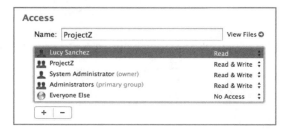

3   Click Done to save these settings.

Confirm that Maria Miller and Gary Pine can create and edit items in the ProjectZ share point, and that the Sales VP (Lucy Sanchez) cannot create, edit, or remove items.

1   On your administrator computer, in the Finder, choose File > New Finder Window.

2   If there is an Eject button next to your server in the Finder sidebar, click it to eject any mounted volumes from that server.

3   If your server appears in the Finder sidebar, select your server. Otherwise, if there are so many computers on your network that your server does not appear in the Shared section of the Finder sidebar, click All, and then click your server.

   If Guest access is enabled for any share point, you are automatically connected as Guest.

4   In the Finder window, click Connect As.

5   At the authentication window, provide credentials for Maria Miller (Name maria; Password net).

   NOTE ▶ Do not select the checkbox to remember the password, otherwise you will need to use Keychain Access to remove the password before you can connect as a different user.

6   Click Connect.

   After you successfully authenticate, you see all the share points that the user Maria Miler has access to read.

7 Open the ProjectZ folder.

8 Press Command-Shift-N to create a new folder, and enter the name **Folder created by Maria**.

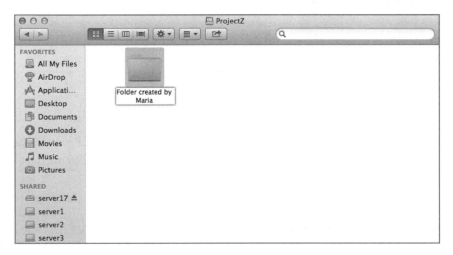

9 Press Return to stop editing the folder name.

You won't do anything else with this folder in the exercise, but you confirmed that Maria Miller has permission to create a folder.

Create a text file as Maria Miller; you will eventually confirm the following:

▶ Gary Pine can also edit that document.

▶ Lucy Sanchez can read, but cannot change, that document.

▶ Other users cannot see that the ProjectZ share point exists.

1 In the Dock, click Launchpad, and then open TextEdit.

2 If you do not see a new blank document, create a new blank document by pressing Command-N or choosing File > New.

3 Enter the following text: **This is a file started by Maria.**

4   Save the TextEdit document by pressing Command-S or choosing File > Save.

5   If necessary, click the triangle next to the Save As field to reveal more options.

6   In the Shared section of the Save As window sidebar, select your server, and then select the folder ProjectZ.

7   In the Save As field, name the file Maria Text File.

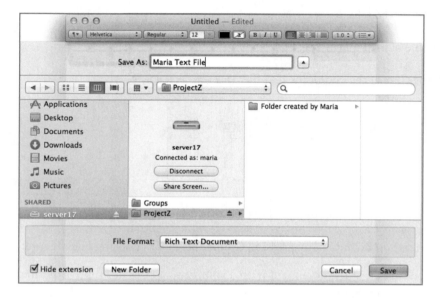

8   Click Save.

9   Close the TextEdit document by pressing Command-W or choosing File > Close.

10   If no Finder window is still open, in the Finder press Command-N to open one.

11   In the Finder sidebar, click the Eject button next to your server.

Connect as the other project member, Gary Pine, and confirm that you can edit files with his credentials.

1   If your server appears in the Finder sidebar, select your server.

Otherwise, if there are so many computers on your network that your server does not appear in the Shared section of the Finder sidebar, click All, and then select your server.

2   In the Finder window, click Connect As.

3   At the authentication window, provide credentials for Gary Pine (Name gary; Password net).

Do not select the checkbox to remember the password.

4   Click Connect.

5   Open the ProjectZ folder.

6   Open the file named Maria Text File.

7   Add another line at the end of the text file: This was added by Gary.

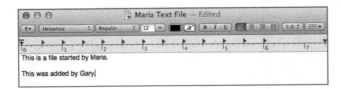

8   Save the TextEdit document by pressing Command-S or choosing File > Save.

9   Close the TextEdit document by pressing Command-W or choosing File > Close.

If you see a dialog that the document is on a volume that does not support permanent version storage and that you will not be able to access older versions of the document once you close it, click OK.

10   In the Finder sidebar, click the Eject button next to your server.

Confirm that you can see, but not edit, a file in the ProjectZ folder when connected as the Sales VP, Lucy Sanchez.

1   If your server appears in the Finder sidebar, select your server.

Otherwise, if there are so many computers on your network that your server does not appear in the Shared section of the Finder sidebar, click All, and then select your server.

2   In Finder window, click Connect As.

3   At the authentication window, provide credentials for Lucy Sanchez (Name lucy; Password net).

Do not select the checkbox to remember the password.

4   Click Connect.

5   Open the ProjectZ folder.

6   Open the file named Maria Text File.

7   Confirm that you can read the text, and that the toolbar contains the text "Locked," indicating that you cannot save changes to this file.

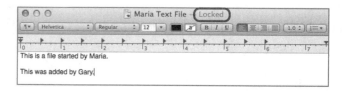

8   Attempt to edit the file by appending text, and note that you see a dialog stating that the file is locked.

9   Click Cancel.

10   Close the TextEdit document by pressing Command-W or choosing File > Close.

Confirm that you cannot create a new folder in the ProjectZ folder as the Lucy Sanchez user, even if you use administrator credentials.

1   In the Finder window, confirm that you are viewing the ProjectZ folder.

2   Choose File > New Folder.

3   You see the dialog "Finder wants to make changes. Type your password to allow this." Provide local administrator credentials and click OK.

You are not able to create a new folder on the network volume, even after providing administrator credentials, because the user Lucy Sanchez has only read permissions.

4   Because you effectively have read-only permissions, you see a dialog that you don't have permission. Click Cancel.

Confirm that you cannot delete an item in the ProjectZ folder as the Lucy Sanchez user.

1   Select Maria Text File and choose File > Move to Trash.

2   At the "Are you sure" dialog, click Delete.

3   Because you effectively have read-only permission, you see a dialog that you don't have permission. Click OK to close the dialog.

Confirm that a different user (Todd Porter, who isn't a member of the ProjectZ group) cannot view items in the ProjectZ folder.

1   In the Finder sidebar, click the Eject button next to your server.

2   If your server appears in the Finder sidebar, select your server. Otherwise, if there are so many computers on your network that your server does not appear in the Shared section of the Finder sidebar, click All, click your server, and then click Connect As.

3   In the Finder window, click Connect As.

4   At the authentication window, provide credentials for Todd Porter (Name todd; Password net).

    Do not select the checkbox to remember the password.

5   Click Connect.

6   Confirm that the ProjectZ folder is not visible.

7   In the upper-right corner of the Finder window, click Disconnect, or if you selected a shared folder, click the Eject button next to your server in the Finder sidebar.

You have successfully managed users and groups, created a share point, and managed the POSIX permissions and ACL for the share point to provide the access that management requested.

However, the company just promoted a new Marketing Vice President, Enrico Baker, who also wants read access to the files.

Rather than adding another individual user to the ACL, at this point in the scenario, it makes more sense to create a group for vice presidents, add appropriate users to that group, and then add an ACE to allow read access for that group. To prevent confusion in the future, you will also remove the original ACE for Lucy Sanchez; her ACE is unnecessary because her user account is part of a group that has an ACE.

Create the Vice Presidents group and add the two users to the group.

1   In the Server app sidebar, select Groups.

2   If there's a pop-up menu visible, set the pop-up menu to Local Network Groups.

3   Click Add (+) to create the following group:

▶ Full Name: **Vice Presidents**

▶ Group Name: **vps**

4   Click Done to create the group.

5   Double-click the Vice Presidents group and click Add (+). Press the Spacebar, click Browse, and drag Lucy Sanchez and Enrico Baker to the Members list.

6   Click Done to finish editing the group.

Update the ACL for the ProjectZ folder using the File Sharing pane.

1   In the Server app sidebar, select File Sharing.

2   Double-click the ProjectZ share point.

3   Click Add (+), enter **vps**, and choose Vice Presidents from the list.

4   Click the permissions pop-up menu for Vice Presidents and choose Read.

5   Select the ACE for Lucy Sanchez and click Delete (–).

The Access section of the Server app should appear like the following figure (the positions of the Vice Presidents ACE and the ProjectZ ACE relative to the other does not matter for the purposes of this exercise).

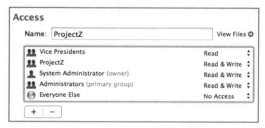

6   Click OK to save the changes to the ACL.

The Server app automatically propagates the updated ACL to items in the share point.

Confirm Enrico Baker , a member of the Vice Presidents group, can read files in the ProjectZ folder.

1   On your administrator computer, in the Finder, if there is no Finder window visible, choose New > New Finder Window.

2   If your server appears in the Finder sidebar, select your server. Otherwise, if there are so many computers on your network that your server does not appear in the Shared section of the Finder sidebar, click All, click your server, and then click Connect as.

3   In the Finder window, click Connect As.

4   Enter credentials for Enrico Baker (Name enrico; Password net).

5   Do not select the checkbox to remember the password.

6   Click Connect.

After you authenticate, you see a list of share points you can access.

1   Open the ProjectZ folder, and open Maria Text File.

2   Confirm that the toolbar contains the text "Locked" to indicate that you cannot make changes to the file.

3   Press Command-W to close the file.

Use the Server app Storage pane's permissions sheet to inspect the ACL for the share point.

1   In the Server app sidebar, select File Sharing.

2   Double-click the ProjectZ share point.

3   Click the arrow next to View Files.

4   Select the ProjectZ folder, and then choose Edit Permissions from the Action (gear icon) pop-up menu.

5   Click the disclosure triangle for ProjectZ to reveal the permissions allowed for the ProjectZ group.

6   Click the disclosure triangle for the Write set of permissions.

The permissions sheet should look like the following figure.

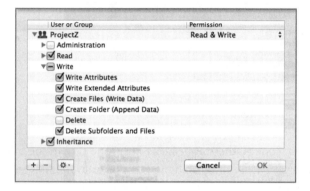

The ProjectZ group has full Read access, and partial Write access (the Delete permission is not allowed, but "Delete Subfolders and Files" is selected, so anyone in the ProjectZ group can effectively delete any item except the ProjectZ share point itself).

Inspect the permissions for the Vice Presidents group.

1   Click the disclosure triangle to hide the detail for the ProjectZ group.

2   Click the disclosure triangle to reveal the permissions for the Vice Presidents group.

3   Click the disclosure triangle for the Read permissions allowed for the Vice Presidents group.

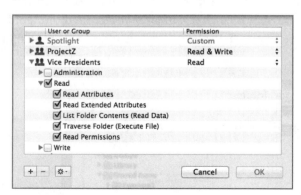

The Vice Presidents group has full read access, and this ACE gets inherited to all new items created in this folder.

4 Click the disclosure triangle to hide the detail for the Vice Presidents group.

5 View the standard POSIX permissions.

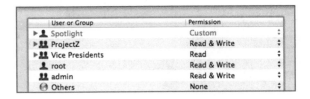

6 Click Cancel to close the permissions sheet.

The POSIX permissions for Others is None (Others appears as Everyone Else in the File Sharing pane of the Server app), so a user will not be able to access or examine files in this share point unless the user is either:

▶ The local user account whose account name is root (Full Name: System Administrator)

▶ In the local group whose group name is admin (Full Name: Administrators)

▶ A member of the ProjectZ or the Vice Presidents group

As long as you don't share any of the shared folder's ancestor folders (in this case, /Shared Items, or the root of the startup volume), no other users will see the existence of the ProjectZ folder (although skilled users could inspect the attributes for a user and see that they are a member of the ProjectZ group).

Inspect the ACL for a folder inside the ProjectZ folder, to show that when you updated the ACL for ProjectZ, the Server app automatically propagated the change. For the ProjectZ folder, you started out with an ACE for Lucy Sanchez, but after you created the "Folder created by Maria" folder, you removed that ACE for Lucy Sanchez and added an ACE for the Vice Presidents group.

1 Select the "Folder created by Maria" folder.

2 Click the Action (gear icon) pop-up menu and choose Edit Permissions.

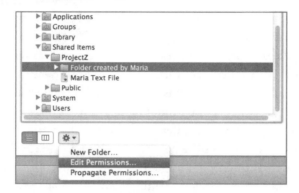

Note in the following figure that there is no ACE for Lucy Sanchez, but there is an inherited ACE for Vice Presidents. It was automatically inherited from the ProjectZ folder's ACL when you used the Server app's File Sharing pane to update the share point's ACL.

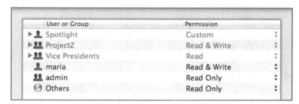

3   Click Cancel to close the permissions sheet for the folder.

Contrast the ways in which the File Sharing pane and the Storage pane's permissions sheet display permissions information for this share point.

1   In the Server app sidebar, select File Sharing.

2   Double-click the ProjectZ share point.

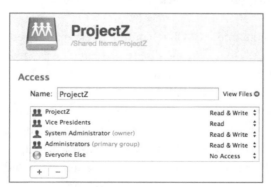

Note that in the Storage pane's permission sheet, you see there is an ACE for Spotlight, but the File Sharing pane simplifies your view and hides that particular ACE. In the Storage pane's permission sheet, you can use the disclosure triangles to configure a custom set of access settings, as well as configure that ACE's inheritance rules; the File Sharing pane offers a pop-up menu with Read & Write, Read, and Write options for an ACE. The File Sharing pane can also display "Custom" for an ACE, but you cannot modify the custom access in the File Sharing pane. Both panes offer Read & Write, Read Only, Write Only, and No Access options for POSIX permissions. The Storage pane permissions sheet lists the POSIX owner and group account names (root and admin), but in the File Sharing pane, the full names are used (System Administrator and Administrators). Additionally, in the File Sharing pane, the name Everyone Else is used instead of the name Others.

Clean Up

Remove the ProjectZ folder; it is not necessary for any other exercises.

1   In the Finder sidebar, click the Eject button next to your server.

2   In the Server app sidebar, select File Sharing.

3   Select the ProjectZ share point, click Remove (–), and at the confirmation dialog, click Remove.

Remove the Vice Presidents group; the group is not necessary for any other exercises.

1   In the Server app sidebar, select Groups.

2   Select the Vice Presidents group.

3   Click Remove (–), and at the confirmation dialog, click Remove.

In this exercise, you used POSIX permissions and an ACL to control access to a shared folder and a text file. You assigned No Access for Everyone Else to prevent all users from accessing the shared folder, and then added an ACE to grant read and write access to a group. You also created an ACE for a particular user, but as the situation evolved, you replaced that ACE with an ACE for yet another group, and noted that this change you made with the File Sharing pane was automatically propagated to existing items. You saw that the File Sharing and the Storage panes offer different views of POSIX ownership and permissions and an item's ACL; the File Sharing pane offers a simple summary and options, and the Storage pane offers more advanced information and options. Finally, the

Server app automatically propagates the share point's ACL whenever you make a change to the share point's ACL or POSIX permissions.

Additional Resources

The following documents provide more information about configuring access to files. Additional resources are available at www.apple.com/osx/server/resources/documentation.html.

OS X Server Administration Guides
OS X Server: Advanced Server Administration
http://help.apple.com/advancedserveradmin/mac/10.8/

Apple Knowledge Base Documents
You can check for new and updated Knowledge Base documents at www.apple.com/support.

Document PH8018, "Lion Server: Permissions in practice"

Document PH8029, "Lion Server: Standard permissions"

Document TS3752, "Can't save to an OS X Server share point that allows write access"

URLs
Welcome to WebDAV Resources: www.webdav.org/

Microsoft Open Specifications: Workgroup Server Protocol Program:
www.microsoft.com/openspecifications/en/us/programs/wspp/default.aspx

Lesson Review

1. When does an ACE for a folder's ACL get propagated to items in the folder?
2. What permissions can you choose for an ACE in the File Sharing pane of the Server app?
3. What permissions can you specify for an ACE in the permissions sheet of the Storage pane of the Server app?
4. In the permissions sheet of the Storage pane in the Server app, what four rules for inheritance can you apply to an ACE?
5. How do you remove an inherited ACE?
6. What might it mean if you see a GUID rather than a user name in an ACL?

Answers

1.   An ACE of a folder's ACL is propagated to a new item that is created in that folder, or copied into that folder from another volume, if the inheritance options for the ACE apply. Also, an administrator can select a folder in the Storage pane of the Server app, choose Propagate Permissions from the Action (gear icon) pop-up menu, select the Access Control List checkbox, and click OK. Finally, if you use the File Sharing pane to modify an ACL that has been inherited, the changes will be propagated.

2.   In the File Sharing pane of the Server app, when you edit an ACE, you can choose Read & Write, Read, or Write.

3.   In the Storage pane of the Server app, when you edit an ACE, you can select checkboxes for 13 kinds of permissions. The categories include Administration, Read, and Write.

4.   Apply to this folder; Apply to child folders; Apply to child files; and Apply to all descendants.

5.   In the Storage pane of the Server app, navigate to the item that has an ACL, click the Action (gear icon) pop-up menu, choose Edit Permissions, click the Action (gear icon) pop-up menu, and choose Remove Inherited Entries.

6.   If you see a GUID instead of a user name in an ACL, it could mean that you removed a user or a group from your server, and the ACE is displaying that user or group's GUID because it cannot map the GUID to a user or a group.

Implementing Deployment Solutions

Lesson 15

Leveraging NetInstall

One significant challenge for OS X administrators today is the deployment of software to multiple computers. Whether it is operating system (OS) releases and updates or commercial applications, installing the software manually is a labor-intensive process. OS X Server provides services and technologies to aid in this deployment. The NetInstall service simplifies OS rollout and upgrades.

Knowing how to use time efficiently is a very important aspect of an administrator's job. When managing several hundred OS X computers, an administrator needs a solution that is both speedy and flexible for performing day-to-day management of computers. When computers need to be set up for the first time, what software should be installed? Should they have the latest software updates? Should they have a full complement of non-Apple software, such as Adobe Creative Suite or Microsoft Office? What about shareware programs and the necessary work-related files? Safety videos? Mandatory PDFs?

GOALS

► Understand the concepts of NetBoot, NetInstall, and NetRestore

► Create an image for deployment

► Configure the NetInstall service

► Configure clients to use NetInstall

► Learn to troubleshoot NetInstall

Before you can push out data to a computer, you must decide *how* to push out that data and in what state. Though there are several third-party tools that complete the tasks of image creation and deployment, Apple has several applications to assist you with this process. These helpful applications include System Image Utility, Apple System Restore (ASR), Apple Remote Desktop (ARD), and NetInstall.

With the advantage of these deployment software tools, you can build an automated system that needs very little user interaction to function. This lesson focuses primarily on the NetInstall service provided by OS X Server.

Creating NetInstall images can be a lengthy process, but most of the time is spent waiting for the image to be processed. Because this lesson includes the creation of two images, you may want to split this lesson over a couple days, or over a dinner break, at either of the two image-creation steps.

Reference 15.1
Managing Computers with NetInstall

Think about the ways in which you start up (or boot) your computer. Most often, your computer starts up from system software located on the local hard disk. This local startup provides you with a typical computer experience of running applications, accessing information, and accomplishing tasks. When you perform an OS installation for versions of OS X prior to Lion, you could start up from a CD-ROM or DVD-ROM disc.

Managing a single standalone computer isn't much of an inconvenience. However, imagine managing a lab of computers. Every time you need to upgrade the operating system or install a clean version of OS X, you would need to boot each computer in the lab from Mountain Lion Recovery. That isn't very practical.

OS X Server provides the NetInstall service, which simplifies the management of operating systems on multiple computers. With NetInstall, client computers start up using system software they access from a server instead of from the client's local hard disk. With NetInstall, the client obtains information from a remote location. With other startup methods, the client boots off a local source, such as the internal hard disk or other device.

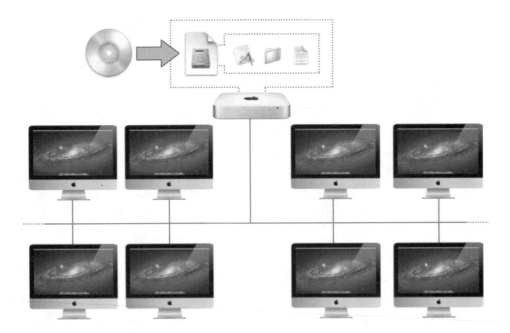

NetInstall is most effective in situations in which there is a high frequency of user turnover and in which a large number of computers are being deployed with a common configuration. The ability to deploy standard configurations across multiple computers makes NetInstall ideal for computing environments such as:

- Classrooms and computer labs—The NetInstall service makes it easy to configure multiple identical desktop systems and repurpose them quickly. With the NetInstall service, you can reconfigure systems for a different class simply by restarting from a different image.

- Corporate workstations—Using NetInstall to install system software allows you to reimage, deploy, and update workstations very quickly. Also, because installation is done over the network, it can even be done in place at the user's desk. A creative way to take advantage of this technology is to create a NetInstall service image with various computer diagnosis and disk recovery software. Booting into a rescue image at a user's desk could save a lot of time for a frustrated user.

- Kiosks and libraries—With the NetInstall service, you can set up protected computing environments for customers or visitors. For example, you can configure an information station with an Internet browser that connects only to your company's website, or set up a visitor kiosk that runs only a database for collecting feedback. If a system is altered, a simple restart restores it to its original condition.

- Computational clusters—The NetInstall service is a powerful solution for data centers and computational clusters with identically configured web or application servers. Similarly purposed systems can boot from a single network-hosted image maintained on a network-based storage device.

- Emergency boot disk—The NetInstall service can be used to troubleshoot, restore, and maintain client computers. The NetInstall service can also help access computers whose boot drives have failed and whose recovery partition is not available.

Hardware Requirements
For NetInstall to function properly, certain minimum hardware requirements must be met:

- 512 MB RAM on the client computer
- 100Base-T Ethernet (up to 10 clients)
- 100Base-T switched Ethernet (10 to 50 clients)
- 1000Base-T switched Ethernet (beyond 50 clients)

Apple has no official test results for configurations beyond 50 clients. Although there are some Mac computers that can use NetInstall over Wi-Fi, it is best to use Ethernet for NetInstall when possible. NetInstall over Wi-Fi is neither supported by Apple nor recommended. For computers shipped without an Ethernet port, such as the MacBook Air, using a USB or Thunderbolt to Ethernet adapter is recommended.

Understanding NetInstall Startup Types

There are three types of NetInstall startup:

▶   A NetBoot startup (using a NetBoot boot image) provides a fairly typical user experience, because clients start up using an operating system they access from a server. Most users won't even know they aren't booted from their computer's hard disk.

▶   A Network Install, also known as NetInstall, startup sequence (using a NetBoot Install image) enables you to quickly perform fresh installations of your operating system. It also allows you to install applications or updates, or install configured disk images. The terms Network Install and NetInstall are used interchangeably in this lesson.

▶   NetRestore is aimed at deploying full system images. Another defining choice is the ability to define a restore image source other than the disk image embedded in the NetInstall set. This allows you to host the image on other servers.

Keep these three types of NetInstall in mind while you work through the remainder of this lesson.

With NetBoot, you create disk images on the server that contain OS X system software. Multiple network clients can use each disk image at once. Because you are setting up a centralized source of system software, you need to configure, test, and deploy only once. This dramatically reduces the maintenance required for network computers.

When you start up from a NetBoot image, the startup volume is read-only. When a client needs to write anything back to its startup volume, NetBoot automatically redirects the written data to the client's shadow files (which are discussed later in this lesson, in the section "Understanding Shadow Files"). Data in shadow files is kept for the duration of a NetBoot session. Because the startup volume is read-only, you always start from a clean image. This is ideal in lab and kiosk situations in which you want to ensure that users never alter the startup volume.

Stepping Through the NetInstall Client Startup Process

When a client computer boots from a NetInstall image, it performs a number of steps to start up successfully:

1. The client places a request for an IP address.

    When a NetInstall client is turned on or restarted, it requests an IP address from a DHCP server. While the server providing the address can be the same server providing the NetInstall service, the two services do not have to be provided by the same computer.

    NOTE ▸ DHCP is a requirement for NetInstall to work.

2. After receiving an IP address, the NetInstall client sends out a request for startup software. The NetInstall server then delivers the boot ROM (read-only memory) file ("booter") to the client using Trivial File Transfer Protocol (TFTP) via its default port, 69.

3. Once the client has the ROM file, it initiates a mount and loads the images for the NetBoot network disk image.

    The images can be served using Hypertext Transfer Protocol (HTTP) or Network File System (NFS).

4. After booting from the NetInstall image, the NetInstall client requests an IP address from the DHCP server.

    Depending on the type of DHCP server used, the NetInstall client might receive an IP address different from the one received in step 1.

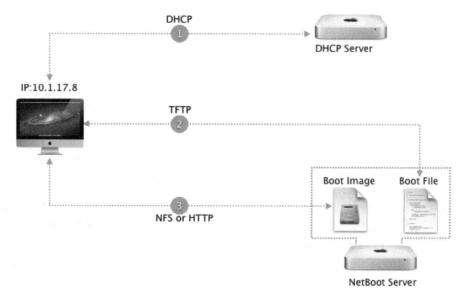

Using Home Folders with NetBoot

When you restart a client computer from a NetBoot image, the client computer receives a fresh copy of the system software and the startup volume. Users cannot store documents or preserve preferences on this startup volume, because it is a read-only image. If the administrator denies access to the local hard disk or removes the hard disk, users might not have any place to store documents. However, if you configure network user accounts to use network home folders, users can store documents and preserve preferences in their network home folders.

When a user logs in to a NetBoot client computer using a network user account, he retrieves his home folder from a share point. Typically, this share point resides on a server other than the NetBoot server, although with a small number of clients, one could perform both duties from the same server.

> **TIP** Using NetBoot places high demands on a server. To prevent performance degradation, store home folders on a different, preferably dedicated, home folder server.

Reference 15.2
Creating Images with System Image Utility

System Image Utility is the tool you use to create all three types of NetInstall images. Available from the Tools menu in the Server app, System Image Utility uses files from a mounted volume, disk image, or the "Install OS X Mountain Lion" application to create a NetInstall image. The actual application is located in /System/Library/Core Services on every Mountain Lion computer.

Each image requires an image ID, or index, which client computers use to identify similar images. If, when a client lists the available NetInstall images in the Startup Disk pane of System Preferences, two images have the same index, the client assumes that the images are identical and displays only one entry. If only one server will serve an image, assign it a value between 1 and 4095. If multiple servers will serve the same image, assign it a value between 4096 and 65535. System Image Utility generates a semi-random index between 1 and 4095, but you can change it if you customize the image.

When creating an image, you specify where to store it. For the NetInstall service to recognize the image, it must be stored in /<volume>/Library/NetBoot/NetBootSP*n*/*imagename*.nbi, where *n* is the volume number and *imagename* is the image name you entered when you created the image. If you have already configured the NetInstall service, the Save dialog includes a pop-up menu listing the available volumes. If you choose a volume from that pop-up menu, the save location changes to the NetBootSP*n* share point on that volume.

TIP In a NetBoot environment, many clients booting from the same NetInstall server can place high demands on the server and slow down performance. To improve performance, you can set up additional NetInstall servers to serve the same images.

System Image Utility also enables you to customize your NetBoot, NetRestore, or Network Install configurations by adding any of the following Automator workflow items:

▶   Add Configuration Profiles

▶   Add Packages and Post-Install Scripts—Allows you to add third-party software or make virtually any customization you desire automatically

▶   Add User Account—Will include additional users in your image. These users could include system administrator accounts or user accounts.

▶   Apply System Configuration Settings—Allows you to automatically bind computers to LDAP Directory servers, along with applying basic preferences such as the computer's host name

▶   Create Image—The basis for all image building

▶   Customize Package Selection—Defines which packages are usable and visible

▶   Define Image Source—Allows the user to pick the source for the image

▶   Define Multi-Volume NetRestore—Allows restoration of multi-boot systems

▶   Define NetRestore Source—Defines the network location of the NetRestore image

▶   Automated Installation—Can assist in doing speedy deployments in which you're dealing with identical configurations and want to do hands-off installation

▶   Filter Client by MAC Address—Restricts which clients can use the network-based images

▶   Filter Computer Models—Restricts which model computers can use the network-based images

▶   Disk partition support—Built in to System Image Utility so you can add a partition automatically in your deployments

Creating NetBoot Image Types

With System Image Utility, you can create two distinct types of NetInstall images:

▶   Boot image—A file that looks and acts like a mountable disk or volume. NetBoot boot images contain the system software needed to act as a startup disk for client computers on the network. When creating a boot image, you can specify a default user account the client can use to access the network disk image. You must specify a user name, short name, and password.

▶ Install or restore image—A special boot image that boots the client long enough to install software from the image, after which the client can boot from its own hard disk. Just as a boot image replaces the role of a hard disk, an install image is a replacement for OS X Recovery or an installation DVD.

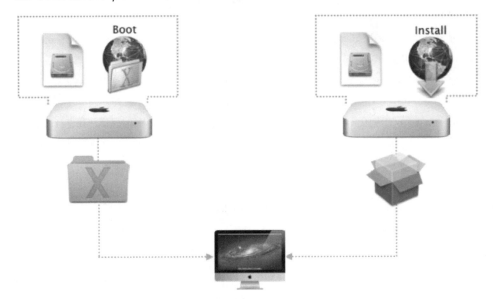

NOTE ▶ There is no real difference between the NetBoot, Network Restore, and Network Install boot processes: A boot image starts up and runs either the Finder or the Installer. The distinction is how the image file is tagged. The tag allows the user to visually differentiate between image file types in utilities such as Startup Disk in System Preferences. What happens after the boot can be very different.

Using Network Install

Network Install is a convenient way to reinstall the OS, applications, or other software onto local hard disks. For system administrators deploying large numbers of computers with the same version of OS X, Network Install can prove very useful. All startup and installation information is delivered over the network. You can perform software installations with Network Install using a collection of packages or an entire disk image (depending on the source used to create the image).

TIP ▶ For installing small packages rather than entire disks, it might be easier to use ARD, because not all packages require a restart. If NetInstall is used to deploy a package, the client will need to be rebooted whether or not the package requires it.

When creating an install image with System Image Utility, you have the option to automate the installation process to limit the amount of interaction from anyone at the client computer. Keep in mind that responsibility comes with this automation. Because an automatic network installation can be configured to erase the contents of the local hard disk before installation, data loss can occur. You must control access to this type of Network Install disk image, and you must communicate to users the implications of using these images. Always instruct users to back up critical data before using automatic network installations. When configuring your NetInstall server, you will be warned about this even if you aren't doing automated installs.

NOTE ▶ Set the default NetInstall image on every server. Images that normal users can select should probably be NetBoot images, not Network Install images. You may also turn off the NetInstall service when you don't need it.

When creating NetInstall images, specify a source for the image in System Image Utility. System Image Utility should only be used to build images of like versions of OS X. You can use OS X Server to serve images of any version of OS X, but if you want to make images of earlier OS X versions, you should use the respective version of OS X and its version of System Image Utility to build the image. You can create images from the following sources:

▶   "Install OS X Mountain Lion," as downloaded from the Mac App Store.

▶   Disk images—Instead of using a configured hard disk as a source, you can use Disk Utility to create a disk image of a configured hard disk, and then use the disk image as a source for creating NetBoot images.

▶   Mounted volumes—When a mounted volume is selected as a source, the entire contents of the volume—including the operating system, configuration files, and applications—are copied to the image. When a client computer starts up from an image created from a mounted volume, the boot experience is similar to that of starting up from the original source volume. A copy of the source volume is written to the client computer's hard disk. A benefit of using volumes for image sources is that the image creation is much faster than when using discs. In addition, installations that use images created from volumes are faster than installations that use disc-created images.

There are additional features available, including external image sources such as a network share or ASR multicast streams available by choosing Customize and the Define NetRestore Source Automator action. This is where you can define that a network share with a disk image made from an existing volume is available.

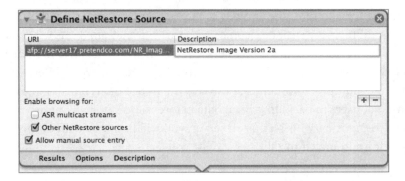

Use the latest version of the operating system when creating NetBoot images. If you are creating OS X 10.8 images, use the imaging tools from OS X 10.8. If you are creating OS X 10.7 images, use the imaging tools on OS X 10.7 or OS X Server 10.7.

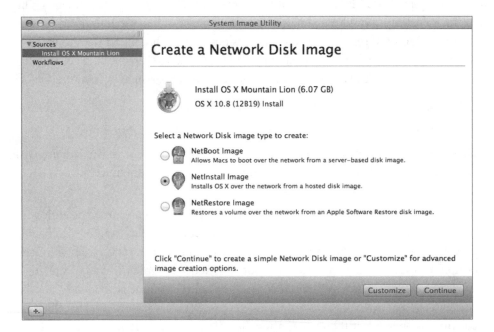

When adding new computers to the NetInstall environment, you may need to update the NetInstall image to support them. Check the OS software version that accompanied the new computer.

Reference 15.3
Understanding Shadow Files

Many clients can read from the same NetBoot image, but when a client needs to write anything (such as print jobs and other temporary files) back to its startup volume, NetBoot automatically redirects the written data to the client's shadow files, which are separate from regular system and application software files. These shadow files preserve the unique identity of each client during the entire time the client is running off a NetBoot image. NetBoot also transparently maintains changed user data in the shadow files, while reading unchanged data from the shared system image. The shadow files are re-created at boot time, so any changes that the user makes to the startup volume are lost at restart.

This behavior has important implications. For example, if a user saves a document to the startup volume, the document will be gone after restart. This preserves the condition of the environment the administrator set up, but it also means that you should configure each network user account to have a network home folder if you want them to be able to save their documents.

For each image, you can specify where the shadow file is stored using the Diskless checkbox in the NetBoot image configuration in the Server app. When the Diskless option for an image is disabled, the shadow file is stored on the client computer's local hard disk at /private/var/netboot/.com.apple.NetBootX/Shadow. When the Diskless option is enabled, the shadow file is stored in a share point on the server named NetBootClients$n$ in /<volume>/Library/NetBoot, where n is the number of the volume that stores the shadow file. With the Diskless option enabled, a NetBoot image enables you to operate client computers that are literally diskless.

> **TIP** Make sure you consider the storage need for shadow files when configuring your server. When running diskless, users may experience delays, since writes to the shadow files take place via the network and not locally.

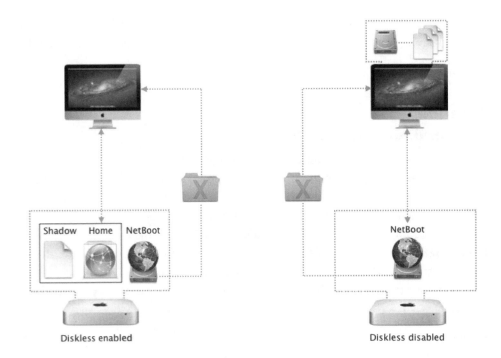

Diskless enabled   Diskless disabled

Reference 15.4
Troubleshooting NetInstall

NetInstall is a fairly straightforward process. If a client does not successfully start up from a NetInstall server, you can troubleshoot the issue by looking into the following areas:

▶ Check the network. The client must have an IP address obtained through DHCP.

▶ Check the server logs for bootpd messages, since the underlying process that serves NetInstall is bootpd. These logs can also identify if you mistyped an Ethernet hardware address or selected the wrong type of hardware for a filter.

▶ Press and hold the Option key as you boot the client, which will indicate whether you have a firmware password configured for the computer. A firmware password requires that a password be entered before any alternate boot sources are used, such as a NetInstall image. A firmware password is applied if a lock command was ever sent to an OS X client.

▶ Check the disk space on the server. Shadow files and disk images may be filling the server's disk space. You may want to add disks with larger capacity or more of them to accommodate these files.

▶ Check for server filters. Do you have filters enabled for IP address, hardware address, and model type? If so, you should disable the filters to allow all computers on the network to start up using the NetInstall service.

▶ Check firewall configurations. NetInstall requires that a combination of DHCP/ BOOTP, TFTP, NFS, AFP, and HTTP ports be open. Temporarily disabling the firewall or adding a rule to allow all traffic from the subnet you're starting up with NetInstall will indicate if you have a firewall configuration problem.

Exercise 15.1
Create NetInstall Images

To create a Network Install image from the "Install OS X Mountain Lion" application as downloaded from the Mac App Store, follow these steps:

1   On your server computer, copy the "Install OS X Mountain Lion" application into the /Applications folder of the server if it isn't already there.

    NOTE ▶ The installer will be available in the Student Materials folder for instructor-led classes or available from the Mac App Store for those who aren't in a classroom situation.

2   Open System Image Utility from the Tools menu in the Server app. The application resides in /System/Library/CoreServices.

3   In the Sources list on the left, select "Install Mac OS X Mountain Lion."

4   Select NetInstall Image.

5   Click Continue.

6   Change the Image Name to My NetInstall v1.

7   Change the Description to NetInstall of OS X 10.8 Version 1.

    TIP ▶ Give your images unique identifiers to help you keep track of which image is which. This process often involves multiple attempts and updates, which you'll want to be able to track.

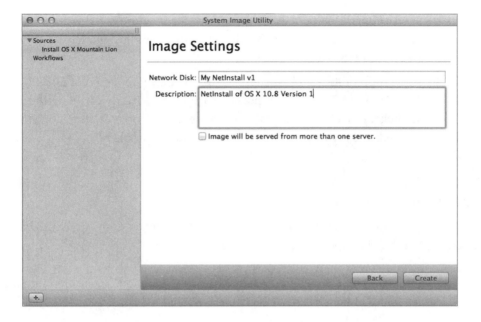

8   Click Create.

9   Agree to the software license agreement.

10 When prompted where to save the image, select your desktop and click Save.

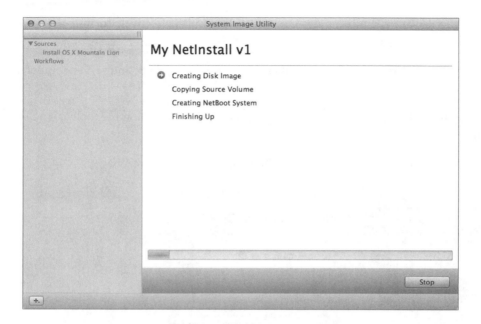

Creating an image can take from 15 minutes to a few hours depending on the size of the source image and the speed of the computer.

Exercise 15.2
Create NetBoot and NetRestore Images

▶ **Prerequisite**

▶ FireWire or Thunderbolt cable as appropriate for the computers.

The NetInstall image you created is a very basic image used for the same purpose as the OS X installation app. In most NetInstall situations in which people are working off the network image, you'll probably want to create a customized environment for them.

NetBoot Image Creation

In this example, you'll take the OS X client computer you've been working on and use it as your template computer for creating a NetBoot image that hundreds of computers could boot and operate from.

1   Hold down the T key on your client computer and power it on. Release the T key once you see a FireWire or Thunderbolt logo on the screen.

This boots your client computer into target disk mode, effectively turning the computer into an external FireWire or Thunderbolt disk enclosure.

2   Connect a FireWire or Thunderbolt cable between your client and server computers.

You should see your client computer's hard disk appear on your server's desktop. If you don't, in the Finder, choose Finder > Preferences, click General in the toolbar, and select the option to show hard disks on the desktop.

3   On your server, open System Image Utility and select NetBoot Image.

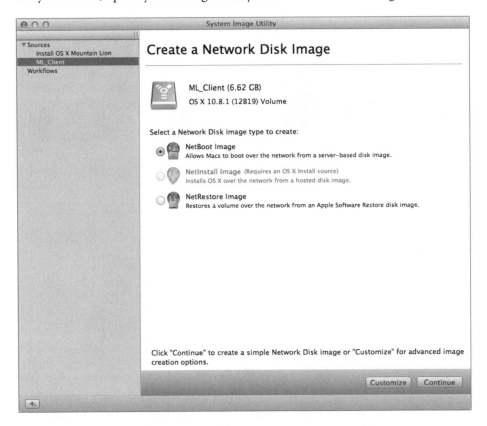

4   Click Customize, and then click Agree when the license agreement appears.

This opens a window containing Automator Library actions related to System Image Utility. This is a feature that allows you to create complex workflows for creating NetInstall images and save them for later repeated use if desired.

5   In the Define Image Source action in the window, identify the Source as your client computer's hard disk.

6   Drag the Add User Account action to the workflow.

7   Configure the Add User Account action as follows:

▶   Name: **NetBoot Admin**

▶   Short Name: **nbadmin**

▶   Password: **nbadmin**

▶   Allow user to administer this computer.

If desired, you could add additional local accounts by adding more Add User Account actions to the workflow.

8   Drag the Apply System Configuration Settings action item to the workflow and configure it as follows:

▶   Generate unique Computer Names starting with **ML_Client**.

▶   Change ByHost preferences to match client after install.

This last setting may or may not be desired in your environment. Certain settings are saved in preference list (plist) files that include a MAC (Media Access Control) or UUID (universally unique) identifier in the filename. You should use this option so these files are correctly applied to target computers.

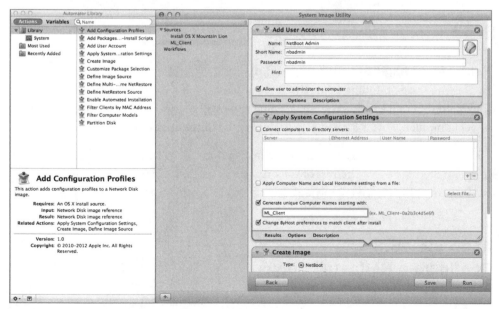

9 Drag the Create Image action to the bottom of the workflow and make sure NetBoot is selected. Fill in:

▶ Image Name: **NetBoot of ML_Client**

▶ Installed Volume: Will already be filled in.

▶ Description: This is the boot image made from a target mode computer.

▶ Index: Pick a number below 4095 that is different from the index of your first image, such as 432.

▶ Save to: Desktop

10 Click Run. Enter the administrator account credentials to create the image.

If you'd like to see more information about what's happening, you can choose View > Show Log.

```
Workflow Started (2012-09-02 17:17:09 -0700)
OS X Server 10.8.1 (12B19), System Image Utility 10.8 (622)
Starting action: Define Image Source (1.4)
Finished running action: Define Image Source
Starting action: Add User Account (1.4)
Finished running action: Add User Account
Starting action: Apply System Configuration Settings (1.5)
Finished running action: Apply System Configuration Settings
Starting action: Create Image (1.7)
Starting image creation process...

Create NetBoot Image

Initiating NetBoot from installed volume.

created: /Users/ladmin/Desktop/NetBoot of ML_Client.nbi/NetBoot.dmg
```

NetRestore Image Creation (Optional)

NetRestore image building is much the same as making a NetBoot or NetInstall image. The main difference is that the image you create will be restored to the hard disk of the target computer. This is a great way to deploy preconfigured images.

To create a NetRestore image, follow the instructions for NetBoot, but choose NetRestore Image in Step 3. Follow the rest of the exercise as written, changing the word NetBoot to NetRestore in the image's name and description as appropriate.

Exercise 15.3
Configure a NetInstall Server

▶ **Prerequisite**

▶ Exercise 15.1, "Create NetInstall Images"

You need to configure your server to offer NetInstall images to your client computers. This, like many other services, is done through the Server app.

1 Open the Server app and connect to your server.

2 In the left column, select the NetInstall service.

3 In the toolbar, click the Settings button.

4 In Access, enable the Ethernet port, if it isn't already enabled.

5 In Edit Storage Settings, select your server's storage volume to serve both Images & Client Data. Click OK.

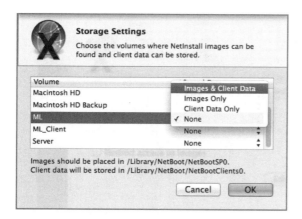

6 Click Save.

Configure NetInstall to Serve an Image
Before you can start the NetInstall service, it has to have an image it can serve, and be configured to use it.

1 After the image is created, copy your NetBoot image (NBI) to the NetBootSP0 folder, if it isn't already there. Do so by dragging the entire My NetInstall v1.nbi folder to the Net-BootSP0 folder (in the Finder, choose Go > Go To Folder, enter **/Library/NetBoot/NetBootSP0** and click Go to open that folder). Provide local administrator credentials when prompted.

2 After it has copied over, return to the Server app.

3 In the left column, select the NetInstall service.

4   Click the Images tab.

5   Double-click your My NetInstall v1 image.

6   Enable the image by selecting the "Make available over" checkbox and choosing NFS from the pop-up menu.

For each image, you can also specify which protocol, NFS or HTTP, is used to serve the image. NFS continues to be the default and the preferred method. HTTP is an alternative that enables you to serve disk images without having to reconfigure your firewall to allow NFS traffic.

7   Click Done.

8   Click the On/Off switch to turn the NetInstall service on.

Verify the Share Points

Your NetInstall service is now configured. The action of selecting a volume to serve the images automatically configured two share points for you. You should verify this now. Running AFP is only needed if you will host diskless NetBoot images.

1   Open the Server app.

2   Select File Sharing.

3   Review the Share Points list.

Notice the addition of two share points: NetBootClients*n* and NetBootSP*n*. These share points are used for the shadow files and NetInstall images, respectively. However, only the NetBootClients*n* share is available over AFP by default. Additionally, this process may not start the file-sharing services, so you should do that now.

Specify a Default Image

Within the Server app, the Images pane lists the available NetInstall images on the server, which can host up to 25 different disk images. Each image can be enabled, allowing client computers to use the image to boot, or each image can be disabled, preventing client computers from accessing the image. While you can have several images, you must specify one of the NetInstall images as the default image. When you hold down the N key on a client computer at startup, if the client has never started up from that NetInstall server before, the server will provide the default image to start up the client; hold down Option-N to use the current default.

1   In the Images pane of the NetInstall service, select the image you want to be the default image.

2   From the Action (gear icon) menu, choose Use as Default Boot Image.

The image is now noted as "(default)" on the right side of the pane.

TIP ▶ Remember that image files can be very large and can take up a significant amount of disk space on the server. Consider using a second volume to hold the images and keep them off the boot volume.

Exercise 15.4
Filter NetInstall Clients

▶ **Prerequisite**

▶ Exercise 15.3, "Configure a NetInstall Server"

Client filtering has changed significantly in OS X Server in its presentation.

The NetInstall Settings pane permits you to allow or deny access to NetInstall services globally or per image based on the client computer's hardware, or MAC, address. Filtering removes the risk of allowing non-NetInstall clients to access unlicensed applications or to accidentally perform a network installation. By maintaining accurate Filters settings, you can seamlessly integrate NetInstall into traditional network configurations.

You also have the ability to set NetInstall filters on a per-image basis in addition to the per-server filters. This could be particularly useful if you have one server for multiple Mac class-rooms. Each classroom could be configured with its own NetBoot image, and use per-image filters to limit which classrooms can access which image. You can also filter by Mac model.

1   Open the Server app on your server computer and select the NetInstall service.

2   In the Images pane, double-click the image.

This pane allows you to perform per-image filters based on hardware type and/or specific Ethernet hardware addresses. It's important to differentiate between the per-image filters and the NetInstall servicewide filters.

3   Select the "Image is visible to" pop-up menu, choose "only some Mac models", and select Allow for your client computer hardware type in the list.

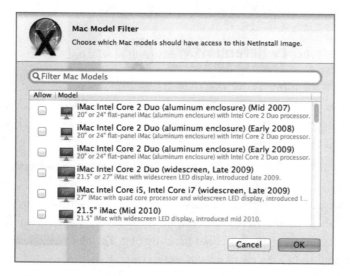

4   Click OK to close the Mac Model Filter pane.

5   Click Done to return to the NetInstall pane.

6   Boot your client computer normally and log in.

7   Open System Preferences.

8   Click Startup Disk.

9   Select the NetInstall image with the filters.

10 Restart your client computer.

It boots from the NetInstall image you just defined.

Exercise 15.5
Configure a NetInstall Client

▶ **Prerequisites**

- ▶ DHCP must be available on your network

- ▶ Exercise 15.3, "Configure a NetInstall Server"

As long as your client computer has the latest version of its firmware and is a supported client computer, you don't need to install any other special software. The Extensible Firmware Interface (EFI) (Intel) boot code contains the software used to boot a computer using a NetInstall image.

There are at least three ways to cause a computer to use NetInstall at startup:

- ▶ Hold down the N key until the blinking NetInstall globe appears in the center of the screen. This method allows you to use NetInstall for a single startup. Subsequent reboots return the computer to the previous startup state. Your client computer will then boot from the default NetInstall image hosted by the NetInstall server.

- ▶ Select the desired network disk image from the Startup Disk pane in System Preferences. The version of the Startup Disk pane included with OS X v10.2 and later presents all available network disk images on the local network. Notice each type of NetInstall image maintains a unique icon to help users differentiate between the types of images. With the desired network disk image selected, you can reboot the computer. The computer then attempts to use the NetInstall service on every subsequent startup.

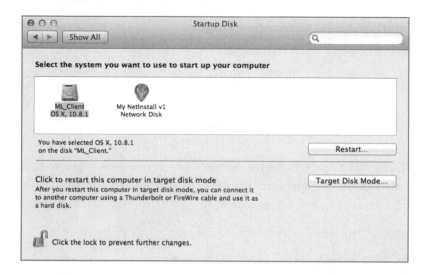

▶ Hold down the Option key during startup. This invokes the Startup Manager, which presents a list of available system folders as well as a globe icon for NetInstall. Click the globe icon and click the advance arrow to begin the NetInstall process. This option doesn't allow you to pick which image you want to boot from. As when holding down the N key, you will get the default image.

It is important to note a couple of things that can upset the NetInstall process:

▶ If no network connection exists, a NetInstall client will eventually time out and look to a local drive to start up. You can prevent this by keeping local hard disks free of system software and denying users physical access to the Ethernet ports on a computer.

▶ Resetting the parameter random-access memory (PRAM) resets the configured startup disk, requiring you to reselect the NetInstall volume in the Startup Disk pane of System Preferences.

You'll try starting up your client computer with NetInstall now.

1 Shut down your client computer.

2 Turn on the computer while holding down the N key until the blinking NetBoot globe appears.

It boots into the OS X Installer from the NetInstall image you just created and enabled. Because you don't actually want to reinstall your computer, just shut down the computer.

Exercise 15.6
Monitor NetInstall Clients

You can monitor NetInstall usage with Server Admin. The Connections pane provides a list of client computers that are booted from the server. It will report the computer's hostname, IP address, its progress in percentage, and status.

Additionally, the NetInstall logs can be useful when monitoring the progress of a NetInstall in action. You can access your NetInstall server logs using these steps:

1   Open the Server app and connect to your server.

2   In the Server app sidebar, under Status, select Logs.

3   In the pop-up menu, choose Service Log.

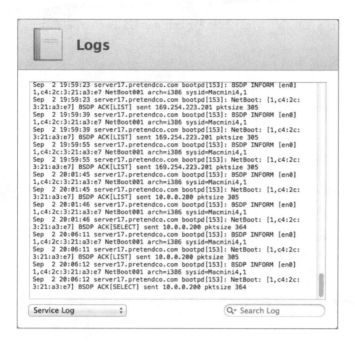

Additional Resources

The following documents provide more information about implementing deployment solutions in OS X Server.

Many other documents are available at www.apple.com/osx/server/resources/documentation.html.

OS X Server Administration Guides

OS X Server: Advanced Administration
http://help.apple.com/advancedserveradmin/mac/10.8/

Apple Knowledge Base Documents

You can check for new and updated Knowledge Base documents at www.apple.com/support/.

Document HT1159, "Mac OS X versions (builds) for computers"

Document HT4178, "OS X Server: Creating a single NetBoot, NetInstall, or NetRestore image for multiple Macs"

Document HT3735, "NetBoot/NetInstall: MacBook Air can use USB Ethernet Adapter for NetBoot or NetInstall"

URLs

Apple System Imaging List: https://lists.apple.com/mailman/listinfo/system-imaging

Lesson Review

1.   What are the advantages of using NetBoot?

2.   What are three ways to configure the network startup disk?

3.   Which network protocols are used during the NetInstall startup sequence? What components are delivered over each of these protocols?

4.   What is a NetBoot shadow file?

5.   What are the major differences between NetBoot, NetInstall, and NetRestore images?

Answers

1.   Because NetBoot unifies and centralizes the system software that NetBoot clients use, software configuration and maintenance are reduced to a minimum. A single change to a NetBoot image propagates to all client computers on the next startup. NetBoot also decouples the system software from the computer, decreasing potential time invested in software troubleshooting.

2.   A client can select a network disk image via the Startup pane within System Preferences, by holding down the N key at startup to use the default NetInstall image, or by using the Option key to enter the Startup Manager.

3.   NetInstall makes use of DHCP, TFTP, NFS, and HTTP during the NetInstall client startup sequence. DHCP provides the IP address, TFTP delivers the boot ROM ("booter") file, and NFS or HTTP is used to deliver the network disk image.

4.   Because the NetBoot boot image is read-only, anything that the client computer writes to the volume is cached in the shadow file. This allows a user to make changes to the boot volume, including setting preferences and storing files; however, when the computer is restarted, all changes are erased.

5.   NetBoot allows multiple computers to boot into the same environment. NetInstall provides a convenient way to install operating systems and packages onto multiple computers. NetRestore provides a way to clone an existing image to multiple computers.

Lesson 16

Implementing Software Update Service

Once you have deployed computers, the question of how to keep the software on them up to date will arise. Built into OS X Server is the ability to mirror the Apple software updates that exist on the Apple Software Update servers onto your local server.

Reference 16.1
Managing Software Updates

With OS X Server, you have the option of mirroring the Apple Software Update servers on your local server. This has two distinct advantages. The first is that you can save Internet bandwidth, and the second is you can control the updates available to your users.

Only software updates to Apple-supplied software can be served by the update services. Third-party software or modified Apple updates can't be added to the service.

When using a Software Update server, all of your client computers will retrieve their software updates from the server on your local network rather than over the Internet, which will also result in faster downloads for your users. The service can be configured to automatically download and make the update available, or the updates can be manually enabled.

The process of manually controlling which updates can be downloaded and made available to your users can be particularly useful when a software update might be incompatible with some software you're using or the update hasn't gone through testing in your environment.

If you have set the service to automatically download and enable updates, obsolete updates will be removed automatically. If you set the service for Manual, you will need to cull outdated updates manually.

GOALS

▶ Understand the concepts of Software Update service (SUS)

▶ Configure the server to provide software updates

▶ Configure a client to use the Software Update service

▶ Configure which updates are provided to the clients

▶ Learn to troubleshoot Software Update service

Clients can be configured to utilize the update service by a manual change to a preference list or by a configuration profile. Configuration profiles with a software update payload are only available for devices and device groups.

For situations where multiple Software Update service implementations are appropriate to use, such as for load balancing across a large number of client computers, a cascade of servers can be created. One main server is created and others are pointed at it to get their updates. This prevents having many Software Update servers from using additional network bandwidth. Refer to Knowledge Base document HT3765, "OS X Server: How to cascade Software Update Servers from a Central Software Update Server."

Reference 16.2
Troubleshooting Software Update Service

If Software Update service doesn't work as expected, you can troubleshoot the issue by looking into the following areas:

▶ Check the network. The client must be able to contact your Software Update server and be able to communicate with it. The default port the service uses is 8088. Enter the URL for the update service into a browser on the client and check that a result is displayed.

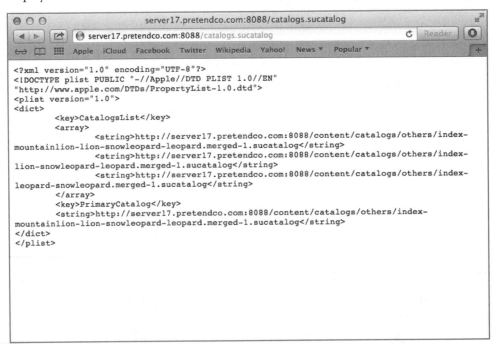

▶ Are the updates listed in SUS? If the updates haven't been downloaded, they won't be available to the client devices. Software Update service can't work through an authenticated proxy if you are using one.

▶ Is space available on the server's disk? Logs will indicate that Software Update will stop synchronizing if the server's volume has less than 20% of its total storage space available.

▶ Is the Software Update service profile installed on the device? If the computer doesn't have a profile containing the Software Update service information, it won't know to look for your Software Update server.

▶ Is the specific update enabled? Check in the list of updates.

▶ Check the Software Update logs (Service, Access, and Error logs).

Exercise 16.1
Configure Software Update

Setting up your Software Update server is easy. Here's how:

1   Open the Server app and connect to your server.

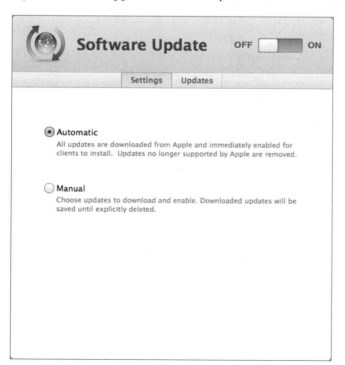

2   In the Server app sidebar, select the Software Update service.

3   Click the Settings tab.

4   Select Automatic to download the updates and enable them unless you are in a class-room situation in which case use Manual.

TIP If you want to control which updates are available to the clients, select Manual. This will download the updates but not automatically enable them.

TIP If you have another storage volume, you may want to consider changing the location of the update packages. The default location is on your startup volume, and the updates can take a considerable amount of room on the volume. You can change the location through the Settings pane for the server in the Server app.

5   Click the On switch. After a period of time, the list of available updates appear in the Updates pane.

This begins mirroring the software updates from Apple. If you have a slow Internet connection, this initial sync takes quite some time, possibly a number of hours. A common situation is turning on the service one day and returning the next to fully downloaded updates.

Enable Individual Updates

You can select which updates to make available to your users from within the list of updates if you use the Manual choice in Settings.

1   In the Server app, select the Software Update service.

2   Select Manual if originally configured as Automatic.

3   In the toolbar, click the Updates button.

     This screen lists all the updates currently available from the Apple servers.

4   Select which updates you want to be enabled.

If the list of updates is empty, it is still being copied down from Apple.

NOTE ▶ The update must be copied down before you can enable it.

You can enable or disable the update by selecting its status entry or by using the Action (gear icon) pop-up menu at the bottom of the pane.

Exercise 16.2
Configure Computers for Your Software Update Service

▶ **Prerequisites**

The following two prerequisites should be listed:

▶ Exercise 11.1, "Enable Profile Manager"

▶ Exercise 16.1, "Configure Software Update"

As with other settings, you'll be using profiles to tell your computer to utilize your local Software Update server instead of Apple's. This preference can be set at the device or device group level. Refer to Lesson 12, "Managing with Profile Manager," for more information on how to build profiles.

1   On your administrator computer, open the Profile Manager web app, and log in with administrator credentials.

2   In the left column, select Device Groups.

3   Click Add (+) to create a new device group. In the device group name field, enter LabGroup, and press the Tab key to save the name change.

4   Under Settings for LabGroup, click Edit.

5 For the Profile Distribution Type, select Manual Download so that you can download this profile on your administrator computer, which is unmanaged.

6 In the Description field, enter Software Update Service settings.

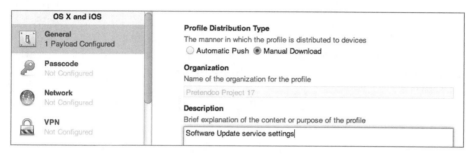

7 Leave the other settings in this pane at their defaults.

8 In the Profile Manager web app sidebar, select Software Update and click Configure.

9 In the Software Update server field, enter http://server*n*.pretendco.com:8088/index .sucatalog (where *n* is your student number).

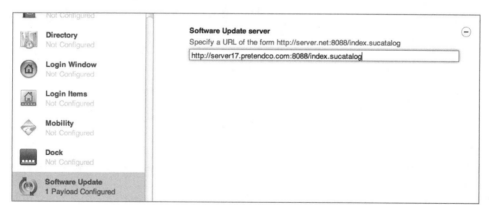

10 Click OK to exit the Software Update payload pane.

11 Click Save to save the changes. In the Save Changes dialog, click Save again.

12 On your administrator computer, in the Profile Manager web app view of the Lab-Group configuration profile, click Download.

13 System Preferences automatically opens the .mobileconfig file and asks if you want to install it. Click Install, then provide administrator credentials.

14 After the configuration profile is installed, inspect the settings in the Profiles pane of System Preferences.

15 On your administrator computer, from the Apple menu, choose Software Update.

16 On your server, check in the Software Update service logs in the Server app. Look for the administrator computer's IPv4 address in the Access log to show that your Software Update service is being used.

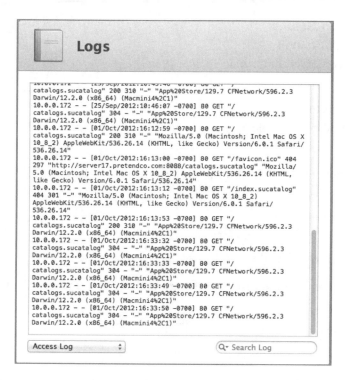

If you are not using Profile Manager, you can use the defaults command in Terminal to point unmanaged client computers to a Software Update server. You must be an administrator to use the defaults command:

sudo defaults write /Library/Preferences/com.apple.SoftwareUpdate CatalogURL *URL*

Replace *URL* with the URL of the Software Update server, including the port number and the name of the catalog file:

sudo defaults write /Library/Preferences/com.apple.SoftwareUpdate CatalogURL
"http://*servern*.pretendco.com:8088/index.sucatalog"

Additional Resources

The following documents provide more information about Software Update service in OS X Server.

Many other documents are available at www.apple.com/osx/server/resources/documentation.html.

OS X Server Administration Guides

OS X Server: Advanced Administration

http://help.apple.com/advancedserveradmin/mac/10.8/

Apple Knowledge Base Documents

You can check for new and updated Knowledge Base documents at www.apple.com/support/.

Document HT3923, "Requirements for Software Update Service"

Document HT5383, "OS X Server: About the Software Update service"

Document HT2794, "OS X Server: Software Update Service compatibility"

Document HT4974, "OS X Server: Changing the service data storage location"

Document HT3765, "OS X Server: How to cascade Software Update Servers from a Central Software Update Server"

Lesson Review

1. What are the advantages of using Software Update?

2. What are three logs available to monitor the service?

3. How can you configure a client to use the update service?

4. What is the default port used?

5. What level of management can Software Update be applied to in Profile Manager?

Answers

1. You can better administer updates to clients and prevent high bandwidth usage from your clients all reaching out to the Apple update servers, keeping the traffic within your network.

2. Service, Error, and Access.

3. Using the defaults command to modify the update plist or a configuration profile.

4. 8088. This is important as it needs to be defined in the catalog URL even though it isn't shown in the configuration panes in the Server app.

5. Devices and device groups.

Providing Network Services

Lesson 17

Offering Time Machine Network Backup

A powerful feature of Time Machine is its ability to use network-based sharepoints as a backup location. OS X Server can be configured to provide this special type of network share.

GOALS

▶ Enable Time Machine service

▶ Configure OS X Server to offer Time Machine services

▶ Restore from Time Machine

Reference 17.1
Time Machine as a Network Service

Time Machine is a powerful backup and restore service available to users of OS X (Mountain Lion, Lion, Snow Leopard, and Leopard); you can use the Time Machine service with OS X Server to provide a backup destination on your server to Time Machine users. You can offer any volume attached to your server, but it's a good idea to use a volume that you dedicate to Time Machine only, because by design Time Machine will eventually fill the volume with backup files.

The File Sharing service must be turned on in order for clients to use the Time Machine service.

> **TIP** The Server app provides no warning that if you turn off the File Sharing service, you will interrupt active Time Machine backups or restores; so, if you offer the Time Machine service, be sure to not turn off the File Sharing service until you have confirmed that no client computers are actively backing up or restoring with the Time Machine service.

After you choose a backup disk, the Server app automatically starts the Time Machine service and the File Sharing service if they were not already on. On the backup disk, OS X Server automatically creates a Shared Items folder on the root of the backup volume and creates a folder named Backups in that folder. Each client computer gets its own sparse disk image (a sparse disk image can grow in size) inside the Backups folder, and there is an automatically configured ACL to prevent anyone from accessing or deleting Time Machine files from the sparse disk image.

If you later change the backup volume, users who use your server Time Machine service will automatically use the new volume. However, OS X Server does not automatically migrate existing backup files, and the next time Time Machine performs a backup on a client computer, it will back up all the files that are configured to be backed up, not just files that have changed since the last time Time Machine ran, so it may take a long time, depending on how much data is backed up.

Remember that you can use the Server app's Users pane to configure individual user access to the Time Machine service (Control-click a user and choose Edit Access to Services from the shortcut menu, and then select or deselect the checkbox for Time Machine).

Exercise 17.1
Enable Time Machine Service

▶ **Prerequisites**

- ▶ Exercise 7.1, "Use Time Machine to Backup OS X Server"

- ▶ Exercise 10.1, "Create and Import Network Accounts"

You will configure your server to be a network destination for Time Machine backups, so client computers can keep a Time Machine backup in a centralized location.

In a production environment, you should use a separate volume as a Time Machine backup destination. In this exercise, you can use the boot volume for testing purposes if you like.

1   On your administrator computer, if you are not already connected to your server, open the Server app and connect to your server.

2   In the Server app sidebar, select Time Machine.

3   Next to Backup destination, click the Edit button to open a window that displays the available volumes.

4   Select the BackupTarget volume to offer to Time Machine users.

> **NOTE ►** If you attach a new volume after you have connected to your server with the Server app, you may need to quit the Server app and connect again to see the new volume appear. The message "This disk drive may not support Time Machine backup over the network" is displayed for external drives. The "more information" is a link to Knowledge Base document TA24910 with more details about using external volumes (basically, do not eject an external volume used for Time Machine).

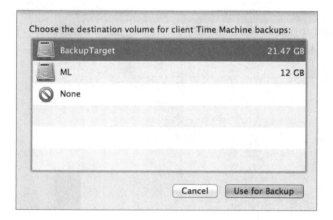

5   Click Use for Backup.

6   Note that the Server app displays which volume is used as the backup destination, and how much space is available on that volume.

The Time Machine service automatically starts but it relies on File Sharing to be running to serve clients. If File Sharing is not on, start it now.

Configure an OS X Computer to Use the Time Machine Destination

Verify that network-based Time Machine works. Configure your administrator computer to use the Time Machine service.

1   On your administrator computer, open System Preferences.

2   Click Time Machine.

3   If the lock in the lower-left corner of System Preferences is locked, click it and provide administrator credentials.

4   Click Select Backup Disk.

> **NOTE ▶** If you are in a classroom environment, do not select another student's server, as this will create unexpected results when their Time Machine service stops.

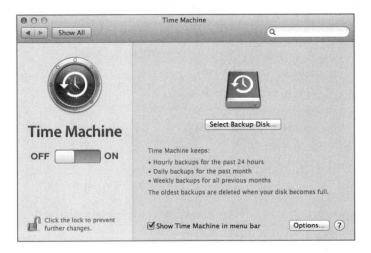

5   Select the item named Backups with your server's computer name. Note that no matter what the destination volume is actually named, the item appears with the name Backups.

6 Click Use Disk.

7 Provide credentials for a user on the server and click Connect. Use Carl's account (carl) and password (net).

Exclude System Files from the Time Machine Backup

Since this is a learning environment, you can reduce the amount of space required for a Time Machine backup by excluding system files, such as the system applications and UNIX tools.

1   Click Options.

2   Click Add (+) to add a folder to be excluded.

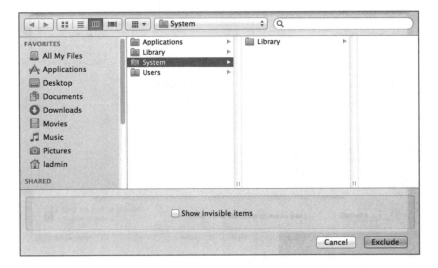

3   Scroll to the left to the point where you are at the "root" of the startup volume to select the System folder and click Exclude.

4   At the notice that you've excluded the System folder, click Exclude All System Files.

5   Also exclude the downloaded Student Materials folder to avoid a long backup period. Click Save.

6   Choose Time Machine > Back Up Now.

Restore from Network Time Machine Destination

To simulate accidentally deleting a file and using Time Machine to restore it, use the following steps to create a file with TextEdit, initiate a Time Machine backup, delete the file, empty the Trash, and then restore the file using Time Machine.

1   Open Launchpad from your Dock and open TextEdit.

2   Enter some text, like This file will be deleted and then restored.

3   Press Command-S to save the file.

4   Press Command-D to choose the desktop as the location to save the file.

5   Name the file DeleteMe (TextEdit automatically adds an appropriate extension such as .rtf or .txt) and click Save. Quit TextEdit.

6   Choose Time Machine > Back Up Now.

7   Wait until the backup has completed (the Time Machine icon stops spinning when the backup is done).

Delete the file and empty the Trash.

1   Drag the DeleteMe file to the Trash (or select DeleteMe and press Command-Delete).

2   In the Dock, click the Trash.

3   If there are any files you do not want to permanently erase, drag them to your desktop or otherwise relocate them from the Trash.

   NOTE ▶ Time Machine does not back up your Trash, so once you empty the Trash, you will not be able to restore files that were in the Trash before you made your first Time Machine backup.

4   Choose Finder > Empty Trash (or press Shift-Command-Delete).

5   At the "Are you sure" message, click Empty Trash.

Enter Time Machine and restore the text file:

1 Choose Time Machine > Enter Time Machine.

2 If the Finder window shows your home folder, open your Desktop folder.

3 Click the arrow to go backward in time until you see your DeleteMe file.

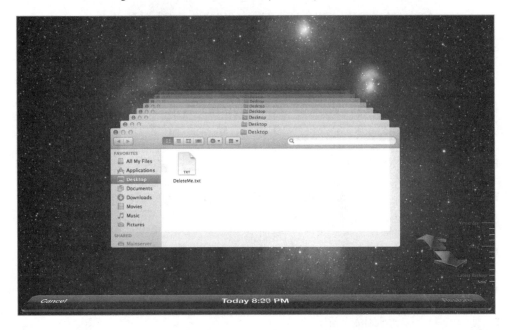

4 Select the DeleteMe file, and click Restore.

5 Open the DeleteMe file to confirm that this was the file you originally created.

6 Quit TextEdit.

7 Delete the DeleteMe file and empty the Trash.

Clean Up

Since this is a test environment, stop using Time Machine from your server.

1 On your administrator computer, open System Preferences.

2 Click Time Machine.

3   If the lock in the lower-left corner of System Preferences is locked, click it and provide administrator credentials.

4   Click Select Disk. Under Backup Disks, select the Time Machine destination you just used and click Remove Disk. Then click Stop Using This Disk.

5   Quit System Preferences.

Configure the Time Machine service to stop offering your server's volume.

1   In the Server app, connect to your server.

2   In the Server app sidebar, select Time Machine.

3   Next to Backup destination, click the Edit button.

4   Select None.

5   Click Use for Backup.

The Server app automatically turns off the Time Machine service.

Additional Resources

The following documents provide more information about Time Machine network backup in OS X Server.

Many other documents are available at www.apple.com/osx/server/resources/documentation.html.

OS X Server Administration Guides
OS X Server: Advanced Administration
http://help.apple.com/advancedserveradmin/mac/10.8/

Apple Knowledge Base Documents
You can check for new and updated Knowledge Base documents at www.apple.com/support/.

Document PH11103, "OS X Mountain Lion: Restore items backed up with Time Machine"

Document PH11193, "OS X Mountain Lion: About excluding system files from backups"

Lesson Review

1. What services must be running for Time Machine to provide a network backup target?

2. If you change the volume that Time Machine is backed up to, what will happen from the client side?

3. Why might you want to exclude certain folders from being backed up?

4. Can you recover what was in the Trash?

Answers

1. File Sharing and Time Machine.

2. An entire backup will occur rather than just the changes from the last backup.

3. To preserve space or to avoid backing up unneeded material.

4. No. The contents of Trash are not backed up.

Lesson 18

Providing Security via the VPN Service

Your may already have a network device that provides VPN service, but if you don't, consider using the OS X Server VPN service, which is both powerful and convenient.

Reference 18.1
Understanding VPN

Even though your server can offer many of its services using SSL to secure the content of data being transferred, some services, like AFP, do not use SSL. In general, for services offered by OS X Server, authentication is almost always secure and encrypted over the network, but the payloads may not be. For example, without a virtual private network (VPN) connection to encrypt traffic, the content of files transferred over AFP are not encrypted. So if an eavesdropper can capture unencrypted network traffic, he might not be able to reassemble credentials, but he can reassemble information to which you probably don't want him to have access.

If your organization does not have a dedicated network device that provides VPN service, you can use OS X Server to provide VPN service using the Layer 2 Tunneling Protocol (L2TP) protocol or L2TP and Point to Point Tunneling Protocol (PPTP). PPTP is considered less secure, but it is more compatible with older versions of Mac and Windows operating systems.

Regardless of what you use for VPN, you can configure your users' computers and devices to use VPN so that when they are outside of your organization's internal network, they have a secure connection to your internal network. Having a VPN connection is like having an impossibly long Ethernet cable from a user's computer or device somewhere else in the world to your internal network; your users can use VPN to encrypt all traffic between their computers or devices and computers inside your organization's internal network.

Don't confuse a firewall and VPN; a firewall can block network traffic based on several different possible criteria, such as the port number and source or destination address, and there is no authentication involved, but a user must authenticate in order to use the VPN service. If you provide VPN service for your users, you can use a firewall to allow services that you provide to all users, like the web and wiki service, but configure your firewall to block outside access to mail and file services. When your users are on the other side of the firewall from your server, they can use the VPN service to establish a connection as if they were on your internal network, and the firewall will not affect them; they can access all the services as if they were not remote.

The most difficult part of establishing a VPN connection falls outside the scope of this guide; you need to be sure that the router passes the appropriate traffic from outside your network to your server so that VPN clients can establish and maintain a VPN connection. See Knowledge Base document TS1629 for more information about well-known ports.

Reference 18.2
Configuring VPN with the Server App

The VPN service is configured and ready for you to start with the default options; just click the On/Off switch. This lesson explains the configuration options.

If you have older clients that aren't compatible with L2TP, click the "Configure VPN for" pop-up menu and choose L2TP and PPTP, to allow either protocol.

To allow you the flexibility of using an alternate DNS host name that clients use to access your server's VPN service, you can change the VPN Host Name field. When you modify the field, the status indicator is red if your server has no DNS record available for the host name your enter, and the status indicator is green to indicate the existence of a DNS record. Keep in mind that the host name you specify here will likely by used by people that are external to your local network; the host name you specify should have DNS records available outside of your local network as well.

To ensure confidentiality, authentication, and communications integrity, both the OS X Server VPN service and the VPN clients must use the same shared secret, which is like a passphrase. In order to establish a VPN connection, a user must still authenticate with her username and password. By default, OS X Server generates a random string of characters for the shared secret. You can change the string to something else, but it's best if this is a random string. This shared secret is included if you create a configuration profile and distribute to users. If you change the shared secret, each of your users needs to update their VPN client configuration. Some ways of accomplishing this include:

▶ Save the configuration profile again, distribute it to your users, and have them install the new configuration profile.

▶ Use the Profile Manager service to distribute a configuration profile that includes VPN configuration, and update the shared secret in the configuration profile.

▶ Instruct your users to manually enter the new shared secret at their VPN client.

Understanding Advanced Configuration Options

When a VPN client successfully connects to your OS X Server VPN service, the VPN service assigns the VPN client an IP address for your local network.

Be sure that no other devices on your local network use an IPv4 address in the range that the VPN service issues to clients; you should configure your local network's DHCP service to not offer IPv4 addresses in the same range, and ensure that there are no devices with statically assigned IPv4 addresses in the same range.

When you hover your pointer over the "Starting at" field, the Server app displays the VPN protocol and effective IPv4 address range, as shown in the following figure.

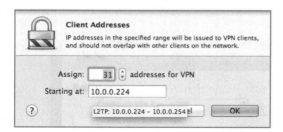

You can assign internal DNS servers for VPN clients to use, if you have DNS records that are available for clients on your internal network only. Similarly, you can assign one or more default search domains that are appropriate for clients on your internal network.

If you have complex network configuration, you can specify additional routes and whether they are private or public. One example would be if you have multiple private subnets, as shown in the figure below.

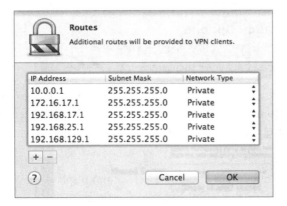

Saving a Configuration Profile

After you've configured your VPN settings, you can create a configuration profile for your users; just click the Save Configuration Profile button in the VPN pane.

The configuration profile uses the VPN Host Name that you specify in the Server app's main configuration pane for the VPN service.

Having a configuration profile for a computer (OS X Lion or Mountain Lion) or iOS device makes it easy to set up a VPN connection; you don't need to enter the information that you would otherwise need to manually enter, such as the service type, VPN server address, and shared secret. By default, the configuration profile file name has a suffix of .mobileconfig.

You can also use the OS X Server Profile Manager service to create and distribute a configuration profile that contains VPN configuration information. If the VPN service is started, it is automatically included in the "Settings for Everyone" configuration profile. See Lesson 12, "Managing with Profile Manager," for more information.

Reference 18.3
Troubleshooting

The VPN service writes log messages to /var/log/ppp/vpnd.log, but when you use the Server app to view the logs, you don't need to know the log locations; just open the Logs pane and choose Service Log in the VPN section of the pop-up menu.

You might not understand all the information, but you might compare information about a trouble-free connection with information related to someone experiencing problems. In general, it is a good idea to keep examples of "known good" logs, so that you can use them as a reference when you are using logs to troubleshoot problems.

Exercise 18.1
Configure the VPN Service

▶ **Prerequisite**

> ▶ Exercise 10.1, "Create and Import Network Accounts"; or create a user with Full Name Barbara Green, Account Name barbara, and a password of net.

The VPN service is easy to configure and turn on. You will configure the VPN service on the server, save a profile with that configuration information, install the profile on your administrator computer, and start a VPN connection. In the instructor-led environment, we do not have the ability to configure the classroom router to allow VPN service for each student's server, so you will make a VPN connection from inside the classroom network, which is still a valid connection.

1   On your administrator computer, if you are not already connected to your server, open the Server app, connect to your server, and authenticate as a local administrator.

Be sure you are using your administrator computer so that you can install the configuration profile in the next exercise.

2   In the Server app sidebar, select VPN.

3   In the instructor-led environment, confirm that the VPN Host Name is your server's host name.

If you are performing the exercises independently, and your router forwards all traffic, or all traffic on VPN-related ports, to your server's IPv4 address, you could configure the VPN Host Name to be a host name that maps to your server's publicly available IPv4 address.

4   Select the "Show shared secret" checkbox.

Assign the range of client addresses.

You will assign addresses between 10.0.0.n6 and 10.0.0.n9, where n is your student number. For example, student 1's range is 10.0.0.16 through 10.0.0.19, and student16's range is 10.0.0.166 and 10.0.0.169.

1   Next to Client Addresses, click the Edit button.

2   Enter 4 in the "Assign addresses for VPN" field.

3   Enter 10.0.0.*n*6 (where *n* is your student number) in the "Starting at" field.

4   Hover your pointer over the "Starting at" field, until the range of IP addresses appears. Confirm that the range is what you expect.

5   Click OK to save the changes.

Turn on the VPN service.

1   Click the On/Off switch to turn on the service.

Save the configuration profile. The Save Configuration Profile button appears only when the service is on.

1   Click Save Configuration Profile.

2   Press Command-D to change the destination folder to your desktop.

3   Click Save.

See Lesson 12, "Managing with Profile Manager," for more information about distributing configuration profiles to computers and devices.

Install the VPN Profile on Your Administrator Computer

On your administrator computer, open and install the VPN configuration profile, and then open a VPN connection.

1   On your administrator computer, from the desktop, open the mobileconfig file (the default name is VPN.mobileconfig).

2   When System Preferences opens the mobileconfig file, click Show Profile.

3   Scroll through the profile and inspect its settings.

Note that in the following figure, the Description field uses the organization that was specified during the process of configuring this server as an Open Directory master. You do not need to configure your server as an Open Directory server in order to provide the VPN service; if you did not configure your server as an Open Directory server, your information will look slightly different.

4 Click Continue.

5 When asked to confirm, click Continue.

6 In the "Enter settings for 'VPN'" pane, leave Username blank, so that each user of this computer will be required to enter his own user name, and click Install.

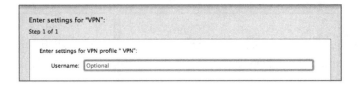

7 When prompted, provide local administrator credentials and click OK.

The profile appears in the Profiles preferences list of profiles.

Configure the VPN icon to appear in the menu bar so that users can start a VPN connection without opening System Preferences.

1 Click Show All to return to the list of all preferences.

2 Click Network.

3 In the list of interfaces, select the newly installed VPN entry.

4 Select the "Show VPN status in menu bar" option.

5 Click Connect.

6 At the VPN Connection pane, provide credentials for a local user or a local network user on your server and click OK.

You can use the username barbara, and a password of net.

If you successfully authenticate and make a VPN connection, Status is shown as Connected, and you see connection information (Connect Time, IP Address, and Sent and Received traffic meters).

You also see the connected time in the menu bar.

7 If you are not in an instructor-led environment, and your Mac is outside your local network, confirm that you can access internal resources. For example, if your server's Websites service is not already on, then on the server computer, use the Server app's Websites pane to turn the service on. Then on your administrator computer, open Safari, and in the Location field, enter your server's publicly-available IPv4 address.

8 Click Disconnect.

Examine Logs

Use the Server app to inspect information related to the VPN service. You'll examine the information for a successful connection.

1   On your administrator computer, if you are not already connected to your server, open the Server app, connect to your server, and authenticate as a local administrator.

2   In the Server app sidebar, select Logs.

3   In the pop-up menu, choose Service Log under the VPN section.

     When you enter text in the search field, the Server app highlights entries that contain the text you entered.

4   In the search field, enter the name of the user you specified when making a VPN connection earlier.

     Note that the text you enter is highlighted as you type it.

5   Press Return to highlight the next instance of your search terms.

In this exercise you configured the VPN service with the Server app, used a configuration profile to quickly configure a VPN client, used System Preferences to quickly establish a VPN connection, and used the logs to view the VPN service log.

Exercise 18.2
Clean Up

▶ **Prerequisite**

   ▶   Exercise 18.1, "Configure the VPN Service"

On your administrator computer, remove the VPN Profile to prepare for the other exercises.

1   In the Network preferences, deselect the checkbox labeled "Show VPN status in menu bar."

2   Click Show All.

3   Open Profiles.

4   Select the VPN profile.

5   Click the Remove (–) button.

6   Click Remove to remove the profile.

7   If asked, provide your local administrator credentials and click OK.

Note that when there are no profiles, Profiles is not displayed in the available preferences.

8   Quit System Preferences.

9   In the Server app, click the On/Off switch for the VPN service to turn it off.

10   In the Finder, drag VPN.mobileconfig to the Trash, and then choose Finder > Empty Trash, and click Empty Trash.

Additional Resources

The following documents provide more information about providing VPN service. Additional Resources are available at www.apple.com/osx/server/resources/documentation.html.

OS X Server Administration Guides
OS X Server: Advanced Server Administration
http://help.apple.com/advancedserveradmin/mac/10.8/

Apple Knowledge Base Documents
You can check for new and updated Knowledge Base documents at www.apple.com/support/.

Document HT1424, "iOS: Setting up VPN"

Document HT2585, "AirPort Extreme base station: How to enable Cisco VPN connections"

Document HT5078, "OS X Server: How to connect to VPN service from Windows"

Document PH10755, "OS X Mountain Lion: Connect to a VPN automatically"

Document PH11138, "OS X Mountain Lion: Set advanced VPN options"

Document TS1629, "Well known TCP and UDP ports used by Apple software products"

Microsoft Knowledge Base Documents

How to configure an L2TP/IPsec server behind a NAT-T device in Windows Vista and in Windows Server 2008, http://support.microsoft.com/kb/926179

Lesson Review

1. What kind of users would benefit from using the VPN service?

2. What is an easy way to help your users running OS X to quickly configure their computers to use your server's VPN service?

3. What two protocols does the OS X Server VPN service support?

4. What are the differences between the two supported VPN protocols?

5. If the shared secret becomes discovered, does this mean that anyone in the world can now use your server's VPN service?

6. What do you need to do if you decide to change the shared secret?

Answers

1. Users who are away from your local network can use the VPN service to securely access resources available on your local network.

2. In the Server app sidebar, select VPN, click Save Configuration Profile, and distribute the resulting mobileconfig file to your users. When a user of a computer running OS X Lion or Mountain Lion opens the mobileconfig file, the Profiles preferences automatically opens and prompts the user to install the configuration profile. You can also distribute the mobileconfig file to users of iOS devices.

3. L2TP and PPTP.

4. L2TP is more secure, but PPTP is compatible with older VPN client software.

5. Not necessarily; even if the shared secret becomes published, users still need to authenticate with a username and password to establish a VPN connection.

6. If you change the shared secret, all your VPN service users must change the shared secret in their VPN configurations. You can facilitate this change by saving a new configuration profile and distributing the new mobileconfig file to your users.

Lesson 19

Understanding DHCP

You can use the OS X Server DHCP (Dynamic Host Configuration Protocol) service to dynamically configure network settings for computers and devices, so that you don't have to manually configure them. The word "Host" in "Dynamic Host Configuration Protocol" refers to the computers and devices that are DHCP clients. Although many networks now provide DNS and DHCP service as part of their basic infrastructure, you may want to use the OS X Server DHCP service because it is easier or more convenient to administer DHCP with the Server app than it is to administer with your network router's interface. Additionally, you can dedicate one or more of your server's network interfaces to providing DHCP, DNS, and NetInstall services to an isolated or dedicated NetInstall subnet (as Lesson 15, "Leveraging NetInstall," explains, NetInstall clients require DHCP service on the network in order to successfully start up from a network image).

GOALS

- ▶ Learn the function of DHCP
- ▶ Use the Server App to configure and manage the DHCP service
- ▶ Understand static addresses
- ▶ Identify current clients of OS X Server DHCP services
- ▶ Display the log files for the DHCP service

Warning: If your network's infrastructure already provides DHCP service, *do not* turn on the OS X Server DHCP service; otherwise client computers on your local network may no longer be able to function on the network (for instance, they may obtain an IPv4 address from your server's DHCP service that another DHCP service has already assigned, or they may start using a DNS server that isn't configured properly). You should not have more than one DHCP service active on the same network. Of course, it is possible for multiple DHCP servers to coordinate with each other, but the OS X Server DHCP service is designed as a standalone service.

Reference 19.1
Understanding How DHCP Works

The process followed by a DHCP server granting an address to a client is well documented. The interaction occurs in this order:

1. A computer or device (host) on the network is configured to obtain network configuration information via DHCP. It broadcasts a request over its local network to see if a valid DHCP service is available.

2. A DHCP server receives the request from the host and responds with the appropriate information. In this example, the DHCP server proposes that the host use an IPv4 address of 172.16.16.5, along with some other network settings, including a valid subnet mask, router, DNS servers, and default search domain.

3. The host replies to the first DHCP offer it sees on the network; it sends a request for the IPv4 address of 172.16.16.5, the setting that the DHCP server just offered it.

4. The DHCP server formally acknowledges that the host can use the settings it requested. At this time, the host has a valid IPv4 address and can start using the network.

A key benefit provided by the DHCP server in this example is the assignment of configuration information to each host on the network. This negates the need to manually configure the information on each computer or device. When the DHCP server provides this configuration information, you are guaranteed that users will not enter incorrect information when configuring their network settings. If a network has been engineered properly, a new user can take a new Mac out of the box, connect to either a wired or wireless network, and automatically configure the computer with appropriate networking information. The user can then access network services without any manual intervention. This capability provides a simple way to set up and administer computers.

Understanding DHCP Networks

You can use OS X Server to offer DHCP service on multiple network interfaces. It is likely that each network interface will have different network settings, and that you will want to offer a different set of information to DHCP clients depending on what network they are on.

OS X Server uses the term "networks" to describe a set of DHCP settings; a network includes the network interface on which you offer DHCP service, the range of IPv4 addresses you offer on that interface, as well as the network information to offer, including lease time, subnet mask, router, DNS server, and search domain. For clarity, this guide refers to this kind of network as a DHCP network. The DHCP network is the foundation of the DHCP service in OS X Server.

If you need to offer multiple ranges of IPv4 addresses per network interface, you can create multiple DHCP networks per network interface.

MORE INFO ▶ Other DHCP services use the word "scope" to describe DHCP networks.

As part of your planning process, you should decide whether you need multiple DHCP networks or whether a single DHCP network will suffice.

Understanding Leases

A DHCP server leases an IPv4 address to a client for a temporary period, the lease time. The DHCP service guarantees that the DHCP client can use its leased IPv4 address for the duration of the lease. Halfway through the lease time, the host requests to renew its lease. The host relinquishes the address when the network interface is no longer in use, such as when the computer or device is shut down, and the DHCP service can assign that IPv4 address to another host if necessary. In the Server app, you specify a lease time of 1 hour, 1 day, 7 days, or 30 days.

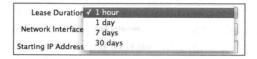

If mobile computers and devices use your network, it's likely that they don't all need to be on your network at the same time. Leasing allows an organization to support a larger number of network devices than there are available IPv4 addresses by reusing IPv4 addresses over time. If this is the case for you, the lease time is one of the key options to consider when implementing a DHCP service; if network devices come and go often, consider a short lease time, so that once a network device leaves the network, its IPv4 address becomes available for a different network device more quickly.

Even if you have more available IPv4 addresses than devices, the fact that hosts need to periodically renew their DHCP leases means that you can make a change to the DHCP information you hand out, and hosts will eventually receive updated information when they renew their lease. If it is a big change, like an entirely different set of network settings, you can force a lease update by rebooting clients or by briefly disconnecting and then reconnecting their network connections.

Understanding Static and Dynamic Assignments

You can use the DHCP service to dynamically or statically assign IPv4 address to individual computers and devices. Each computer or device's network interface has a unique

MAC (Media Access Control) address, which is a physical attribute that cannot be easily changed; it uniquely identifies the network interface. The DHCP service associates a lease with a MAC address. The MAC address is also known as a physical or network address; an example of a MAC address is c8:2a:14:34:92:10. Understand the difference between a dynamic and a static address:

▶ Dynamic address—An IPv4 address is automatically assigned to a computer or device on a network. The address is typically "leased" to the computer or device for a specific period of time, after which the DHCP server either renews the lease of the address to that computer or device, or makes the address available to other computers and devices on the network.

▶ Static address—You assign an IPv4 address to a specific computer or device on the network, and rarely change it. Static addresses can be applied to a computer or device manually, or by configuring the DHCP server to provide to a MAC address the same IPv4 address every time the computer or device with that MAC address logs onto the network.

It is possible that you will have a combination of statically and dynamically assigned addresses on your network. One of the determining factors as to which address type is most appropriate is the use of the computer or device. For example, if the computer or device is a server, network appliance, or printer, you should consider a static address, whereas mobile computers and devices that come and go on your network would likely be assigned dynamic IPv4 addresses.

Understanding Serving Multiple Subnets

The location of the DHCP server has a direct impact on the viability of a DHCP implementation. When a network client asks for DHCP service, it uses the BootP (Bootstrap Protocol) network protocol. By default, routers do not forward BootP traffic beyond network borders, whether physically separate subnets, or programmatically separated VLANs (virtual local area networks). In order for network clients to receive DHCP service, the DHCP server must be providing DHCP service on the subnet via a network interface on that subnet, or the router must be configured to relay BootP traffic between subnets; this is sometimes referred to as configuring a helper address or a DHCP relay agent.

Reference 19.2
Configuring DHCP Service

This section details the necessary steps for using the Server app to configure OS X Server.

NOTE ▶ Do not turn on the DHCP service at this time; refer to the optional exercise for complete instructions.

The process for configuring DHCP with the Server app involves the following steps:

1. Configuring your server's network interface(s)

2. Editing and creating networks

3. Starting the DHCP service

4. Monitoring the DHCP service

Configuring Your Server's Network Interface

Before you can offer any services on a network interface, it needs to be configured and active. Use the Network preferences on your server to configure each network interface on which you intend to serve DHCP. The following figure shows a Mac mini configured with two extra USB to Ethernet adapters, so it can offer DHCP service on multiple networks.

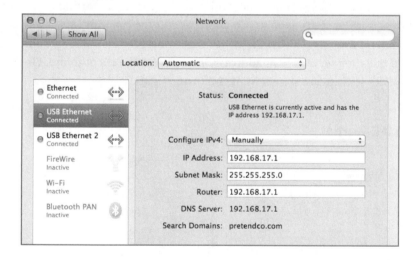

Editing a Subnet

Your next step is to edit one or more subnets. This process includes the configuration of any optional settings such as DNS information.

By default, when you open the DHCP pane in the Server app, the Networks tab displays one DHCP network, based on your server's primary network interface.

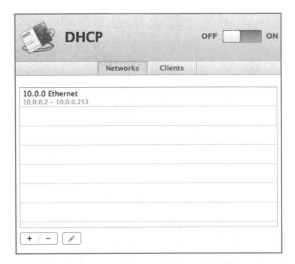

If you double-click this default DHCP network to edit it, you'll see that the name is based on the IPv4 address of your server's primary network interface, and the starting IP address and ending IP address is just a starting point. You need to edit the range of IPv4 addresses that DHCP service offers; your server's own IPv4 address is included in the range, and you do not want to hand out your server's IPv4 address to a client for the client to use. One default DHCP network's settings are shown in the following figure:

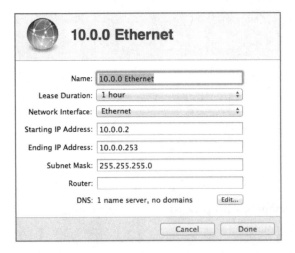

As you can see, the information you can specify for a DHCP network includes:

▶ Name

▶ Lease duration

▶ Network interface

▶ Starting IP address

▶ Ending IP address

▶ Subnet mask

▶ Router

Also, if you click the Edit button next to DNS, you can specify the following:

▶ DNS name server

▶ DNS default domain

The DNS fields are automatically populated from the values of the network interface the network uses.

> **NOTE** ▶ If you specify your server's IPv4 address to be a name server, be sure to enable the checkbox to "Perform lookups for clients on the local network" in the DNS pane of the Server app. The term "the local network" includes each network that is local to each network interface on your server. For example, in the exercises, the 10.0.0/24 network is local to your built-in Ethernet network interface, and if you use a USB to Ethernet adapter to configure an additional network interface with an IPv4 address of 192.168.17.1 and a subnet mask of 255.255.255.0, the 192.168.17/24 network is local to that network interface. However, note that OS X Server does not perform routing; it will not pass traffic from an otherwise isolated network out to the Internet.

In the Networks pane, you can configure multiple subnet ranges. For example, you can add an additional subnet range for a second range on an existing network interface or for a range on a different network interface. When you create a new DHCP network, the Server app will not allow you to specify a range of IPv4 addresses that another DHCP network already includes.

Click Add (+) to create a new DHCP network, and click Remove (–) to remove an existing DHCP network. Here's an example of the Server app displaying three DHCP networks, with two on the same subnet:

Starting the DHCP Service

To start the DHCP service; click the On/Off button to turn on the service.

> **NOTE** ▸ Do not turn on the DHCP service at this time; refer to the optional exercise for complete instructions.

Monitoring and Configuring the DHCP Service

You can use the Server app to view information about the DHCP clients associated with the DHCP service. To view the DHCP client information, click the Clients tab.

> **TIP** ▸ You can change the size of the columns in the Server app window to display more information for a particular column.

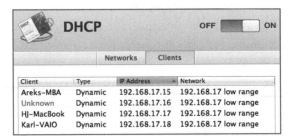

The Clients pane provides the following information:

▶ Client (for Macs, this is the client's computer name)

▶ Type (Dynamic or Static)

▶ IP Address

▶ Network (DHCP network)

> **NOTE** ▶ The DHCP Client ID, an optional value (in OS X, you can specify it in Network preferences), does not appear in the Server app's Clients pane. The DHCP Client ID may provide an administrator more information about which host is assigned a specific IPv4 address. Some service providers may require a valid client ID before providing an IPv4 address from their DHCP server.

Assigning Static Addresses

In the Clients pane, the DHCP service allows you to create a static IPv4 address for a client; the Server app refers to this as a static address (some other DHCP servers call this a reservation). This allows you to benefit from the ease of using DHCP to configure network settings like subnet mask and DNS servers, while assigning static IPv4 addresses to key equipment (such as servers, printers, and network switches) automatically.

If you already know a network device's MAC address, it's simple to create a static address for it. In the Clients pane, click Add (+), assign a name, choose the DHCP network, assign an IPv4 address, and specify the MAC address:

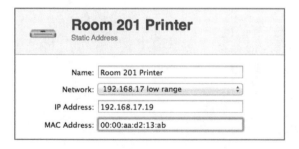

But what if you don't know the MAC address? You can create a static address for a DHCP client that already has a lease. In the Clients pane, select the client in the list, click the Action (gear icon) pop-up menu, and choose Create Static Address. In the following figure, the Unknown entry is a printer.

After you choose Create Static Address, you can specify the Name, Network, and IP Address; the MAC Address is pre-populated.

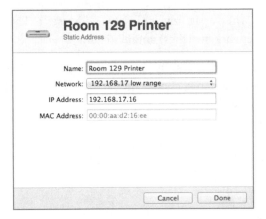

Reference 19.3
Troubleshooting DHCP

As with many network services, it is sometimes difficult to exactly locate the cause of a DHCP problem. At times, configuration errors will be present on client systems. Other times, problems with the network infrastructure will prevent the computers and devices on the network from communicating with the DHCP server. On occasion, issues arise when the DHCP server has not been configured correctly or is not behaving in an expected manner.

To think through the troubleshooting process, imagine that a specific computer or device on your network is unable to obtain a DHCP address from your server. First, troubleshoot the client, and then troubleshoot the server.

Ask the following questions when you are troubleshooting DHCP issues for OS X:

▶ Is the computer or device configured correctly on the network? Check physical network issues, such as cabling, broken routers or switches, and limitations of the physical subnet.

▶ Can you establish any network connection? Can you ping another host? Can you see another host over Bonjour?

▶ Is the configuration properly set up? Are you using addresses dynamically assigned via DHCP or manually assigned static address? If the problem is with DHCP, would a static address work?

▶ Is an IPv4 address assigned via DHCP or is the address self-assigned (169.254.x.x range)? Can you ping another host via both IPv4 address and host name? Can you perform a DNS lookup?

In this imaginary situation, you were able to connect to an external website by manually configuring the network interface with a static address, so you have concluded that the issue must lie with the server.

Ask the following questions when you are troubleshooting DHCP issues for OS X Server:

▶ Is the DHCP server configured correctly on the local network? Is the server reachable on the network via ping? Does the server have the proper IPv4 address?

▶ Is the DHCP service configured properly? Is the DHCP service turned on?

▶ Does the Server app show the expected DHCP client activity?

▶ Do the DHCP log entries match the expected DHCP client activity?

Examining the Logs

DHCP log entries are contained in the main System Log file. You can view the System Log using other utilities such as the Console app; but if you use the Server app's Logs pane to view the DHCP Service Log, only the DHCP entries will be displayed.

> **TIP** You can change the size of the Server app window to display log entries on a single line.

Apple's implementation of DHCP relies on BOOTP. That's why the DHCP process that runs on the server is listed as the bootpd process.

You can look for specific events by entering them in the search box at the top right of the pane. Note the specific DHCP entries and the general flow of the events for DHCP:

▸ DHCP DISCOVER—A DHCP client sends a discover message to look for DHCP servers.

▸ OFFER—A DHCP server responds to a client DHCP DISCOVER message.

▸ DHCP REQUEST—A DHCP client requests DHCP configuration information from the DHCP server.

▸ ACK—A DHCP server responds with DHCP configuration information for the DHCP client.

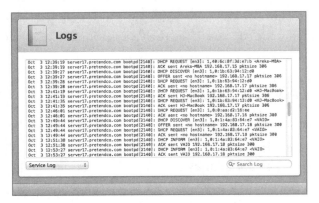

You can remember this chain of events with the acronym DORA: Discover, Offer, Request, Acknowledge.

You can also determine whether a client has received an IPv4 address from a DHCP server. If the DHCP server has run out of available network addresses, or no DHCP service is available, the client will automatically generate a self-assigned link-local address. Link-local addresses are always in the IPv4 address range of 169.254.x.x and have a subnet mask of 255.255.0.0. The network client will automatically generate a random link-local address and then check the local network to make sure no other network device is using that address. Once a unique link-local address is established, the network client will be able to establish connections only with other network devices on the local network.

Exercise 19.1
Configure DHCP Service (Optional)

NOTE ▸ Skip this exercise if you do not have an additional isolated network, and an additional network interface, or if you cannot disable DHCP on the router for the isolated network you are using with this guide.

Do not enable the DHCP service on a network that already has DHCP service.

Follow along with the steps in this exercise to configure an additional network interface on your server computer, disable the default DHCP network, and create a new DHCP network for an additional isolated network.

You will use your administrator computer as a DHCP client on an isolated network, as shown in the following figure:

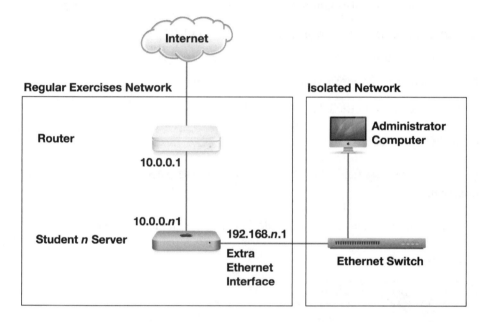

Start out by making sure your extra isolated network is ready.

1   If you have a Mac Pro with multiple Ethernet ports, you can use the Ethernet port that you are not already using. Otherwise, connect the USB to Ethernet adapter, or the Thunderbolt to Gigabit Ethernet adapter, to your server computer.

2   Use an Ethernet cable to connect the Ethernet adapter (or your Mac computer's other network port) to an isolated network Ethernet switch.

Now that your server computer's other network interface is connected to an Ethernet switch, configure that network interface.

1   On your server computer, log in as a local administrator if you are not already logged in as a local administrator.

2   Open System Preferences.

3   Select Network.

4   Select the newly added, or unconfigured, network interface.

5   Click the Configure IPv4 pop-up menu and choose Manually.

6   Enter the following information:

IP Address: 192.168.*n*.1 (where *n* is your student number)

Subnet Mask: 255.255.255.0

Router: 192.168.*n*.1 (where *n* is your student number)

7   Click Advanced to set the DNS server and search domains.

8   Click the DNS tab.

9   For the DNS Servers field, click Add (+) and enter 192.168.*n*.1 (where *n* is your student number).

10   For the Search Domains field, click Add (+) and enter pretendco.com.

11   Click OK to save the changes.

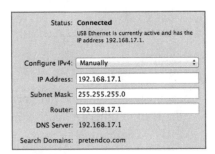

12   Click Apply.

Configure the DHCP service.

1   In the Server app sidebar, select DHCP.

2   Select the default DHCP network, which is based on your server's primary network interface.

3   Click Delete (–), and then click Delete.

4   Click Add (+) to create a new DHCP network.

5   Enter Extra Net in the Name field.

6   Click the Lease Duration pop-up menu, and choose 1 hour.

7   Click the Network Interface pop-up menu and choose the network interface you just configured at the beginning of this exercise.

8   Enter the following information:

Starting IP Address: 192.168.n.50 (where n is your student number)

Ending IP Address: 192.168.n.55 (where n is your student number)

9   If necessary, enter the following information:

Subnet Mask: 255.255.255.0

Router: 192.168.n.1 (where n is your student number)

10   For DNS, click Edit, and enter the following information, if necessary:

Provide these name servers to connected clients: 192.168.n.1 (where n is your student number).

Provide these search domains to connected clients: pretendco.com.

11   Click OK to dismiss the DNS Settings sheet.

12   Review the settings.

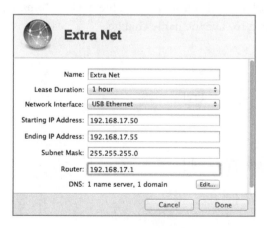

13   Click Done to save the changes.

Start the DHCP service

1   Click the On/Off button to start the DHCP service.

Connect your administrator computer to the extra isolated network, and allow it to obtain a DHCP address. Create a new network location for your administrator computer to use DHCP, and prepare to switch networks. A network location is a collection of all the settings for all your network interfaces, and switching between network locations allows you to quickly change network settings for different circumstances. See Lesson 23 in *Apple Pro Training Series: OS X Support Essentials* for more information on network locations.

1   On your administrator server, quit the Server app if it is open.

2   In the Finder, press Command-N to open a new Finder window.

3   If there are any eject icons for network volumes in the Finder window sidebar, click them to eject all network volumes.

4   Connect your administrator computer's Ethernet cable to the isolated network's Ethernet switch.

Preserve your current network location so you can quickly return to it.

1   On your administrator computer, if the current network location already has an appropriate name, move on to the next steps.

   If your current network Location is still named Automatic, double-click Automatic, enter Server Essentials, and press Return to save the name change.

Create a new network location.

1   On your administrator computer, open System Preferences.

2   Choose View > Network.

3   Click the Location pop-up menu, and choose Edit Locations.

4   Click Add (+).

5   Enter DHCP as the new Location name, and then press Return to save the name change.

6   Select the DHCP location and click Done.

This dismisses the Location sheet and makes DHCP the location the Network pane displays.

7   Confirm that the Location pop-up menu is set to DHCP.

8   Click Apply.

9   Leave the Network pane open so you can change locations again at the end of this exercise.

Without any configuration of your new location, each network interface is set to use DHCP. Wait for your administrator computer's Ethernet interface to receive a new IPv4 address assigned by DHCP.

Monitor the service and view the logs.

1   On your server computer, in the DHCP pane, click Clients.

Confirm that your administrator computer is listed.

2   In the Server app sidebar, select Logs.

3   Click the Logs pop-up menu and choose the Service Log under the DHCP section.

Confirm that you can see the Discover, Offer, Request, and Acknowledge (Ack) traffic.

Clean Up

Change back your administrator computer's network location, reconnect to the network for the rest of the exercises, and turn off the DHCP service.

1   On your administrator computer, click the Location pop-up menu and choose Server Essentials.

2   Click Apply.

3   Disconnect your administrator computer's Ethernet cable from the isolated network switch.

4   Connect your administrator computer's Ethernet cable to the network switch you were using before this lesson.

5   In the Server app sidebar, select DHCP, and click the On/Off switch to turn off the service.

Confirm that the status indicator next to DHCP in the Server app sidebar disappears, indicating that the service is off.

You enabled the DHCP service on a network interface that's connected to an isolated network. You confirmed that a client (your administrator computer) can obtain an IPv4 address from your server's DHCP service, and you viewed the DHCP service logs.

Additional Resources

The following documents provide more information about providing DHCP service with OS X Server. Additional resources are available at www.apple.com/osx/server/specs/.

OS X Server Administration Guides
OS X Server: Advanced Administration
http://help.apple.com/advancedserveradmin/mac/10.8/

Apple Knowledge Base Documents
You can check for new and updated Knowledge Base documents at www.apple.com/support/.

Document HT5412, "OS X Server: About the DHCP Service"

RFC Documents
Access the RFC (Request for Comment) documents at: www.ietf.org/rfc#### (#### = RFC Number).

RFC 2131, "Dynamic Host Configuration Protocol"

RFC 1632, "The IP Network Address Translator (NAT)"

RFC 3022, "Traditional IP Network Address Translator (Traditional NAT)"

Lesson Review

1. If a host computer or device is on an active network with other clients receiving DHCP addresses, why might this specific computer or device not get an IPv4 address?

2. How can you determine whether a host has a routable IPv4 address or a link-local address?

3. Before you can statically map an IPv4 address to a specific client, what must you know about that client before you can create a static address for that client?

4. Where would you find log entries related only to the DHCP service?

Answers

1. If other computers and devices on a given network are able to secure DHCP addresses, it is likely that the server has run out of DHCP leases.

2. Because a link-local address must fall in the 169.254.x.x range, checking the current IPv4 address of the client will provide the answer.

3. You must know the MAC address of the client; if the client already has a DHCP lease, simply create a static address from that client's entry in the Clients pane.

4. You would find log entries only related to the DHCP service in the Server app's Logs pane, in the Service Log under the DHCP section.

Lesson 20
Hosting Websites

OS X Server provides a simple interface for providing web hosting services. Based on open source, popular, and well-understood Apache, the OS X Server hosting facilities allow even a new administrator to bring a website online.

GOALS

▶ Define the OS X Server web engine

▶ Understand how to manage the web service

▶ Control access to websites

▶ Configure multiple websites and locate site files

▶ Examine website log files

▶ Locate and use secure certificates for websites

Reference 20.1
Web Service Software

This lesson helps you understand, manage, and secure the various aspects of the Apple web services, including managing high-bandwidth connections, sharing files, and locating log files for access, viewing, and troubleshooting.

The OS X Server web service is based on Apache, open source software commonly used in a variety of operating systems. It is a well-accepted and well-understood web server that is serving more than 60% of all the websites on the Internet.

As of this writing, the version installed in OS X Server is Apache 2.2.22.

To provide web hosting that is available to users on the Internet, proper DNS entries for external hosts must be registered and the OS X Server exposed to the Internet via a DMZ (demilitarized zone), also known as perimeter networking or port forwarding.

Reference 20.2
Understanding Basic Website Structure

Before you manage any websites, it is important to know where critical Apache and website files are stored. All Apache and Apple configuration files for web services are located in /private/etc/apache2/, which is normally hidden from view in the Finder. Apache modules—including Apple-specific modules (pieces of code that perform

Apple-specific functions in Apache)—are located in /usr/libexec/apache2/, which is also normally hidden from view in the Finder. Apache modules will not be covered in this guide, but additional information can be found in external Apache documentation. The default location for the OS X Server website is located in /Library/Server/Web/Data/Sites/.

All website files and the folders in which they normally reside must be at least read only for Everybody or the "_www" user or group, otherwise users won't be able to access the files with their web browsers when they visit your site.

Enabling and Disabling Websites

When managing websites on OS X Server, you use the Server app. You also use the Server app to manage file and folder permissions, thus allowing or restricting access to folders that are to be seen by web browsers, such as Safari.

Because OS X Server has preconfigured web services for the default website, all you need to do to start exploring is turn on the web service.

To disable a website, you simply remove it from the list of websites in the Server app. This does not remove the site files, just the reference to the site in the web service configuration files.

Managing Websites

To allow multiple websites to be hosted on one server, domain name, IP address, and port are used to separate sites from one another. For example, you can have two sites on the same IP address as long as their ports are different. You can also have two sites with the same IP address and different domain names. By editing and ensuring that one of these three parameters is unique, you are logically separating your sites. The URL to reach a server's webpage is its IP address, or fully qualified domain name (FQDN), such as:

▶   http://10.0.0.171

    or

▶   http://server17.pretendco.com

This can be modified by adding a port definition such as:

▶   http://server17.pretendco.com:8080

    or

▶   http://server17.pretendco.com:16080

Users visiting the site may need to be told the port value in order to access the site. Ports 80 and 443 are known by most browsers and do not require additional typing when entering the address.

Reference 20.3
Monitoring Web Services

Apache has excellent logging capabilities and uses two main files when logging website information: the Access log and the Error log. The log files can store all kinds of information, such as the address of the requesting computer, amount of data sent, date and time of transaction, page requested by the visitor, and a web server response code.

Log files, named access_log and error_log, are located inside /var/log/apache2/ and are readable via the Server app. The Apache logs are parsed to display the access and error logs per site. While the logs are also viewable in the Console app, they are not parsed and they will need to be filtered to find entries for specific sites.

Reference 20.4
Troubleshooting

To troubleshoot web services, it helps to understand how the service works and what pieces control what aspects of the service. Here are some areas to investigate:

▶   Check if Web service is running by verifying that a green status indicator dot appears next to the service in the Server app.

▶   Check that the website is pointing to the location where the website files are stored.

▶   Verify that the website files and directory can be read by _www or the group Everybody.

▶   Check if there are site restrictions as to who can access the site.

▶   Check that the appropriate networking ports aren't blocked to the server (80 for http, 443 for https, and any others that may have been defined for a specific website).

▶   Check that the proper IP address has been set for the website.

▶   Use Network Utility to check that DNS resolves properly for the website's fully qualified domain name (FQDN).

Exercise 20.1
Enable Web Services

▶ **Prerequisites**

- ▶ Exercise 3.1, "Configure DNS Services"

- ▶ Exercise 10.1, "Create and Import Network Accounts"

Web services is very easy to configure and use. This exercise will get OS X Server prepared to host websites.

Start the Web Service

To use the web service, you must first enable it as a service in the Server app.

1   Open Safari on your administrator computer, and connect to http://10.0.0.*n*1 (where *n* is your student number). Observe the page, and then in the Location field, enter the FQDN (http://server*n*.pretendco.com, where *n* is your student number), and make sure you can observe the page again. Refresh the page if necessary.

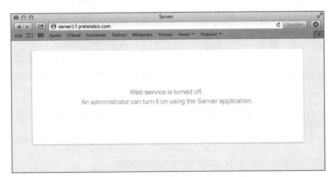

2   Note that even though you haven't turned on the Websites service, a basic webpage appears telling you that the web service is not on.

3   Open the Server app, and in the sidebar select Websites.

4   Click the On/Off switch at the top of the window to turn on the service.

5   Again, open Safari on your administrator computer, and connect to http://10.0.0.n1 (where *n* is your student number). Observe the page, and then enter the FQDN (http://server*n*.pretendco.com, where *n* is your student number), and make sure you can observe the page again. Refresh the page if necessary.

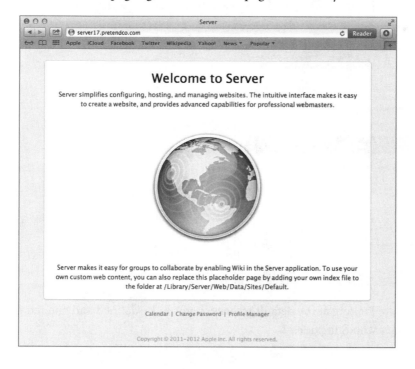

> **NOTE ▶** Notice that you did not configure the website in any way. The OS X Server web service is set to serve up the default webpage automatically.

6   Once more, open Safari on your administrator computer, and connect to **https://10.0.0.**n**1** (where *n* is your student number). Observe the page, and then enter the FQDN (**https://** **server**n**.pretendco.com**, where *n* is your student number), and make sure you can observe the page again. Refresh the page if necessary. This connects to the SSL protected version site.

View Website Parameters

Understanding what parameters OS X Server sets for the default website is helpful, as you will often want to adjust or change some of them on your other sites.

1   In the Server app, select the Websites service.

2   Select the default website, and click the Edit field (pencil icon) below the Websites field.

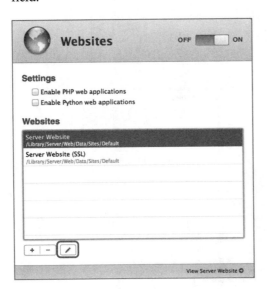

Although you are looking at the default website, items to be defined and entered for any new websites would include:

▶ Store Site Files In—The location of the files served up by the selected site. The arrow button opens a Finder window at the location where the site files are stored.

▶ Who Can Access—Allows the site to require authentication for access

▶ Additional Domains—Alternate domain names for the site

▶ Redirects—Sends requests to other URLs

▶ Aliases—Makes folders accessible via URLs

▶ Index Files—The index files used when not defined when entered in a browser

▶ Edit Advanced Settings—Set site advanced preferences

3   Click Done.

Create a New Website

Now that you have viewed the general parameters, you will create a secondary website based on a second IP address, FQDN, and port number.

NOTE ▶ OS X Server can have multiple IP addresses on a single interface, or more than one network interface. Therefore, it is important to distinguish IPv4 addresses as mapped to certain sites. Entering this information limits the site to just the entered parameters.

NOTE ▶ Port 443 assumes SSL access to a site, which you will enable later.

1 On your server, open System Preferences, click Network, click Add (+), choose your primary network interface in the Interface pop-up menu, and click Add. Select the new interface, click the Configure IPv4 pop-up menu and choose Manually. Assign the IP Address of **10.0.0.***n***5** (where *n* is your student number) with a Subnet Mask of **255.255.255.0**, Router **10.0.01**, and DNS at **127.0.0.1**.

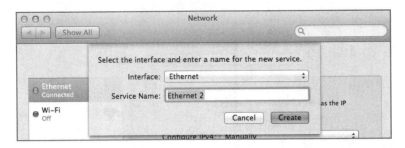

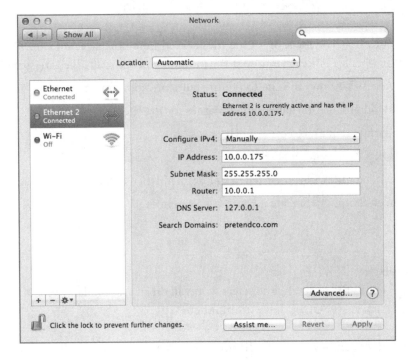

2 Still on the server, open TextEdit and create a new document. In the document, add the text **My New Website!** Press Command-S to save the file. In the Save As field, enter

index.html. Press Command-D to set the Where pop-up menu to Desktop, click the File Format pop-up menu and choose Web Page (.html), and click Save.

3   Use the Finder to navigate to /Library/Server/Web/Data/Sites and make a new folder called **MyNewWebsite**.

4   Drag index.html into /Library/Server/Web/Data/Sites/MyNewWebsite. Provide administrator credentials when prompted.

5   On your server, in the Server app Websites pane, click the Add (+) button to create a new site, and enter the following information:

▶   Domain Name: **server*n*.pretendco.com** (where *n* is your student number)

▶   IP Address: Any

▶   Port: **8080**

▶   SSL Certificate: None

▶   Store Site Files In: Click Other and navigate to /Library/Server/Web/Data/Sites/ MyNewWebsite and then click Choose.

▶   Who Can Access: Anyone

6   Click Done and when prompted, click Use server*n*.pretendco.com (where *n* is your student number).

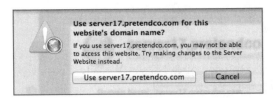

7   In Safari, enter http://server*n*.pretendco.com:8080 (where *n* is your student number) in the address bar and press Return to contact the site.

Your edited webpage appears from your directory over the port you chose, 8080.

NOTE ▸ You can see the proper site because you have defined a different port from the default server website.

8   If you try accessing http://www.pretendco.com, you'll see it defaults back to the original OS X Server default page.

Modify the website so that it responds to a different host name. Lesson 3, "Providing DNS," contains directions for creating the appropriate DNS records for www.pretendco .private at 10.0.0.*n*5 (where n is your student number). The following figures illustrate the necessary DNS records.

9 Click the Edit button for the website and change the following:

Domain Name: **www.pretendco.private**

IP Address: 10.0.0.*n*5 (where *n* is your student number)

Port: **80**

Click Done and when prompted, click Use 10.0.0.*n*5 (where *n* is your student number).

10 In Safari, enter http://www.pretendco.private in the address bar and press Return to contact the site.

Your edited webpage from your directory appears. This works because you have defined a specific IP for that site to respond to and a DNS record that responds with that IP address when using the FQDN for www.pretendco.private.

11 Quit Safari.

Verify Folder Access

For proper website behavior, it is imperative that folder permissions (and file permissions, to some extent) be set up with adequate access, as well as appropriate controls. At a minimum, the Everyone group must have read access for Apache to serve the files. It is also acceptable for the www user or group to have read-only access.

To check if permissions are read only for All:

1   Open the Server app on the server computer and navigate to the Web service.

2   Select any site, click the Edit button, and then click the arrow icon.

This opens a Finder window at the site folder.

3   View the standard permissions on the folder via Get Info (Command-I or secondary click) in the lower half of the window. Notice that for everyone, permissions are set to Read Only. This allows all users, including www, to access that folder.

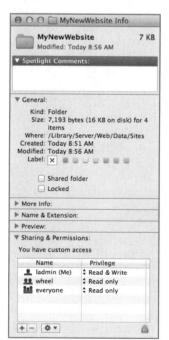

Manage Website Access

OS X Server provides a mechanism to control access to a whole website or portions of the site that can only be accessed by certain users or groups.

Controlling access can be incredibly useful when dealing with websites that contain sensitive information or sections of a site that should only be accessible to one person or group. For example, you could set up a website so that only those users in a given group can access the site. You could also set up a portion of the site so that only a department has access to those particular pages. In most cases, access limitations are set up after users and groups are created, because the access to certain web directories is based on users and/or groups.

1   In the Server app, use the Groups pane to create a new group with the Full Name of **Web Access**. Edit the Web Access group to add Sue Wu as a member.

2   In the Server app, use the Websites pane to select the www.pretendco.private site. Click the Edit button.

3   Set Who Can Access to Web Access. Click Done and accept the IP warning.

4   In Safari, enter http://www.pretendco.private in the address bar and press Return to contact the site.

5   Authenticate with Sue Wu and her password net. Members of the Web Access group will be able to access the site. Try again with a user who isn't a member of the Web Access group. You may need to Quit Safari and reopen it to allow another login attempt.

6   Quit Safari.

Exercise 20.2
Secure Your Website

▶ **Prerequisite**

▶   Exercise 20.1, "Enable Web Service"

Most web traffic travels across the network in clear text, meaning that the content can be viewed by anyone who captures the web data. For many situations this is acceptable, but any time sensitive information is sent across the wire a method of protection is required.

It's very easy to encrypt the web traffic using SSL (Secure Sockets Layer) and a certificate.

Use SSL

OS X Server makes it easy to turn on SSL for a website. During the process of turning on SSL, the default port of the website changes from 80 to 443. You will create a new website using the host name ssl.pretendco.private. Lesson 3, "Providing DNS," contains directions for creating the appropriate DNS records for ssl.pretendco.private at 10.0.0.*n*3 (where *n* is your student number).

1 Using the same technique as you did with Exercise 20.1, use the Network system preference to create a new IPv4 address using your primary network interface. Assign the address of 10.0.0.*n*3 (where *n* is your student number).

2 Open the Server app and connect to your server again.

3 Open TextEdit and create a new document. In the document, add the text My New SSL Website! Press Command-S to save the file. In the Save As field, enter index.html. Press Command-D to set the Where pop-up menu to Desktop, click the File Format pop-up menu and choose Web Page (.html), and click Save.

4 Use the Finder to navigate to /Library/Server/Web/Data/Sites and make a new folder called MyNewSSLWebsite.

5 Drag index.html into /Library/Server/Web/Data/Sites/MyNewSSLWebsite. Provide administrator credentials when prompted.

6 In the web service, click the Add (+) button to create a new site, and enter the following information:

NOTE ▶ You may need to close and reopen the Server app for the new IP address to show up in the list.

▶ Domain Name: ssl.pretendco.private

▶ IP Address: 10.0.0.*n*3 (where *n* is your student number)

▶ Port: 80

▶ Store Site Files In: Click Other and navigate to /Library/Server/Web/Data/Sites/MyNewSSLWebsite and then click Choose.

▶ Who Can Access: Anyone

7 Click Done.

8   In Safari, enter http://ssl.pretendco.private in the address bar and press Return to contact the site.

Your edited webpage from your directory appears.

NOTE ▶ Notice that the site isn't protected by SSL yet as you haven't provided an SSL certificate for the website to use.

9   In the Server app, select the SSL website you just made and click the Edit button.

10 Choose the available SSL certificate in the SSL Certificate pop-up menu.

NOTE ▶ In the example shown, a self-signed certificate that was automatically gener-ated by the server is being used, but this will cause a certificate warning to appear in users' browsers since it is untrusted. To prevent this, consider buying a certificate from a known certificate authority, using the hostname of the server requested

11 View the details of the ssl.pretendco.private website in the Server app, and notice that the port has been changed to 443 from 80. Click Done.

12 In Safari, access https://ssl.pretendco.private. Click the lock to the left of the URL and click Show Certificate to see the details of the certificate used to secure the website.

Exercise 20.3
Monitor Web Services

When administering a website, it is important to understand how OS X Server handles Apache log files, where they are stored, and how to view them.

To view Apache log files for a given site:

1   Open the Server app and select Logs. Choose Access Log (www.pretendco.private) from the pop-up menu.

> Websites
> Access Log (default)
> Access Log (secure default)
> Access Log (ssl.pretendco.private)
> ✓ Access Log (www.pretendco.private)
> Error Log (default)
> Error Log (secure default)
> Error Log (ssl.pretendco.private)
> Error Log (www.pretendco.private)

2   On your administrator computer, open /Utilities/Terminal and enter

ab -n 10000 -c 50 http://www.pretendco.private/

and press Return.

This is an Apache test tool that tells your OS X computer to ask for 10,000 (the -n parameter) requests run concurrently by 50 (the -c parameter) pretend users' concurrent connections.

3   View the log and watch the requests get logged.

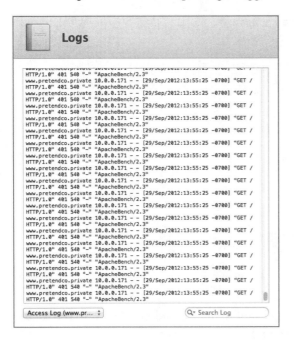

4   On your administrator computer, open Safari and type the following:

http://servern.pretendco.com/nada.html (where *n* is your student number)

This page does not exist; therefore, it will log an error.

5   Using Logs, check the error log for the error by searching for "nada." You will see an error generated by the bad request.

Exercise 20.4
Disable a Website

▶ **Prerequisite**

   ▶   Exercise 20.2, "Secure Your Website"

There is no button or checkbox to disable a website. You must remove the website from the Websites service, but when you do that, it leaves the files in place.

1   Open the Server app and select Websites.

2   Select the ssl.pretendco.private site and click the Remove (–) button at the bottom of the pane. Click Remove to confirm.

3   In the Finder, navigate to /Library/Server/Web/Data/Sites/MyNewSSLWebsite and confirm that the files still exist for the site.

Additional Resources

The following documents provide more information about managing web services in OS X Server.

Many other documents are available at www.apple.com/osx/server/resources/documentation.html.

OS X Server Administration Guides

OS X Server: Advanced Administration
http://help.apple.com/advancedserveradmin/mac/10.8/

Apple Knowledge Base Documents

You can check for new and updated Knowledge Base documents at www.apple.com/support/.

Document HT5382, "OS X Server: Upgrading Websites service from previous versions"

URLs

Apache Organization site: http://httpd.apache.org

Apache log formatting information: http://httpd.apache.org/docs/2.2/logs.html

http://httpd.apache.org/docs/2.2/mod/mod_log_config.html

Lesson Review

1. On what software is the OS X Server web service based?

2. Which permissions are necessary on a web folder to ensure that visitors to the site can access the pages?

3. What are access controls?

4. Where is the default location for the Apache log files?

5. What is the advantage of using SSL on a website?

Answers

1. The web service is based on Apache, the open source web server software.

2. The everyone or www group must have read access to the web files.

3. Access controls are paths to folders that can be restricted based on group.

4. The default location for Apache log files is /var/log/apache2/access_log and /var/log/apache2/error_log.

5. SSL helps protect the traffic traveling to and from the website by encrypting the data.

Using Collaborative Services

Lesson 21
Providing Mail Services

OS X Server provides a simple interface for setting up a capable and standards-based email service. While setting up email servers in the past has been fraught with complication, the configuration of this service in OS X Server has been simplified, yet still allows administration of the deeper details.

GOALS

► Set up the mail service

► Configure email accounts for users

► Filter email for viruses and spam

Reference 21.1
Hosting Mail Services

Email is one of the fundamental services on the Internet. OS X Server includes a feature-rich email service you can use to send, receive, and store email for your organization. Aside from the obvious reason of hosting an email server to gain an Internet identity, a number of other factors make hosting your own mail service advantageous. If you have a small office with a slow Internet connection, you may find that keeping all of your email within the building rather than using external email servers makes better use of your network bandwidth. This is especially true if typical messages within your organization include large attachments. Additionally, many organizations are required to keep the information held in their email messages secure for regulatory or competitive reasons. Hosting your own email server in-house can keep confidential data from falling into the wrong hands. You may also find that various third-party email services don't offer the exact services you want. By running your own mail servers, you can customize various options to meet the needs of your organization.

The mail service in OS X Server is based on two open-source email packages:

► Postfix handles acceptance and delivery of individual messages.

► Dovecot accepts connections from individual users downloading their messages to their mail client. Dovecot is a replacement for Cyrus, found in 10.5 and earlier versions of OS X Server.

In addition to these programs, the mail service in OS X Server makes use of a number of other packages to provide features, such as spam and virus scanning. Each of these is discussed in this lesson, but first you must learn how email works.

Understanding Mail

Although email is one of the oldest and simplest systems on the Internet, it is composed of a number of different protocols. The primary protocol is the Simple Mail Transfer Protocol (SMTP), which is responsible for delivering a message from the sender to the sender's email server and between email servers. When a message is sent, the outgoing mail server first looks up the address of the destination's Mail eXchange (MX) server using DNS. A given Internet domain can have multiple MX servers to help balance the load and provide redundant services. Each MX server is assigned a priority. The highest-priority servers are assigned the lowest number and are tried first when delivering mail via SMTP. In the following image, the priority number follows right after the record type (for example, the first MX record has a priority of 20).

To look up information about a domain's MX servers, you can use the Network Utility found in /Applications/Utilities on a Mac OS X computer.

An individual email message may travel through many servers while en route to its final destination. Each server that a message passes through will tag a message with the name of the server and the time it was processed. This is done to provide a history of which servers handled a given message. To examine this trail using the Mail application, you can choose View > Message > Long Headers while viewing the message.

```
Received:  from cooper ([127.0.0.1]) by localhost (cooper.pretendco.com [127.0.0.1]) (amavisd-new, port
           10024) with ESMTP id 09379-03 for <david.pugh@pretendco.com>; Sat, 21 Sep 2002
           15:31:32 -0400 (EDT)
Received:  from mail-out4.apple.com (mail-out4.apple.com [17.254.13.23]) by cooper (Postfix) with
           ESMTP id 5D5B9B7C672 for <david.pugh@pretendco.com>; Sat, 21 Sep 2002 15:31:32
           -0400 (EDT)
Received:  from relay14.apple.com (relay14.apple.com [17.128.113.52]) by mail-out4.apple.com (Postfix)
           with ESMTP id 292BD251CA2; Sat, 21 Sep 2002 15:31:31 -0700 (PDT)
Received:  from relay14.apple.com (unknown [127.0.0.1]) by relay14.apple.com (Symantec Mail Security)
           with ESMTP id 0E96B20A4C; Sat, 21 Sep 2002 15:31:31 -0700 (PDT)
Received:  from [17.09.21.02] (sep21-2002.apple.com [17.09.21.02]) (using TLSv1 with cipher AES128-
           SHA (128/128 bits)) (No client certificate requested) by relay14.apple.com (Apple SCV relay)
           with ESMTP id E1B20A24685; Sat, 21 Sep 2002 15:31:30 -0700 (PDT)
```

Once the email message is delivered to the recipient's mail server, it will be stored there for the recipient to receive the message using either of the two available protocols:

▶ Post Office Protocol (POP) is a common email retrieval protocol used on mail servers where disk space and network connections are at a premium. POP is preferred in these environments because a mail client will connect to the server, download the email, remove it from the server, and disconnect very quickly. Although good for the server, POP mail servers are typically less user-friendly because they don't support server-side folders and may cause difficulties for a user connecting from multiple computers.

▶ Internet Message Access Protocol (IMAP) is commonly used by mail services that want to provide more features to the user. IMAP allows the storage of all email and email folders on the server, where they can be backed up. Additionally, a mail client will often remain connected to the mail server for the duration of the user session. This can result in quicker notification of new messages. The downside to using IMAP is that it puts more load on the resources of the mail server.

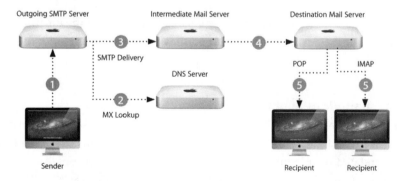

Configuring DNS for Mail

When you send an email, you'll need to ensure that DNS is configured for your domain so that mail can be delivered to the proper address. DNS can be provided by a DNS hosting company or by using your own DNS servers. While the examples here will rely on the basic DNS service provided by the OS X Server, additional DNS would be needed for a "real-life" email server setup.

Specifically you will need to set up an MX record for the domain. The MX record is how the sending email server knows where to send the email. Without an MX record, the server will utilize an A record for the domain listed. Considering that often the email server will be a different server than used for hosting a domain's website, this may not be a good situation, as the mail might be delivered to the wrong location.

Relaying Outgoing Mail

The OS X Server email service has the option to relay outgoing email through another SMTP server. This can be important if you don't want to run your own SMTP service with the attendant issues with blacklists, or if the ISP you use doesn't allow you to host your own SMTP server.

Most likely you'll need user credentials to connect to the ISP's SMTP server. If your ISP allows non-authenticated connections to the SMTP server, it will most likely be tagged an open relay at some point in the blacklists. If your ISP doesn't require credentials to connect, find a new SMTP service that does to prevent problems down the line.

Enabling Mail Quotas for Users

To enable a mail storage quota for a user, the Server app provides a simplified management tool as compared to earlier versions of Server. A difference with OS X Server is that the same quota is applied to all users.

A quota can be helpful to manage the amount of mail users can retain on the email server, but it can also limit them if they exceed their limit and they miss email because of full mailbox errors.

Enabling Incoming Mail Virus Scanning

A common concern when running a mail server is how to protect your users from viruses. The OS X email service uses the ClamAV virus scanning package for this purpose. The virus definitions are updated on a regular basis using a process called freshclam. Any email that has been identified as containing a virus is stored in the /Library/Server/Mail/Data/scanner/virusmails folder and is deleted after a period of time. An alert is sent to the defined recipients in the Server app Alert notifications.

Enabling Incoming Mail Blacklists and Junk Filtering

Blacklists are lists of domains known to host junk mail or other unwanted email servers. By subscribing to a blacklist, your email server will scan the incoming email, compare the host IP from where it came, and allow it to pass or not based on whether or not that host IP is listed. By default, the OS X Server email service utilizes the blacklist hosted by The Spamhaus Project, but you can change this to any other blacklist.

The danger of using a blacklist is that sometimes innocent hosts can get listed, and thus proper and desired emails can get blocked from delivery to your users. Getting off blacklists can be daunting and may result in lost email.

The OS X Server email service can also use the SpamAssassin software package to scan incoming email and rank its likelihood of being spam. The text of the message is analyzed using a complex algorithm given a number that reflects how likely it is to be spam. This can be remarkably accurate unless the email contains terms and words commonly applied to spam. To counteract this, you can manage the service by adjusting what score is considered spam. Certain types of organizations, such as a school, might need to use higher scores, while others, like a medical office, might user a lower score.

The levels of score are:

▶   Aggressive—The filter tolerates few signs of being junk mail.

▶   Moderate—The filter tolerates some signs of being junk mail.

▶   Cautious—The filter tolerates many signs of being junk mail.

Messages that are tagged as spam have the subject appended by ***JUNK MAIL*** and sent on to the recipient. The recipient can then either delete the mail, open it, or possibly configure a filter in the mail client to move it to a junk folder.

Reference 21.2
Troubleshooting Mail Services

To troubleshoot the mail service as provided by OS X Server, it helps to have a good understanding of how email works in general. Review the previous sections to make sure you understand each of the working pieces.

Here are some common problems and suggestions for rectifying them:

▶   DNS problems—If the domain doesn't have proper MX records associated with it, other email servers may not be able to locate your email server to deliver the messages. You can utilize Network Utility to do a DNS lookup of your domain.

▶ Service issues—Utilize the Logs tab in the Server app to review the Mail log for clues to why the service might not start or work properly.

▶ Can't send or receive email—Review the SMTP log for problems with users not being able to send mail, and the POP and IMAP logs for problems with users not being able to receive mail.

▶ Too much spam being sent to the users—Increase the spam filtering rating in the filtering preferences in the Mail service in the Server app.

▶ Too many real emails being marked as spam—Decrease the spam filtering rating in the filtering preferences in the Mail service in the Server app.

Exercise 21.1
Enable the Mail Service

▶ **Prerequisites**

▶ Exercise 3.1, "Configure DNS Services"

▶ Exercise 10.1, "Create and Import Network Accounts"; or use the Server app to create users Barbara Green and Todd Porter, each with an account name that is the same as their first name in lowercase, and a password of net.

The OS X Server email service is configured using the Server app. The interface is very elegant and relatively complication-free.

1   Open the Server app and connect to your server.

2   Select your Server. Click Settings and edit the SSL certificates to apply your server certificate to the mail services. Click OK when done.

3 Select the Mail service in the left column. Click Edit next to "Provide mail for" and enter the domain (pretendco.com). Click OK.

4 Turn on the mail service.

Relay Outgoing Mail

To set up the option to relay outgoing email through another SMTP server:

1 In the Mail service pane in the Server app, select the "Relay outgoing mail through ISP" option.

2   Click the Edit button.

3   If needed, fill in the SMTP server information provided by your ISP, including the user credentials, and click OK. This is not needed for the exercise. If you are performing this exercise in an instructor-led environment, this is not necessary, so click Cancel.

Enable Mail for a User

Unlike in earlier versions of OS X Server, enabling email services for a user is a one-step process. You simply need to provide an email address for the user in the user's record.

1   When editing an existing user or making a new user, add in an email address for the user in the Email Address field and save the change. Enter email addresses for Barbara Green and Todd Porter (**barbara@server*n*.pretendco.com** and **todd@server*n*.pretendco.com**, where *n* is your student number).

Enable Mail Quotas for Users

Setting up quotas for the Mail service is very simple and quick:

1   In the Mail service pane in the Server app, select the checkbox for "Limit mail to."

2   Enter a quota in MB and click out of the checkbox to make it active.

Enable Incoming Mail Virus Scanning

Almost every email server will have some level of virus scanning enabled. This is how to enable it in OS X Server:

1   In the Mail service pane in the Server app, click the Edit Filtering Settings button.

2   Select the "Enable virus filtering" option to make it active.

Enable Incoming Mail Blacklists and Junk Filtering

Here's how to enable blacklists and junk mail filtering for OS X Server Mail service:

1   In the Mail service pane in the Server app, click the Edit Filtering Settings button.

2   Select the "Enable blacklist filtering" option to make it active. You can use the default zen.spamhaus.org blacklist service or replace it with another. Deselect the checkbox to turn off blacklist filtering.

3   Select the "Enable junk mail filtering" option to make active. Move the slider to the score desired for junk mail sensitivity. Click OK when done.

Exercise 21.2
Send and Receive Mail

In this exercise you'll use the Mail, Calendar, and Contacts preferences to configure the Mail app for Todd Porter, so you will create an account for, and log in as, Todd Porter on your administrator computer. You'll see how easy it is to send mail and reply to it.

Set Up the Mail Application with the Mail, Calendar, and Contacts Preferences

Use the Mac, Calendar, and Contacts preferences for Todd Porter.

1   On your administrator computer, create a new user named Todd Local (Name toddlocal, Password net) blue in the Users and Groups System Preferences pane.

2   On your administrator computer, log out.

3   Log in as Todd Local; you may need to complete the Mac OS X Setup Assistant.

4   If the iCloud preferences open automatically, click Show All in the System Preferences toolbar.

5   If System Preferences is not already open, open System Preferences.

6   Open Mail, Contacts & Calendars.

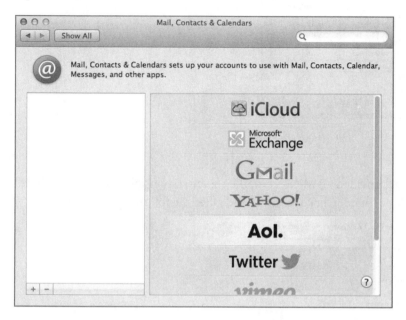

7   Scroll down in the right pane to Add Other Account and click it.

8   In the account type pane, select "Add a Mail account" and click Create.

9   Provide the following information:

Full Name: Todd Porter

Email Address: todd@server*n*.pretendco.com (where *n* is your student number)

Password: net

10 Click Create.

11 If you have not provided an MX record, the server responsible for email for Todd's account won't be found. Click Continue and enter the following information:

Full Name: Todd Porter

Email Address: todd@server*n*.pretendco.com (where *n* is your student number)

Password: net

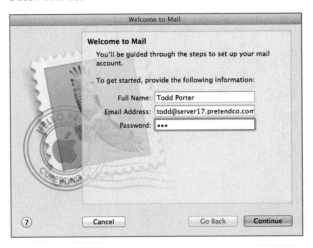

12 In the next pane, enter the following information:

▶ Account Type: IMAP

▶ Description: **Server 17**

▶ Incoming Mail Server: **server*n*.pretendco.com** (where *n* is your student number)

▶ User Name: **todd**

▶ Password: **net**

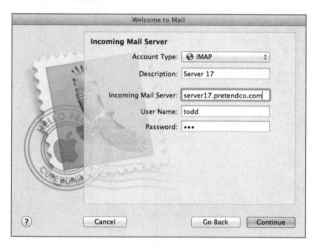

13 In the next pane, enter the following information:

▶ Description: **Server *n*** (where *n* is your student number)

▶ Outgoing Mail Server: **server*n*.pretendco.com** (where *n* is your student number)

▶ User Name (Use Authentication box selected): **todd**

▶ Password: **net**

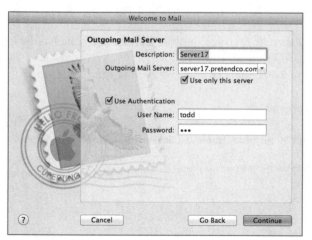

14 At the Account Summary pane, make sure all the information is correct and the "Take account online" option is selected. Click Create. Quit System Preferences.

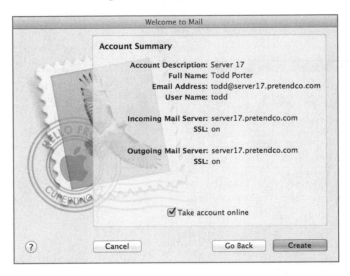

15 Repeat this process on your server computer using the Barbara Green account. You don't have to log in as Barbara; just configure the email account. Now you have two computers with two accounts configured ready to communicate with each other.

Use the Mail Application as Todd Porter

Use the Mail application as Todd Porter to send mail to Barbara Green.

1 On your administrator computer, open Mail by clicking it in your Dock.

2 In the toolbar, click the "Compose new message" button (looks like a pencil and paper).

3 In the To field, enter barbara@server*n*.pretendco.com (where *n* is your student number).

4 In the Subject field, enter Hi Barbara!

5 In the Main mail window, enter Hi Barbara. Hope you are having a great trip. –Todd.

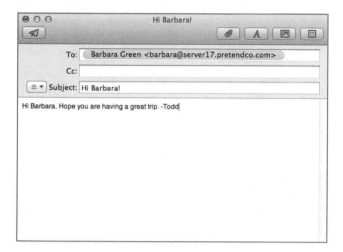

6   Click the Send message button in the upper-left corner of the message window.

7   Leave Mail open and running.

Use the Mail Application as Barbara Green

Use the Mail application as Barbara Green to send mail to Todd Porter.

1   On your server computer, open Mail by clicking it in your Dock.

2   See that the message from Todd was received.

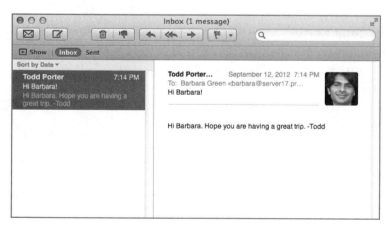

3 Select the message from Todd Porter.

4 In the toolbar of the Mail window, click "Reply to sender" (a tab with a curved arrow pointing to the left).

5 In the main body of the message, enter the message, Hi Todd. Thanks! I'm staying an extra week since I can work remotely. See you soon. –Barbara.

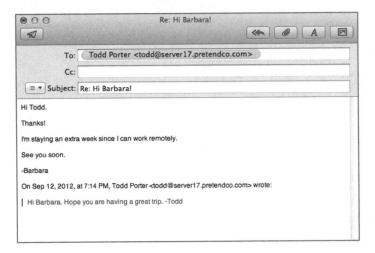

6 Click the Send message button.

7 Once the message is sent successfully, quit Mail.

Check the Reply as Todd Porter
In the Dock on your administrator computer, note that Mail has a red badge with the number 1 in it to indicate that you have one new mail message.

1 In Mail, click the new message from Barbara Green.

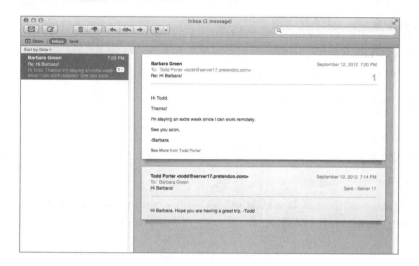

2   Press Command-Q to quit Mail.

3   On your administrator computer log out and log back in as Local Admin.

Additional Resources

The following documents provide more information about managing mail services in OS X Server.

Many other documents are available at www.apple.com/osx/server/resources/documentation.html.

OS X Server Administration Guides

OS X Server: Advanced Administration
http://help.apple.com/advancedserveradmin/mac/10.8/

Apple Knowledge Base Documents

You can check for new and updated Knowledge Base documents at www.apple.com/support/.

Document HT5032, "OS X Server: Enabling and disabling email auto-forwarding"

Lesson Review

1. What protocols can Mail service utilize?
2. What kind of DNS record should be set up for a mail server in production use?
3. What tools are used for filtering the Mail service?

Answers

1. POP, IMAP, and SMTP.
2. An MX record for the domain.
3. SpamAssassin filters for spam. ClamAV provides virus scanning. An external blacklist server can be set for junk mail filtering.

Lesson 22

Configuring the Wiki Service

OS X Server provides a simple interface for providing Wiki services. Wikis are growing in popularity as they offer an easy, cross-platform method to share information to many users.

GOALS

► Set up the Wiki service
► Allow users and groups to manage a wiki

Reference 22.1
Understanding and Managing a Wiki

A wiki is a collaborative web-based tool that allows users and groups to post information in a manner that promotes the logical progression of an idea, project, theme, or any other focal point of discussion within an organization. Wikis are central to the idea of all users within a given group being able to post, edit, review, and discuss material without interference from other groups or departments within an organization. This can benefit the group whose wiki is hosting a confidential project or sensitive information. OS X Server wikis also keep a detailed history of a group's posts, so you can retrieve older information if necessary.

Wikis have a few layers of access control. You can administratively control the users and groups you allow to create wikis. Once a user creates a wiki, she can specify who can read it and who can edit it, all without any intervention from an administrator.

Once users have access to a wiki, they can post articles, images, and files for downloading, link pages together, and format the pages to their liking. Media such as images, movies, and audio are presented right on the webpage and do not need to be downloaded by the user.

Similar to wikis are blogs. Blogs permit users and groups to catalog their experiences surrounding a project or theme. Whereas wikis are collaborative, blogs tend to be singular in nature and organized in a chronological format; however, with group blogging, shared experiences may be posted together.

The files for the Wiki service are stored at /Library/Server/Wiki.

Reference 22.2
Troubleshooting the Wiki Service

Here are some common problems and suggestions for rectifying issues with the Wiki service:

▶ If your users can't connect to the Wiki service on the server, check that the clients are using a DNS server that is providing the proper name resolution for the server.

▶ If users can't connect to the Wiki website, check that ports 80 and 443 are open to the server. Check that the Wiki service is running.

▶ If users can't authenticate to the Wiki service, check that the users are using proper passwords. Reset if needed. Check that the users are allowed access to the service as per the access controls.

For additional information on troubleshooting web issues, refer to Lesson 20 "Hosting Websites."

Exercise 22.1
Enable the Wiki Service

▶ **Prerequisites**

▶ Exercise 3.1, "Configure DNS Services"

▶ Exercise 10.1, "Create and Import Network Accounts" ; or use the Server app to create a user with Full Name: Carl Dunn, Account Name: carl, and a password of net, who is a member of a group named Contractors.

Enabling the Wiki service on OS X Server is simply done by turning on the service in the Server app.

In this exercise, you will enable the service, and then limit who can create wikis. You will ensure that your site uses SSL to protect it.

> **NOTE** ▶ Make sure you have the Contractors group and users available from Lesson 10.

1   In the Server app sidebar, select Wiki.

2   Turn the service on by clicking the On/Off switch.

3   Wiki creation can be limited to specific groups by adding the groups to the Wiki Creators menu. Choose "only some users" and add the Contractors group to the list. Click OK.

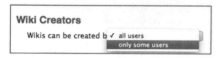

4   In Safari, navigate to server*n*.pretendco.com (where *n* is your student number) to view the default site, and then click Wikis to see the interface. This connection isn't protected by SSL.

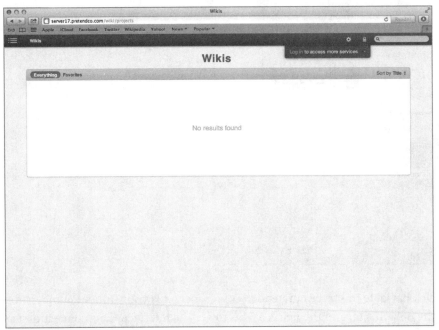

5   To protect the site with SSL automatically, in the Server app select Web. Edit the non-SSL default website and set up a redirect where "This website" is redirected to "Server Website (SSL)."

This sends any requests on HTTP to the SSL-protected HTTPS site.

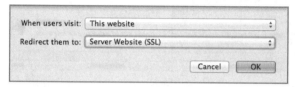

6   On your administrator computer in Safari, navigate to server*n*.pretendco.com (where *n* is your student number) to view the default site again, but notice that a certificate dialog appears, since a self-signed certificate was used. (You will not see this if you use a certificate signed by a known certificate authority.) Click Continue, and then click Wikis to see the interface.

7   Log in as Carl Dunn, a member the Contractors group, click the Add (+) pop-up menu at the top of the page, and choose New Wiki. Give it a name and description. Click Continue.

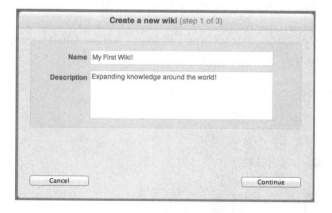

8   In the Set Permissions pane, start typing Contractors into the Permissions field. When the Contractors group appears, choose it and set the permissions to Read and Write. For all logged-in users, set permissions to Read Only, and for "All unauthenticated users," set permissions to No Access. Click Continue.

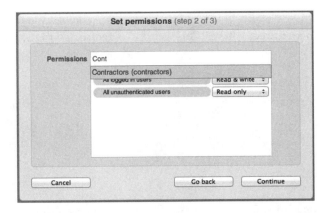

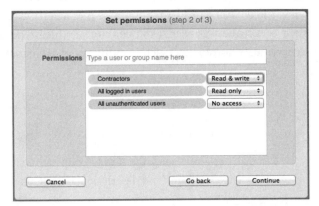

9 In the "Set appearance" pane, pick the color scheme and icon you like. Click Create, and then click "Go to Wiki" at the "Setup complete" pane.

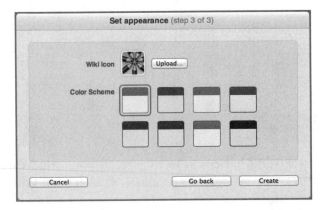

10 Review the various menus and choices in the wiki to get used to the interface.

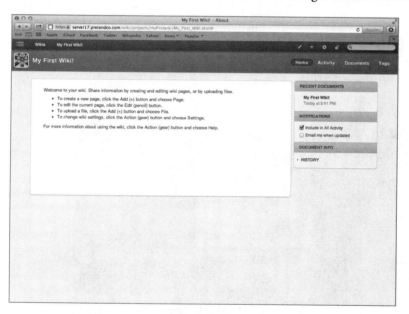

Exercise 22.2
Create a Wiki

> **Prerequisites**

> ▶ Exercise 22.1, "Enable the Wiki Service"

Users that you authorized to create wikis can begin the process of creating a wiki. Because wikis are web based, you can use any browser on any platform to authenticate users to start the process of wiki creation. In this exercise, you'll use network user credentials to create a wiki, manage access to it, and create some content.

1   Log into the wiki as Carl, and then click the Edit button (a pencil icon).

2   Click at the end of the existing text, press Return for a new line, and then click the Attachment icon (a paper clip).

3   Click Choose File, navigate to your Downloads folder, select About Downloads.pdf, and then click Choose.

4   Click Upload to attach the file.

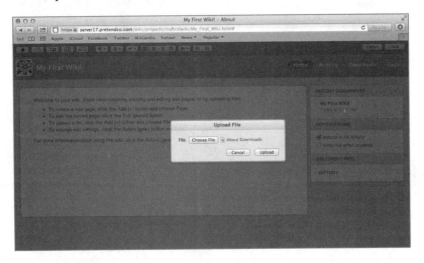

5   Click Save to save the edits to the page.

6   View the results of the edit. Additional media can be uploaded using the appropriate buttons in the toolbar. The media will be presented right on the webpage and won't require downloading for use by the reader.

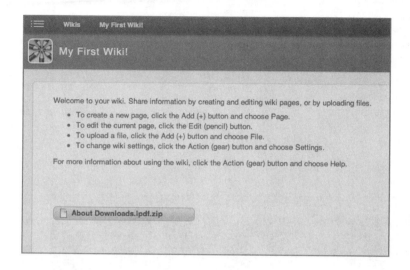

7 To turn on the blog, click the Action (gear icon) pop-up menu and choose Wiki Settings. Under the General tab, toggle the blog on and click Save. Once the blog is on, click the Add (+) button to add a new blog post within the wiki.

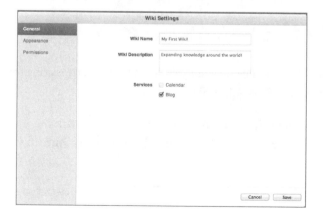

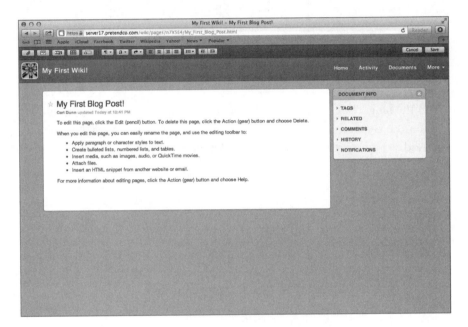

8 Enter Wiki Settings again and click the Permissions tab. Modify the permissions for "All unauthenticated users" to Read Only. Click Save.

9 To delete the wiki, click the Wiki name to move back to the Wiki itself, click the Action (gear icon) pop-up menu and choose "Delete Wiki." You will be asked to confirm your choice.

10 Click "log out," and then quit Safari.

Additional Resources

The following documents provide more information about managing Wiki services in OS X Server.

Many other documents are available at www.apple.com/osx/server/resources/documentation.html.

OS X Server Administration Guides

OS X Server: Advanced Administration
http://help.apple.com/advancedserveradmin/mac/10.8/

Apple Knowledge Base Documents

You can check for new and updated Knowledge Base documents at www.apple.com/support/.

Document HT5082, "OS X Server: Migrating and copying wiki data between servers"

Lesson Review

1. What is a wiki? What is a blog?
2. What tools can an administrator use to specify users that are allowed to create wikis?
3. How does a network user specify which users and groups are allowed to edit a wiki?

Answers

1. A wiki is designed to be read and edited by many. A blog is designed to be read by many but created by an individual.
2. Administrators can use the Wiki Creators list in the Wiki service settings in Server app.
3. When creating a wiki with a web browser, a user can specify permissions for users and groups to access and edit the wiki.

Lesson 23
Implementing Calendar Service

One of the core collaboration services, Calendar provides a standards-based method of scheduling tasks and resources.

Reference 23.1
Calendar Service Data Locations

Like most other services, the data repository for Calendar service is located at /Library/Server. Within that directory is a folder containing data specific to the Calendar service at /Library/Server/Calendar and Contacts.

Within that folder is a Config folder that has the main configuration file, caldavd.plist, for the caldav daemon.

Logs are stored at /var/log/caldavd/access.log.

GOALS

▶ Understand features of Calendar

▶ Explore the usage of the service

▶ Understand the underlying processes of the service

Reference 23.2
Using the Calendar Service

OS X Server contains a calendaring service based on several open source initiatives, mainly the Calendar Server Extensions for WebDAV (CalDAV) calendaring protocol. The Calendar service uses HTTP for access to all of its files. Users who want to use the calendaring service can take advantage of several handy features:

▶ Scheduling rooms or items that can be checked out, such as projectors

▶ Enabling access control for delegation of scheduling and/or restricted viewing of your calendar(s)

▶ Allowing multiple calendars per user

▶ Permitting the attachment of files to events

▶ Sending invitations to events, regardless of whether or not the recipient is a user on the Calendar server

▶   Checking to see if users or meeting locations are available for a certain event

▶   Privately annotating an event with comments that only they and the event organizer can access

▶   Using push notification to support immediate updates for computers and mobile devices

And these under-the-hood features should make administrators happy:

▶   Integration with Open Directory in OS X Server, Microsoft's Active Directory, and LDAP directory services, requires no modification to user records.

▶   Service discovery makes it easy for users to set up Calendar when you choose "Create Users and Groups" or "Import Users and Groups" during your initial server setup.

▶   Server-side scheduling frees up client resources for better client performance and more consistent scheduling results.

Once the Calendar service is started, users can create and manipulate their events and schedules with Calendar (v4.0 or higher), Calendar for iPhone and iPod touch, and wiki calendar pages. A number of third-party applications also work with the Calendar service; you can locate them by doing a web search for CalDAV support.

The Calendar service provides a way to create and use resources (like a projector or a set of speakers) and locations (such as a building or a meeting room). If no delegate has been set, the Calendar service automatically accepts the invitation for the location or resource if it is free, and makes the free/busy information available to users. You can also define a delegate to moderate the availability of the resource or location.

Delegates can have two functions based on whether you set Automatic or With Delegates Approval. If you set Automatic, the resource will automatically accept the invitation, but the delegate can view and modify the resource's calendar. If With Delegates Approval has been selected, the delegate must accept or deny the invitation. The delegate can also view and modify the resource's calendar.

You add locations and resources with the Server app in the Calendar pane.

Reference 23.3
Troubleshooting the Calendar Service

To troubleshoot the Calendar service provided by OS X Server, it helps to have a good understanding of how the Calendar Service works in general. Review the preceding sections to make sure you understand each of the working pieces.

Here are some common problems and potential solutions:

▶ If your users can't connect to the Calendar service on the server, check that the clients are using a DNS server that is providing the proper name resolution for the server.

▶ If users can't connect to the Calendar service, check that ports 8008 and 8443 are open to the server.

▶ If users can't authenticate to the Calendar service, check that the users are using proper passwords. Reset if needed. Check that the users are allowed access to the service as per the service access controls.

Exercise 23.1
Configure and Start the Calendar Service

▶ **Prerequisites**

▶ Exercise 3.1, "Configure DNS Services"

▶ Exercise 10.1, "Create and Import Network Accounts"

▶ Exercise 21.1, "Enable the Mail Service"

You use the Server app to start and manage the Calendar service. The parameters you can adjust are limited to the following:

▶ Enabling or disabling of email invitations and various related settings

▶ Locations and resources

Starting the Calendar service with the Server app is very simple, but you will want to gather the email server information you'll use with email invitations.

1 In the Server app sidebar, select Calendar.

2 Select the "Enable invitations by email" option, and then click the Edit button next to it.

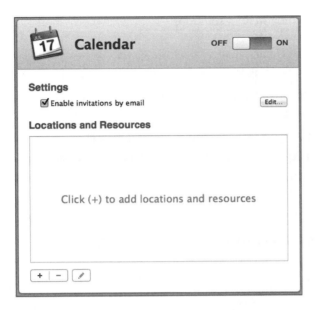

3   Enter the email address you want to use for sending email invitations, and then click Next.

The default email account for the user com.apple.calendarserver, a system account, is filled in for you. If you like, you may use another account, but don't use an email account that is utilized for normal email transactions.

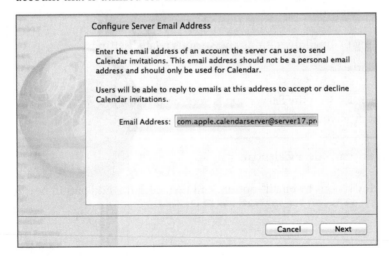

4   Enter the appropriate incoming email server information for your email server, and then click Next. By using localhost as the mail server address, the local OS X Server will be used.

5   Enter the appropriate outgoing email server information for your email server, and then click Next. By using localhost as the mail server address, the local OS X Server will be used.

6   Review the Mail Account Summary page and click Finish.

7 Start the Calendar service.

8 To secure communications between the Calendar service and the clients, set an SSL certificate for the service in the Server app by selecting the server under Hardware. Click the Settings tab, and then click the Edit button next to SSL Certificate. Select the server certificate for Calendar and Contacts service, and then click OK.

Exercise 23.2
Use the Server App to Add Resources and Locations

▶ **Prerequisites**

 ▶ Exercise 23.1, "Configure and Start the Calendar Service"

To add a location and a resource with the Server app:

1   In the Server app sidebar, select the Calendar service.

2   Under the Locations and Resources section, click the Add (+) button, and then choose Location from the pop-up menu.

3   Enter and/or change the following data for your new location:

▶   Name: Conference Room A

▶   Accept Invitations: Automatically

▶   Delegate: Sue Wu (It populates with choices as you type a name.)

4   Click Done to save the changes to the location.

You have now added a location that will be visible when you add or modify an event on a calendar hosted by the Calendar service.

5   Click the Add (+) button, and then choose Resource from the pop-up menu.

6   Enter and/or change the following data for your new resource:

▶   Name: Demo iPad

▶   Accept Invitations: Automatically

▶   Delegate: Lucy Sanchez (It populates with choices as you type a name.)

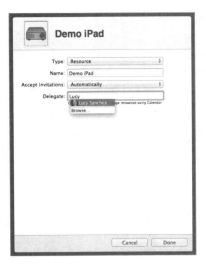

7 Click Done.

You have now added a resource you can invite to an event.

Exercise 23.3
Access the Calendar Service as a User

Users can create and modify events with iCal, a web browser, and mobile devices. In this exercise, you will open iCal, add a network Calendar account, change who can access the account as a delegate, create an event with a location and a resource, and then create one more event and access the free/busy feature.

1 On your administrator computer, open Calendar (in /Applications).

2 Choose Calendar > Preferences, and then click Accounts.

3 Click the Add (+) button to add a Calendar service account, and enter the following data:

    ▶ Account Type: Automatic

▶ Email Address: lucy@server*n*.pretendco.com (where *n* is your student number)

▶ Password: net

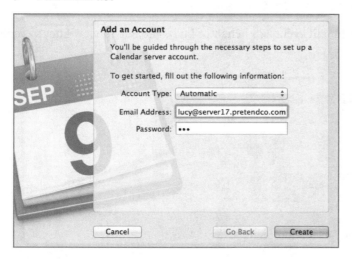

4   Click Create to add the account. You might get a certificate warning if you used a self-signed SSL certificate.

5   Delegate other users to access the calendar to edit and review the events. Click the Delegation tab. Notice that Demo iPad already is showing up in the list of accounts the user can access.

6   Click Edit.

7   Click the Add (+) button.

8   Enter sue, and then choose Sue Wu from the list. Make sure you click the name to choose it.

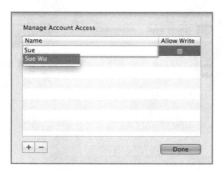

9   Click the Add (+) button, enter Carl, and then choose Carl Dunn from the list.

10 Select the Allow Write checkbox for Carl.

This setup allows Carl to edit events on behalf of Lucy, and Sue to view Lucy's events.

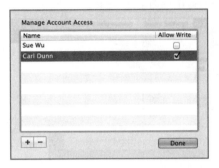

11 Click Done to close the Delegation pane.

12 Click the General tab and choose the calendar for server*n* (where *n* is your student number) to be your Default Calendar.

13 Close the Preferences window.

14 Choose File > New Event, or click the Create Event (+) button, to create a quick event.

15 Enter an event name, such as Status Update, and press Return.

16 In the location field, enter only the first few characters of Conference Room A. Choose Conference Room A when it appears, and then press Return.

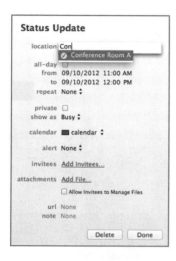

17 Click Add Invitees, and then enter only the first few characters of Sue Wu. Choose Sue Wu when it appears, and then press Return.

18 While still in the invitees field, enter only the first few characters of Demo iPad. Choose Demo iPad when it appears, and then press Return.

19 Click Add File, navigate to your Downloads folder, select About Downloads.lpdf, and then click Open.

20 Click Send to save the changes to this event.

This causes Demo iPad to automatically accept the event, and Sue Wu will get an invitation to the event. The automatic accept occurred because the resource was configured to do that.

21 Click the event you just created. Choose Edit > Duplicate, which creates a new event at the same time as your original event.

22 Choose Edit > Edit Event.

23 Note that Demo iPad has an unavailable icon, because you already scheduled an event for this time that is using the Demo iPad.

24 Click Available Meeting Times to choose a new meeting time that works for the location and invitees (which includes people and resources).

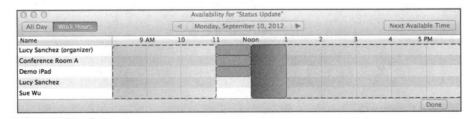

Note that free/busy information is listed for each participant invited to the event, including the location, people, and resources. The unavailable times are blocked out in gray, and the available times are displayed with the color assigned to your calendar.

25 Click Next Available Time, and note that the event moves to the next time that is not busy for each of the invitees.

26 Click Done to close the Availability window and use the new time selected.

27 Click Send to save the changes to the event and notify the invitees of the event. Locations and resources automatically accept invitations.

28 Quit iCal, or try out some of the other features.

Even though you used Calendar in this exercise, you could also use the web calendar link available at the bottom of the default server home page (https://server*n*.pretendco.com/ webcal, where *n* is your student number). Of course, the Calendar service works with Calendar for iPhone and iPod touch through the CalDAV configuration option.

Calendars can also be added to wikis by creating a wiki, and in the General settings selecting the Calendar checkbox.

Since the Calendar service relies on HTTP or HTTPS to transfer data from server to client and vice-versa, standard web troubleshooting applies, such as checking for open and available ports. On a client, Calendar app discovers the Calendar server via DNS lookup so DNS problems could prevent Calendar from working as expected.

Additional Resources

The following documents provide more information about Calendar in OS X Server.

Many other documents are available at www.apple.com/osx/server/resources/ documentation.html.

OS X Server Administration Guides

OS X Server: Advanced Administration
http://help.apple.com/advancedserveradmin/mac/10.8/

Apple Knowledge Base Documents

You can check for new and updated Knowledge Base documents at www.apple.com/ support/.

Document HT3767, "OS X Server: Enabling Calendar and Contacts service access for users of Active Directory or third-party LDAP servers"

Document HT3660, "OS X Server: Enabling Calendar service access for users of Active Directory or third-party LDAP servers"

Lesson Review

1. What protocol does Calendar use?

2. How does a user specify which users are allowed to edit and/or view his calendar?

3. What is the transport protocol for the Calendar service and how can that impact the troubleshooting of the service?

Answers

1. CalDAV, which is an extension of WebDAV.

2. In the Calendar app preferences, he can designate delegates and their rights.

3. CalDAV and WebDAV utilize HTTP as a transport and as a result the troubleshooting of it is similar to web services. You need to make sure DNS is correct and the proper ports are open.

Lesson 24
Providing Messages Service

One of the common collaboration services, Messages provides a standards-based method of communicating with one or many other users.

Reference 24.1
Managing the Messages Service

Messages, previously known as iChat, allows users to collaborate in real time. Messages users can use the following features to quickly share information without the delay associated with email messages and wiki posts:

▶ Exchange text messages instantly.

▶ Send files to each other.

▶ Set up an instant audio conference (using the microphone built into many Macs or an external unit).

▶ Initiate a face-to-face video conference using video cameras (including the iSight or FaceTime camera built into many Macs).

▶ Allow another Messages user to take control of a Mac (using screen sharing).

▶ Use Messages Theater to share many kinds of documents, including text files, PDFs, photos, QuickTime movies, Keynote slide shows, and iPhoto albums.

Unlike a telephone call, which you must either answer immediately or allow to go to voicemail, you can accept an instant text message but answer it when you are ready to process it.

By running your own Messages service, you gain these advantages, plus others like chat transcript archives and the ability to keep all messages secure and private.

Users who chat with each other can use the Messages service to keep those chats within their organization and control the text of the chats. Like many other services on OS X Server, the Messages service can be restricted to certain users or groups, permitting chats to be private and controlled. Chats can also be secured through encryption and logged, permitting them to be searched later. The Messages service is based on the open source Jabber project. The technical name for the protocol used is the Extensible Messaging and Presence Protocol (XMPP).

Various ports are used for the Messages service, depending on whether the service is used internal to your network or exposed to other networks. Refer to Table 24.1 for port usage information.

Table 24.1 Messages Port Usage

Port	Description
1080	SOCKS5 protocol use for file transfers
5060	iChat Session Initiation Protocol (SIP), used for audio or video chats
5190	Only required for basic Instant Messenger (IM) use
5222 TCP	Used only for TLS connections if an SSL certificate is enabled. If no SSL certificate is used, this port is used for nonencrypted connections. TLS encryption is preferred to legacy SSL connections as it is more secure.
5223 TCP	Used for legacy SSL connections when an SSL certificate is used
5269 TCP	Used for encrypted TLS server-to-server connections, as well as non-encrypted connections. TLS encryption is preferred to legacy SSL connections as it is more secure.
5678	UDP port used by Messages to determine the user's external IP address
5297, 5298	Used by Messages versions older than v10.5 for Bonjour IM. v10.5 and later use dynamic ports.
7777	Used by the Jabber Proxy65 module for server file transfer proxy
16402	Used for SIP signaling in OS X 10.5 and later
16384–16403	These ports are used by OS X 10.4 and earlier for audio or video chat using RTP and RTCP. Traffic was exchanged in .Mac (MobileMe) to determine the user's external port information.

Messages Logging

The Messages service can be used for all sorts of purposes, among them group chatting related to projects. There may be a need to review the chat archive of a conversation, perhaps for auditing or administrative purposes. The Messages client application can archive an individual's chats for review.

The Messages service can log all chat messages. The default directory is located in /Library/Server/Messages/Data/message_archives/. Even if the communications between the Messages users are encrypted, the archives will be kept in plain text.

Messages Federation

Your organization may have more than one computer running OS X Server. If both of those servers use the Messages service, it is possible to join them together, allowing users and groups in both Open Directory masters to engage each other in instant messaging. The process of joining different Messages service servers together is called federation. Federation not only allows two servers running Messages services to join, it also allows any other XMPP chat service, such as Google Talk, to join as well. The Messages service federation is enabled by default.

> **NOTE ▸** You can enable secure encryption for the federation if you are already using an SSL certificate. This forces all communications between the servers to be encrypted, similar to the way in which the communications between Messages and the Messages server are encrypted when using that certificate. For archiving purposes, messages are always decrypted on the server.

Reference 24.2
Troubleshooting the Messages Service

To troubleshoot the Messages service provided by OS X Server, it helps to have a good understanding of how the Messages service works in general. Review the preceding sections to make sure you understand each of the working pieces.

Here are some common problems and suggestions for rectifying them:

▸   If your users can't connect to the Messages service on the server, check that the clients are using a DNS server that is providing the proper name resolution for the server.

▸   If users can't connect to the Messages service, check that the appropriate ports are open to the server as listed in Table 24.1 earlier in the section.

▶ If users can't authenticate to the Messages service, check that the users are using proper passwords. Reset if needed. Check that the users are allowed access to the service as per the service access controls.

Exercise 24.1
Set Up the Messages Service

You use the Server app to enable the Messages service like most of the other services on OS X Server. Once enabled, the service is managed in a fashion similar to that of the other services.

1   To protect Messages with SSL, select your server in the Server app sidebar, click Settings, and click Edit next to the SSL Certificate field. Apply the server certificate to the Messages service and click OK.

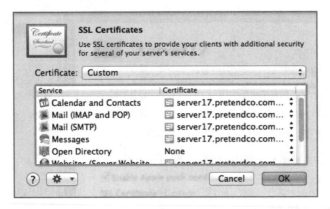

2   In the Server app, select the Messages service and turn on.

Manage Messages Service Archiving

To enable Messages service logging:

1   In the Server app sidebar, select Messages, and then select "Archive all chat messages."

2   To view any logged messages, you must be the root user or escalate privileges and navigate to /Library/Server/Messages/Data/message_archives/. You can then use any text editor to view the log files and search them for relevant keywords.

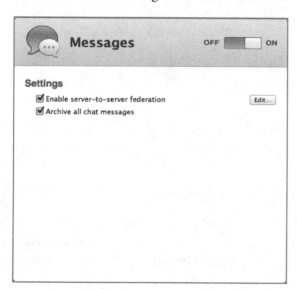

Configure Messages Service Users

After the Messages service has been set up, you can permit users to join the Messages service (called Jabber in the interface). The Messages service account is a user's short name, the @ symbol, and a Messages service's host domain. For example, the user Chat User1 would set up the Messages application as chatuser1@server17.pretendco.com.

To enable a Messages account to use the Messages (Jabber) service:

1   On your administrator computer, click the Messages icon in your Dock. At the iMessage Setup dialog, click Not Now, and then click Skip.

2   At the Account Setup dialog, choose Jabber from the Account Type pop-up menu.

3   Enter sue@server*n*.pretendco.com (where *n* is your student number) in the Account Name field, and enter the password net in the Password field.

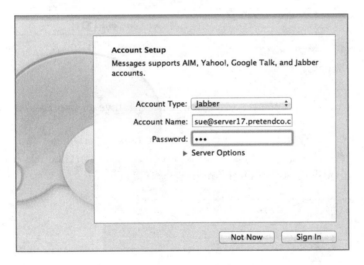

4   Click Sign In.

Messages opens. To see your Messages (Jabber) service buddy list, choose Window > Buddies. In the header at the top of the window, Messages displays the full name of the user logged in on OS X.

5   On your server, repeat steps 1 through 4 with user Carl.

You can add Jabber buddies (other users with whom you want to chat and whose names you want to appear in a list for easy access) to your buddy list as you normally would when using Messages for any other non-Jabber account. You can optionally add a buddy who exists in your Open Directory database. Be sure to include the person's full name when adding a Messages (Jabber) service buddy.

6   On your administrator computer, click the Add (+) button in the Buddy List window to add a buddy. Enter Carl's information (**carl@server***n***.pretendco.com**, where *n* is your student number). Click Add.

7   On the server, a message appears asking permission for Sue to add Carl to her buddy list. Accept the request.

Once you add a buddy, that person receives a notification when he logs in to Messages (Jabber) asking if he would like to be added to your buddy list

Once you have authorized the listing of your name in that person's buddy list, he will see you every time you log in to the Messages (Jabber) service.

8   Simulate a chat between the users.

9   Close Messages.

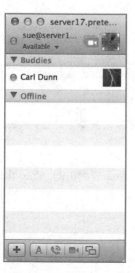

Restrict Messages Service Users

You can also restrict who is permitted to use the Messages service by using service access controls. As with many other services, you can restrict user access via the Server app.

To restrict users from chatting with others on the Messages service:

1   In the Server app sidebar, select Users.

2   Select Sue Wu, and then click the Action (gear icon) pop-up menu and choose "Edit Access to Services."

3   Deselect the Messages service checkbox to disable the user's access to Messages. Click OK.

4   Open Messages on your administrator computer (with Sue Wu's account). Note that she is asked for a password, but you still can't log in as her.

5   Enable Sue's Messages service again and try connecting.

Restrict Messages Federation

By default, federation is allowed with any other Messages service running on any other server or Jabber server. However, you can restrict the Messages service federation to approved Messages servers only. To do so:

1   In the Server app sidebar, select the Messages service. Make sure that "Enable server-to-server federation" is selected, and then click the Edit button.

2   Select the "Restrict federation to the following domains" option and click the Add (+) button to add only those domains you want to participate within the federation. As an example, use the hypothetical **server18.pretendco.com**.

3   To keep communication secure between federated servers, apply an SSL certificate to the Messages service and select the "Require secure server-to-server federation" option. Click OK to close the dialog.

View Messages Service and Chat Logs

1   To view the connection logs for the Messages service, use Server app to view the Messages Service log. Simply enter **session started** in the search field, and you'll see all users, dates, and times that sessions have begun.

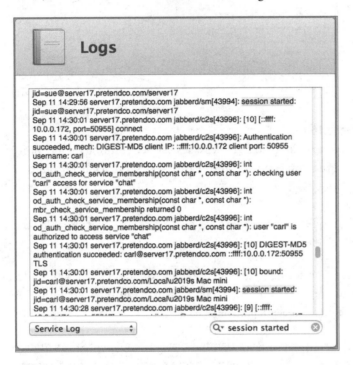

The Messages service reports in the system log can also log any errors that may occur, and you can search for them using the search field in the toolbar.

2   To view the chat transcripts, open Terminal (click LaunchPad, click Others, and click Terminal) on your server computer and enter all on one line

```
sudo more /Library/Server/Messages/Data/message_archives/jabberd_user_messages.log
```

and press Return. You will be prompted for the admin password. Enter it and press Return. The chat transcripts appear; look for the conversation Carl and Sue had.

You must have root access to view the jabberd_user_messages.log file, which contains all the messages your users have exchanged using your server's Messages service. The sudo command gives you the root access you need on a temporary basis. While it is possible to go and change permission on the message_archives folder and the log it contains so you can use a GUI text editor to view the file, it is safer and more secure to use the command-line tools in Terminal to view the file.

Additional logs are available in the Logs section of the Server app.

```
server17:caldavd ladmin$ sudo more /Library/Server/Messages/Data/message_archives/jabberd_user_messages.log
# This message log is created by the jabberd router.
# See router.xml for logging options.
# Format: (Date)<tab>(From JID)<tab>(To JID)<tab>(Message Body)<line end>
Tue Sep 11 13:53:20 2012        carl@server17.pretendco.com/Local's Mac mini      sue@server17.pretendco.com
you ready for the meeting?
```

Additional Resources

The following documents provide more information about Messages in OS X Server.

Many other documents are available at www.apple.com/osx/server/resources/documentation.html.

OS X Server Administration Guides

OS X Server: Advanced Administration
http://help.apple.com/advancedserveradmin/mac/10.8/

Apple Knowledge Base Documents

You can check for new and updated Knowledge Base documents at www.apple.com/support/.

Document TS1629, "Well known TCP and UDP ports used by Apple software products"

Lesson Review

1. What protocol is used for the Messages service?
2. How would you limit access to Messages service on OS X Server?
3. How would you enter the Messages name for the user Jet Dogg (short name: jet) on server17.pretendco.com?

Answers

1. The Messages service uses the Extensible Messaging and Presence Protocol (XMPP).
2. Through "Edit Access to Services" per user available in the Server app.
3. The Messages name format for Jet Dogg is jet@server17.pretendco.com.

Lesson 25
Managing Contacts Service

OS X Server provides a simple interface for providing Contacts services. Contacts allows the central storage of information and makes it available to many clients.

GOALS

► Configure Contacts service

► Understand protocols used

► Connect to the Contacts service

Reference 25.1
Understanding the Contacts Service

The Contacts service enables users to store contacts on the server and to access those contacts with multiple computers and devices. The following applications are compatible with the Contacts service:

► Contacts and Address Book

► Mail

► Messages

Another feature of Contacts allows you to enable the Contacts service to provide LDAP searches of the directory servers your server may be bound to, so your users do not have to configure their Contacts preferences to include various LDAP servers. This option is not available for configuration unless the server is bound to another directory service.

The Contacts service uses open source technologies, including CardDAV (an extension to WebDAV), HTTP, and HTTPS, as well as vCard (a file format for contact information).

When you create a contact with the Contacts service, you use CardDAV, not LDAP, to copy the changes to the server.

Reference 25.2
Troubleshooting the Contacts Service

Here are some common problems with the Contacts service and how they might be rectified:

▶   If your users can't connect to the Contacts service on the server, check that the clients are using a DNS server that is providing the proper name resolution for the server.

▶   If users can't connect to the Contacts service, check that the ports 8800 and 8843 are open to the server.

▶   If users can't authenticate to the Contacts service, check that the users are using proper passwords. Reset if needed. Also check that the users are allowed to use the service based on the service access controls.

Exercise 25.1
Configure the Contacts Service with the Server App

▶ **Prerequisites**

▶   Exercise 3.1, "Configure DNS Services"

▶   Exercise 10.1, "Create and Import Network Accounts"

There is very little to configure in the Contacts service. The Server app allows you to:

▶   Turn the service on and off.

▶   Enable directory contacts for search.

In this exercise, before you start the Contacts service, you will specify an SSL certificate for the service to use.

This exercise requires that the OS X Server be set up as an Open Directory master with the sample users imported.

1   To secure communications between the Contacts service and the clients, set an SSL certificate for the service. In the Server app sidebar, select the server under Hardware. Click the Settings tab, and then click the Edit button next to SSL Certificate. Choose the server certificate for the Calendar and Contacts service.

2   In the Server app, select the Contacts service.

3   Select "Include directory contacts in search."

   NOTE ▶ This box will be dimmed if the server is not bound to another directory service or is not an Open Directory master. If it is dimmed, you can still use the Contacts service but be limited to local users resident on the server.

4   Turn on the Contacts service.

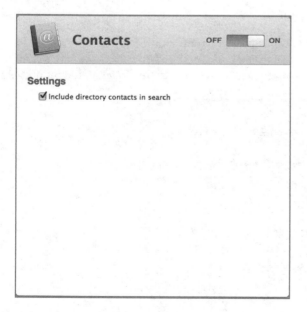

Exercise 25.2
Configure OS X to Use the Contacts Service

> **Prerequisite**
>
> ▶ Exercise 25.1, "Configure the Contacts Service with the Server App"

The Contacts application in OS X is designed to work with the Contacts service on OS X Server.

1   From the Launchpad, open Contacts on your client computer and choose Contacts > Preferences.

2   Click Accounts.

3   Click the Add (+) button.

4   Leave the Account type as CardDAV, as the Contacts service implements CardDAV.

5   In the User name field, enter `gary`.

You must use the user's short name.

6   In the Password field, enter the proper password `net`.

7   In the Server address field, enter `servern.pretendco.com` (where `n` is your student number).

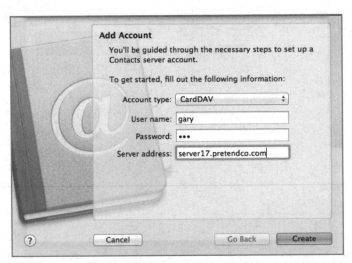

8   Click Create.

9   If a Verify Certificate dialog appears, click Show Certificate, select the checkbox for "Always trust," and authenticate with administrative credentials.

The new account appears in the Accounts list.

Of course, in a production environment, you would populate client computers to trust your known good SSL certificates, and then train users to alert an administrator when they see an unknown-certificate message.

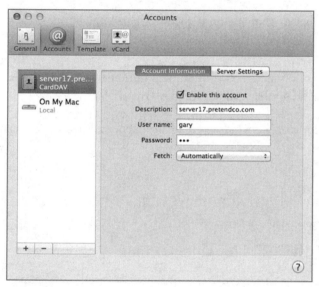

10   Click the General tab.

11   From the Default Account pop-up menu, choose server*n*.pretendco.com (where *n* is your student number).

Now when you create a new contact, it will automatically be created on the server account.

12 Close the Preferences window.

13 Notice in Contacts the three sections under All Contacts: On My Mac, server*n*. pretendco.com (where *n* is your student number), and Directories. The latter one is due to the Contacts service having the "Include directory contacts in search" option configured.

> **NOTE ▶** If the Contacts pane isn't showing on the left side, click the leftmost view button at the bottom of the left pane.

14 Choose server*n*.pretendco.com (where *n* is your student number) and click the Add (+) button to create a new contact that will be stored on the server.

15 Enter sample information for a user, including email and Jabber addresses. You can use the following values:

   ▶ First: Jet

   ▶ Last: Dogg

   ▶ Email (work): jet@example.com

   ▶ Chat (work): jet@jabber.example.com

16 Click Done to save your changes.

The contact you just created is synced locally on your OS X computer for offline use, and it is also stored with the Contacts service, so you can access it from other computers and devices.

Messages also supports your Contacts service account. Use the following steps to demonstrate that you can use your Contacts service account with Messages. If you haven't already configured Messages with your network user account, refer to "Managing the Messages Service" in Lesson 24.

17 If Messages is not already running, open Messages (in /Applications).

18 If the *servern* List window is not already displayed, choose Window > server*n*.pretendco.com List (where *n* is your student number).

19 Click the Add (+) button, and choose Add Buddy.

20 Click the disclosure button to reveal additional choices.

21 Click the entry you created (Jet Dogg).

22 Click Cancel.

In a production environment, you would click Add to add this user to your buddy list. Do not click Add now, because this would create an authorization request for the foreign Jabber server, and you are on an isolated network.

23 Quit Messages.

The contacts you create with your Contacts service account are available to you on other OS X computers, as long as you configure Contacts with your Contacts service account. You can also access your contacts with any application that uses CardDAV.

Additional Resources

The following documents provide more information about Contacts services in OS X Server.

Many other documents are available at www.apple.com/osx/server/resources/documentation.html.

OS X Server Administration Guides

OS X Server: Advanced Administration
http://help.apple.com/advancedserveradmin/mac/10.8/

Apple Knowledge Base Documents

You can check for new and updated Knowledge Base documents at www.apple.com/support/.

Document HT3767, "OS X Server: Enabling Calendar and Contacts service access for users of Active Directory or third-party LDAP servers"

Lesson Review

1. On what protocols is the Contacts service based?

2. How can the information contained in a directory service the server is bound to be included in the Contacts searches?

3. Where is SSL for the Contacts service configured for use?

Answers

1. The OS X Server Contacts service is based on CardDAV (an extension to WebDAV), HTTP, and HTTPS, as well as vCard (a file format for contact information).

2. Make sure the "Include directory contacts in search" option is selected in the configuration of the Contacts service.

3. In the Settings pane of the Hardware tab in the Server app under SSL Certificate.

Index

Apple Certification
Fuel your mind.
Reach your potential.

Stand out from the crowd. Differentiate yourself and gain recognition for your expertise by earning Apple Certified Pro status to validate your OS X Server skills.

This book prepares you to pass the OS X Server Essentials 10.8 Exam and in conjunction with the OS X Support Essentials 10.8 Exam, earn Apple Certified Technical Coordinator (ACTC) status. The exam is available at Apple Authorized Training Centers (AATCs) worldwide. ACTC certification verifies knowledge of OS X and OS X Server core functionality, including the ability to configure key services and perform basic troubleshooting on OS X and OS X Server.

Three Steps to Certification

1 Choose your certification path.
More info: training.apple.com/certification.

2 All Apple Authorized Training Centers (AATCs) offer all OS X and Pro Apps exams, even if they don't offer the corresponding course. To find the closest AATC, please visit training.apple.com/locations.

3 Register for and take your exam(s).

"Knowing that I am Apple Certified gives my clients the confidence to trust me with their most complex projects. It makes my life easier: my Apple Certifications open a whole new world of trust. Apple Certified professionals have already proven that they know their craft."

— Luisa C. Winters, Multimedia Specialist/Graphic Artist, VideoTrainers

Reasons to Become an Apple Certified Pro

· **Raise your earning potential.** Studies show that certified professionals can earn more than their non-certified peers.

· **Distinguish yourself from others in your industry.** Proven mastery of an application helps you stand out from the crowd.

· **Display your Apple Certification logo.** Each certification provides a logo to display on business cards, resumes and websites.

· **Publicize your certifications.** Publish your certifications on the Apple Certified Professionals Registry (apple.com//certification/verify) to connect with schools, clients and employers.

Training Options

Apple's comprehensive curriculum addresses your needs, whether you're an IT or creative professional, educator, or student. Hands-on training is available through a worldwide network of Apple Authorized Training Centers (AATCs). Self-paced study is available through the Apple Pro Training Series books, which are also accessible as eBooks via the iBooks app. Video training and video training apps are also available for select titles. Visit training.apple.com to view all your learning options.

Meet Creative Edge.

A new resource of unlimited books, videos and tutorials for creatives from the world's leading experts.

Creative Edge is your one stop for inspiration, answers to technical questions and ways to stay at the top of your game so you can focus on what you do best—being creative.

All for only $24.99 per month for access—any day any time you need it.

creative edge

creativeedge.com